Human Rights Today – 60 Years of the Universal Declaration

HUMAN RIGHTS TODAY – 60 YEARS OF THE UNIVERSAL DECLARATION

Edited by

Miodrag A. Jovanović & Ivana Krstić

eleven international publishing

Published, sold and distributed by Eleven International Publishing
P.O. Box 358
3500 AJ Utrecht, The Netherlands
Tel.: +31 30 231 0545
Fax: +31 30 225 8045
info@elevenpub.com
www.elevenpub.com

Sold and distributed in USA and Canada
International Specialized Book Services
920 NE 58th Avenue, Suite 300
Portland, OR 97213-3786, USA
Tel: +1 800 944 6190 (toll-free)
Fax: +1 503 280 8832
orders@isbs.com
www.isbs.com

Printed on acid-free paper.

ISBN: 978-90-77596-84-5

Printed in The Netherlands

Table of Contents

PART III: DEVELOPMENTS AND CHALLENGES IN HUMAN RIGHTS LAW

List of Contributors

The Editors

Miodrag Jovanović
Associate Professor in Introduction to Jurisprudence, Faculty of Law, University of Belgrade

Ivana Krstić
Senior Lecturer in Public International Law, Faculty of Law, University of Belgrade

The Authors

Anne van Aaken
Max Schmidheiny Foundation Tenure-Track-Professor for Law and Economics, Public, International and European Law

Abdullahi Ahmed An-Na'im
Charles Howard Candler Professor of Law, School of Law, Emory University, Former Executive Director for Human Rights Watch/Africa in Washington, D.C.

Daphne Barak-Erez
Stewart and Judy Colton Professor of Constitutional and Administrative Law and Chair of Law and Security at the Faculty of Law, Tel Aviv University, chairperson of the Israeli Association of Public Law

Henk Botha
Professor of Constitutional Law and International Law at the Faculty of Law, Stellenbosch University

Ian Brownlie
CBE Q.C, has been practicing in public international law and human rights since 1967, and has appeared in a full range of international tribunals, including the ICJ, the ECtHR, and the ECJ. He has also acted as an arbitrator in a number of major cases, and has re-elected for his third five-year term to the ILC

Thomas Fleiner
Professor of Constitutional, Administrative and Public International Law, Faculty of Law, University of Fribourg, former Director of the Swiss Institute of Federalism (1984-2008)

Aleksandra Gajić
Assistant Lecturer in Public International Law, Faculty of Law, University of Belgrade, Practicioner before the ICTY

Mathias Hartwig
Researcher for Comparative Public Law and Public International Law, Max-Planck-Institut, Heidelberg

Jasminka Hasanbegović
Full Professor in Introduction to Jurisprudence and Legal Philosophy, Faculty of Law, University of Belgrade

Dragoljub Popović
Judge of the European Court of Human Rights, former Ambassador of the State Union Serbia and Montenegro to Switzerland

Patrick Thornberry
Professor of International Law at the School of Politics, International Relations and Philosophy, Keele University, current member of the UN Committee on the Elimination of Racial Discrimination, Chairman of Minority Rights Group

Introduction

Miodrag A. Jovanović & Ivana Krstić

Human Rights in the 21st Century: Between Crisis and a New Beginning

In the introduction to his 1989 book, which is in itself a remarkable theoretical exposition of the structure of international legal argument, Koskenniemi attempts to justify his decision to treat international law "as the classical law of peace, concerned with the relations of sovereign States *vis-à-vis* each other," thus leaving aside themes relating to war, human rights and international organizations. He finds one of the principal reasons for this move to be in the fact that any meticulous treatment of both the law of war and the law of human rights will instantly lead to a murky philosophical discussion of a just war or fundamental rights, and that is exactly what international legal scholars try to avoid. Therefore, Koskenniemi stresses that, although he is convinced of the importance of justice at war and individual rights, he shall, nonetheless, "set these issues aside as they so obviously conflict with the mainstream understanding of what is significant in international law."[1]

Despite the fact that one can provide some arguments to support Koskenniemi's approach, it is hardly deniable that precisely the issue of human rights was the one around which the post-World War II international legal order recuperated. As early as in 1942, the Allied forces, which were named after Roosevelt – the United Nations – produced their Declaration, whose preamble justified the coordinated military efforts of the signatory states upon the claim that

> complete victory over their enemies is essential to defend life, liberty, independence and religious freedom, and to preserve human rights and justice

1 M. Koskenniemi, From Apology to Utopia – The Structure of International Legal Argument, xxv (1989).

Miodrag Jovanović & Ivana Krstić (Eds.), Human Rights Today – 60 Years of the Universal Declaration, 3-17.

> in their own lands as well as in other lands, and that they are now engaged in a common struggle against savage and brutal forces seeking to subjugate the world.[2]

No wonder then that after the defeat of the Axis powers, one of the corner stone documents of a newly emerging international legal order was the 1948 Universal Declaration of Human Rights. In Ignatieff's words, this document was "part of a wider reordering of the normative order of postwar international relations, designed to create fire walls against barbarism."[3] It was later followed with the two 1966 legally binding international human rights covenants. Significantly new and certainly positive features of that order concerned the international legal recognition of individuals and their rights, as well as the emergence of what has become known as a 'global civil society' – local and international non-governmental organizations that actively participate in domestic and international affairs by vigorously advocating the human rights cause. Over the course of time, and in particular after the disappearance of a bipolar world in the 1990s,[4] these new actors on the international scene have managed to profoundly reshape the traditional perception of the international legal order to the extent that few scholars nowadays would be ready to follow Koskenniemi's 1989 exposition of "the mainstream understanding of what is significant in international law," in which there is no room for human rights law.

In fact, Koskenniemi himself would no longer acquiesce to the claim that human rights law is only "supplementary to the main body (of international law), or derivative from it."[5] On the contrary, in the capacity as the Chairman of the Study Group of the International Law Commission, which has recently prepared a comprehensive report on the process of the "fragmentation of international law,"[6] he often refers to human rights law as an example of the so-

---

[2] *Declaration by United Nations*, 1 January 1942, at http://www.ibiblio.org/pha/policy/1942/420101a.html.

[3] M. Ignatieff, Human Rights as Politics and Idolatry 5 (2001).

[4] Ignatieff notes:

> After forty years of deference toward the sovereignty of states, the United Nations decided in the 1990s to create its own cadre of human rights activists under the leadership of the High Commissioner for Human Rights.

Id., at 11.

[5] Koskenniemi, *supra* note 1, at xxv.

[6] *Fragmentation of International Law. Problems Caused by the Diversification and Expansion of International Law, Report of the Study Group of the International Law Commission*, finalized by Martti Koskenniemi A/CN4/L.682, 13 April 2006. The final 42 conclusions are contained in *Fragmentation of International Law: Difficulties Arising From the Diversification and Expansion of International Law: Report of the Study Group of the International Law Commission*, A/CN.4/L.702, 18 July 2006, at 7-25.

called 'self-contained' legal regime that exists within a system of international law.[7] This report, in general, points to the problem

> that such specialized law-making and institution-building tends to take place with relative ignorance of legislative and institutional activities in the adjoining fields and of the general principles and practices of international law. The result is conflicts between rules or rule-systems, deviating institutional practices and, possibly, the loss of an overall perspective on the law.[8]

One might argue that this trend of 'fragmentation' of general international law is best reflected exactly in the field of human rights law. Namely, human rights experts often tend to treat their discipline as superior to the 'rest' of international law. Take, for example, Reisman's statement that "the international human rights program is more than a piecemeal addition to the traditional corpus of international law, more than another chapter sandwiched into traditional textbooks of international law."[9] While it is true that international human rights law brought with it a novel function similar to the one of constitutional law[10] (insofar as it put limits on what states may do to citizens within their jurisdiction), it nonetheless shares the same essential feature of general international law – it lacks sufficiently effective methods of enforcement. Consequently, human rights law "does not generally bind governments against their will,"[11] and human rights courts with powers of judicial review and compulsory jurisdiction "remain the exception rather than the rule, especially at the global level."[12] On the other hand, where the enforcement of decisions of human rights bodies is more firmly entrenched, as in the case of the European Court of Human Rights, those bodies

7 In the broadest sense,

> whole fields of functional specialization, of diplomatic and academic expertise, are described as self-contained (whether or not that word is used) in the sense that special rules and techniques of interpretation and administration are thought to apply. For instance, fields such as 'human rights law', 'WTO law', 'European law/EU law', 'humanitarian law', 'space law', among others, are often identified as 'special' in the sense that rules of general international law are assumed to be modified or even excluded in their administration.

Fragmentation of International Law. Problems Caused ..., supra note 6, at 68.

8 *Id.*, at 11.

9 M. Reisman, *Sovereignty and Human Rights in Contemporary International Law*, 84 American Journal of International Law 866, at 872 (1990)

10 *See* Van Aaken's contribution to this volume on the function of human rights in the constitutionalization of public international law.

11 S. Gardbaum, *Human Rights as International Constitutional Rights*, 19 The European Journal of International Law 749, at 763 (2008)

12 *Id.*, at 751.

> have developed a steady jurisprudence under which the interpretative principles applicable to human rights treaties differ from principles applicable to other treaties, enabling an activist role by human rights bodies.[13]

This activism illustrates, in fact, a greater level of institutional autonomy achieved by these bodies.[14]

On a more general plane, human rights language tends to become the *lingua franca* even in the functioning of such institutions as the World Bank or International Monetary Fund, which should, by its very nature, be primarily driven by the logic of economic values. This is what Kinley perceives as human rights' '*Reactionary Fundamentalism*', that being "a tendency towards human rights evangelicalism where human rights are touted as a panacea for many or all social, political, legal and economic ills."[15] The problem with this development is that, "as human rights spread wider, their distinctiveness diminishes. The ability to speak a human rights language becomes a coveted *carte blanche*, an unsurpassed marker of legitimacy." As a consequence,

> if all institutions administer some kind of benefits, and if all benefits may be characterized as the rights of those to whom the benefits are due, then fragmentation reaches its apogee as the institutional counterpart of human rights law's complete indeterminacy.[16]

Moreover, with their gaining of power and authority, international human rights' "scope and remit have become increasingly blurred" and this particularly concerns the problems of striking a proper balance between human rights and sovereignty, as well as determining justificatory grounds for so-called humanitarian intervention.[17] Especially after NATO's intervention in Kosovo, it is apparent that these grounds are searched for in the sphere of political morality (*e.g.* 'supreme humanitarian emergency')[18] rather than in the sphere of established international legal rules. In the eyes of many legal scholars, this

---

13 Koskenniemi refers in particular to the case *Belilos v. Switzerland*, 29 April 1988, Series A, Vol. 132, § 50, as a formal challenge to general treaty law in the treatment of reservations. M. Koskenniemi, *Constitutionalism, Managerialism and the Ethos of Legal Education*, 1 European Journal of Legal Studies 1, at 6 (2007). *Cf.* M. T. Kamminga & M. Scheinin (Eds.), The Impact of Human Rights Law on General International Law (2009), in particular chapters 2, 3 and 4.

14 *See* Popović's contribution to this volume on the 'autonomous legal concepts' of the ECHR.

15 D. Kinley, *Human Rights Fundamentalisms*, 29 Sydney Law Review 545, at 547 (2007).

16 M. Koskenniemi & P. Leino, *Fragmentation of International Law? Postmodern Anxieties*, 15 Leiden Journal of International Law 553, at 570 (2002).

17 Ignatieff, *supra* note 3, at 17. An international panel of experts have proposed to use the new phrase 'responsibility to protect', instead of the common one – 'humanitarian intervention', because the latter phrase "necessarily focuses attention on the claims, rights and prerogatives of the potentially intervening states much more so than on the urgent needs of the potential beneficiaries of the action." International Commission on Intervention and State Sovereignty, The Responsibility to Protect 16 (2001).

18 This term was first coined by Nicholas J. Wheeler in his book Saving Strangers: Humanitarian Intervention in International Society (2000).

course of action not only violates the international rule of law,[19] but, as pointed out by Chinkin, "selectivity (also) undermines moral authority." She notes:

> The commitment to human rights that humanitarian intervention supposedly entails does not mean equality of rights worldwide. The human rights of some people are more worth protecting than those of others. Military intervention on behalf of the victims of human rights abuses has not occurred in, inter alia, Sudan, Afghanistan or Ethiopia. It was woefully inadequate and delayed in Rwanda.[20]

Those who are at the forefront of worldwide human rights activism are domestic and international NGOs, as well as various specialized international organizations. As noticed by Ignatieff, they are often inclined to portray their activism "as an antipolitics, in defense of universal moral claims designed to delegitimize 'political' (i.e. ideological or sectarian) justification for the abuse of human rights." Yet, what actually happens in practice is that

> impartiality and neutrality are just as impossible as a universal and equal concern for everyone's human rights. Human rights activism means taking sides, mobilizing constituencies powerful enough to force abusers to stop.

Consequently, "human rights activism is bound to be partial and political."[21] This would not be an insurmountable obstacle as such, if human rights activists, in particular those engaged in places other than their own, were to take their role with due responsibility. Unfortunately, this is at times not the case. Recall, for instance, recent live coverage on CNN of a representative from a prominent international human rights NGO who visited one heavily bombed Palestinian location – supposedly a strongpoint of Hammas – that had dozens of civilian casualties. When asked for a comment, she firmly responded that, though she had not spent much time in the area, the case in point was *prima facie* for war crimes. Such hasty and negligent proclamations, instead of thorough fact finding,[22] are what make many commentators point to the problem of accountability of NGOs' activities. Not only are they themselves not parties to international human rights treaties,[23] but they are also composed of small groups of people, "their management as well as the articulation of their concerns are generally in the hands of a tiny elite." As a result, "no

---

[19] *See* Brownlie's contribution to this volume concerning the politics of human rights in relation to the international rule of law.

[20] C. M. Chinkin, *Kosovo: A 'Good' or 'Bad' War?*, 93 The American Journal of International Law 841, at 847 (1999).

[21] Ignatieff, *supra* note 3, at 9.

[22] On the importance of fact funding as the necessary precondition for an independent judiciary, which is the best guardian of human rights, *see* Fleiner's contribution to this volume.

[23] As Gardbaum says, it is "surely a significant limitation" to the constitutionalist paradigm of international law. Gardbaum, *supra* note 11, at 763.

accountability exists towards the public at large, and even accountability towards the membership is sometimes poorly organized."[24]

Another source of potential crisis to human rights today concerns its claim to universality.[25] As put by Ignatieff: "Human rights doctrine is now so powerful, but also so unthinkingly imperialist in its claim to universality, that it has exposed itself to serious intellectual attack."[26] Although the main body of criticism comes from Islam and East Asia and to a lesser degree from the West itself,[27] serious challenges to the universality of the concept could be found in other parts of the world as well. One should distinguish though between the two types of criticism. Whereas in the first set of cases the very foundation of the human rights doctrine is taken into question for its Western, individualistic origin,[28] in a number of other places the claim to universality is frequently seen as a convenient ideological tool for promoting the particular political interests of Western countries in those parts of the world.[29]

Concerns about a Westernized reading of the content of the "universal human rights" concept was expressed as early as in 1947, when the American Anthropological Association submitted a notice of apprehension to the UN Commission on Human Rights, stressing that "the rights of man in the Twentieth Century cannot be circumscribed by the standards of any single culture or be dictated by the aspirations of any single people."[30] In a less stringent form, this message was reiterated in the 1999 *Declaration on Anthropology and Human Rights* in which this organization stated that its approach to anthropological principles of respect for concrete human differences "reflects a commitment to human rights consistent with international principles but not

---

[24] C. Tomuschat, Human Rights – Between Idealism and Realism 283 (2008).

[25] *See* An-na'im's contribution to this volume concerning the paradox of universality of human rights.

[26] Ignatieff, *supra* note 3, at 58.

[27] One of the most influential challenges is offered in A. Pollis & P. Schwab, *Human Rights: A Western Construct With Limited Applicability*, *in* A. Pollis & P. Schwab (Eds.), Human Rights: Cultural and Ideological Perspectives 1 (1979).

[28] For an Islamic challenge of this sort, *see, e.g.* S. A. Aldeeb Abu-Sahlieh, *Muslims and Human Rights: Challenges and Perspectives*, *in* W. Schmale (Ed.), Human Rights and Cultural Diversity 239 (1993). For an Asian challenge of this sort, *see, e.g.* O. Yasuaki, *In Quest of Intercivilzational Human Rights: 'Universal' vs. 'Relative' – Human Rights Viewed From an Asian Perspective*, 1 Asia Pacific Journal on Human Rights and the Law 53 (2000). Both articles, nevertheless, tend also to highlight the hypocritical nature of Western policies, which use discourse of human rights, even though they are often in plain contradiction with the very principles they allegedly promote.

[29] This is very often the case in Southeastern European societies. *See, generally* M. A. Jovanović, *On Obstacles to Building a Culture of Human Rights in the South East Europe Region*, 9 Human Rights Tribune 11 (2003).

[30] The Executive Board, American Anthropological Association, *Statement on Human Rights*, 49 American Anthropologist 539, at 543 (1947).

limited by them."[31] The Declaration, thus, urged for the active involvement of anthropologists in the ongoing debate about the foundations of human rights. This debate engages not only human rights specialists, but scholars of general international law, political theorists and philosophers as well.[32]

All aforementioned considered, it seems that it would not be an exaggeration to state that the agenda of human rights – both political and legal – is currently in a state of flux, if not in a full-fledge crisis. Since the adoption of the Universal Declaration, we have been witnessing the juridical, advocacy and enforcement revolutions around the globe that have induced the emergence of a global human rights culture.[33] However, as with all successfully completed revolutions, it is time for human rights devotees of all sorts to abandon exaltation, triumphant rhetoric and self-complacency and to engage in a sober and critical self-reflection of what has been done, what is being done and, in particular, what has yet to be done. At the beginning of this millennium, human dignity is constantly brutally trampled on in all different corners of the world,[34] and human rights in general are faced with serious challenges, the global war on terrorism being only the most frequently mentioned one.[35] In addition to providing a coherent and viable response to this challenge,[36] and to some of the previously mentioned, equally important tasks for human rights scholars concern defining the boundaries of their discipline, as well as the

[31] Committee for Human Rights, American Anthropological Association, *Declaration on Anthropology and Human Rights (1999)*, *in* M. Goodale (Ed.), Human Rights – An Anthropological Reader 101, at 102 (2009).

[32] *See, e.g.* a recent debate, inspired by Jack Donnelly's article *The Relative Universality of Human Rights*, 29 Human Rights Quarterly 281 (2007). It was followed by Michael Goodhart's comment *Neither Relative nor Universal: A Response to Donnelly*, 30 Human Rights Quarterly 183 (2008) and Donnelly's response *Human Rights: Both Universal and Relative (A Reply to Michael Goodhart)*, 30 *Human Rights Quarterly* 194 (2008). For an intriguing philosophical exposition of this problem, *see, e.g.* W. J. Talbott, Which Rights Should Be Universal? (2005).

[33] Ignatieff, *supra* note 3, at 5 *et seq. See* Hasanbegovic's contribution to this volume on the topic of human rights culture.

[34] For instance, at the moment of the writing of this text, the Afghan Supreme Court has confirmed a 20 years imprisonment sentence to a 23-year-old Afghan journalism student, Sayed Perves Kambaksh. He was initially sentenced to death by a local Islamic court just for distributing a critique of those who misinterpret the Koran to justify the oppression of women. No wonder, thus, that on Human Rights Day 2007, the UN Secretary General launched a year-long UN system-wide advocacy campaign, on the occasion of the celebration of the 60th anniversary of the Universal Declaration, with the official motto "Dignity and Justice for All of Us". *See* Botha's contribution to this volume on human dignity as a contested constitutional value.

[35] *See* Barak-Erez's contribution to this volume, discussing what is new in the otherwise well-known challenge of terrorism.

[36] For a genuine human rights activist's approach to this challenge, *see* the speech of the executive director of Human Rights Watch, K. Roth, *Human Rights as a Response to Terrorism*, 6 Oregon Review of International Law 37 (2004). His emphasis is on the former Bush's administration policies in this area.

scope of human rights law application. Hence, what they have to address is, *inter alia*: the relationship between human rights law and humanitarian law;[37] the status of minority rights law, especially the potential conflicts between minority collective rights and individual rights;[38] since states are increasingly acting outside their borders, do their human rights obligations follow them, that is, should human rights treaties be applied extraterritorially and, if so, to what extent (for example, should a state be held responsible for human rights violations by corporations acting outside that state's territory);[39] can the official doctrine of the United Nations, supported both by the General Assembly and by the Office of the High Commissioner for Human Rights on the interdependence and indivisibility of human rights be theoretically and empirically grounded, or is it just "high flown political rhetoric without much content";[40] is it possible, and desirable, for the global monitoring bodies, such as the UN High Commissioner for Human Rights, to design a system of prioritizing human rights violations around the globe,[41] and so on.

* * *

This collection of papers comes as a result of the conference *Universal Declaration – 60 Years After*, which was convened at the Faculty of Law, University of Belgrade, on 22-23 September 2008. It is an attempt to highlight and critically assess some of the aforementioned issues by a distinguished group of academics, researchers and practitioners. The book is divided into three parts. The first one addresses some more general issues of human rights theory and practice, such as the relation of human rights politics and the international rule of law, human rights' claim to universality, the constitutionalization of international law through human rights instruments, as well as problems of human rights culture and/or ideology. The second part deals both with the role of domestic and international courts for the effective protection of human rights and the specific techniques of implementation of human rights law

[37] Orakhelashvili, for instance, argues that humanitarian law cannot function completely as *lex specialis* to human rights law. A. Orakhelashvili, *The Interaction Between Human Rights and Humanitarian Law: Fragmentation, Conflict, Parallelism or Convergence?*, 19 European Journal of International Law 161 (2008). *Cf.* Hartwig's contribution to this volume on human rights in times of war.

[38] *See* Thornberry's contribution to this volume on the problem of the range of persons and communities entitled to protection under the Convention on the Elimination of All Forms of Racial Discrimination.

[39] *See* the panel discussion – *The Extraterritorial Application of Human Rights*, 100 ASIL Proceedings 85 (2006).

[40] J. W. Nickel, *Rethinking Indivisibility: Towards A Theory of Supporting Relations Between Human Rights*, 30 Human Rights Quarterly 984, at 985 (2008).

[41] *See, e.g.* a blueprint for such a system in F. Ni Aoláin, *Looking Ahead: Strategic Priorities and Challenges for the United Nations High Commissioner for Human Rights*, 35 Columbia Human Rights Law Review 469 (2004).

by certain international tribunals. The third part of the book is dedicated to certain developments in this field, such as the growing importance of various forms of minority protection for the general body of human rights norms, as well as with the role that human dignity as a prime constitutional value plays in certain legal systems. Finally, this part also addresses the currently widely debated challenges for human rights law – its status in times of war and in the global fight against terrorism.

In the first essay, Brownlie argues that in the context of international relations as they stand today in relation to the proliferation of human rights instruments and the erosion of the reserved domain of domestic jurisdiction, human rights are used as a tool for hegemonial intervention and the promotion of unequal relations between states, instead of further implementation of the international rule of law. He identifies background elements which are conducive to the abuses and inequalities in the application of the law: the political atmosphere and orthodoxy, the non-effective and non-objective fact finding which leads to the manipulation of key facts, the proliferation of forms of international criminal jurisdiction, and strong political opportunism controlling the human rights milieu. Brownlie further presents some examples where double standards in relation to human rights and humanitarian law were present, such as the cases of Darfur, the Balkans, or the conflict between Ethiopia and Eritrea. He concludes that although the abuse of power is not a new problem, the scale of the abuse has changed. Therefore, the only way for a genuine promotion of human rights is through their further implementation and adherence to the international rule of law.

One important element of possible political manipulation with the content and meaning of human rights law comes with its claim to universality. An-Na'im discusses what he calls "the paradox of universality of human rights", keeping in mind permanent and profound cultural differences that exist among human societies. He argues that to prevent future human rights violations and to make them work effectively, it is necessary to integrate human rights into the culture of all peoples around the world. In other words, the concept of universality of human rights requires the effective participation of all human beings in defining and protecting human rights norms. However, the remaining question is how to achieve universal acceptance in our diverse world? An-Na'im proposes to mediate this paradox in promoting an 'overlapping consensus' among different cultural traditions through both an internal discourse within cultures and a cross-cultural dialogue. This process has already begun with the Universal Declaration, and today is built on existing international human rights treaties and institutions which must be susceptible to further developments and evolution. It is also necessary to deemphasize the dichotomy between internal and external influences. This would imply that human rights advocates must act with sensitivity and respect for the integrity of other cultures, to apply the same standards in all situations and to avoid a "double standard" policy. He concludes that the universality of human rights and their cultural dimension can be compatible and mutually supportive, but it depends on how different actors perceive the matter and respond to them in particular situations. Therefore, the universality of human rights is not a 'given' concept, but rather a '*product of a process*' which depends mainly on the nature of said process, the role of the actors, context, and other conditions.

The third essay provides an analytical perspective into the plausibility of the use of constitutional interpretation in fragmented international law. Van Aeken argues that human rights issues are pervasive in international law, despite the fact that only a few specialized adjudicatory mechanisms exist. She notices that many regimes in Public International Law pursue different goals, but many cases cannot be easily classified into these different regimes. The horizontal function of international human rights system is to provide guidelines to international courts in interpreting non-human rights law. If the object and purpose of one treaty contains human rights, it may be used in a teleological interpretation of the treaty itself, but the problem is that most non-human rights treaties do not contain such a reference. Furthermore, Article 31 (3) (c) of the Vienna Convention on the Law of Treaties, under which an interpretation should take into account "*any relevant rules of international law applicable in the relations between the parties*," is perceived as a general principle of treaty interpretation. However, it provides only an answer of what other international legal instruments can be taken into account when the interpretation of a non-human rights treaty is at stake. She, therefore, argues that the unity of the international legal order can be achieved through constitutional interpretational means, in particular the balancing approach as it is developed in German legal theory, in order to mitigate the tension between human rights law and other issues of Public International Law.

Treating human rights as one important principle and value in a constitutionalized international order would certainly require developing an underlying and supporting culture of human rights. In her essay, Hasanbegović explains why it is difficult to differentiate human rights culture and human rights ideology, as well as human rights rhetoric and human rights reality. She argues that human rights culture must be approached differently than the ideal meaning of civic legal culture. To discover whether one legal order belongs to the civic or to the submissive legal culture, one must explore whether and to what extent the realization of at least minimum standards set up in the Universal Declaration exists. On the other hand, a nuanced approach to different legal cultures includes both an analysis of the factual state of affairs and normative solutions, as well as the influence of political, religious and legal tradition. She believes that the investigation of the factual state of affairs is important because human rights culture today encompasses a minority rights culture too. However, the problem, especially in former real-socialist states, is that even well-crafted normative legal framework is often a product of a pragmatic program of the predominant political elite, rather than an expression of a genuine need of society as a whole. Accordingly, human rights implementation is slow because elites in transitional countries cannot openly refuse to accept values of modern democracy, and yet they are not truly dedicated to those values. Consequently, she argues that the state of affairs in transitional countries can be at best described as 'unfounded normative optimism', since legal norms are not embedded in an adequate human rights culture.

One of the reasons for the aforementioned problems in transitional countries of Eastern Europe concerns the situations in their judiciary and judicial systems in general. The second part of this book starts with Fleiner's paper on the importance of the independence of the judiciary. He argues that even the best catalogue of human rights cannot guarantee justice if the remedies for human rights violations are limited. In this respect, he emphasizes that all international instruments providing for the basic elements of the rule of law give a clear priority to the principle of independent, impartial and competent courts provided by law. The essential elements of the independence of the judiciary include: the procedure of procedure, the institutional organization of the court, the procedure for the election of judges, the protection and guarantee of judges' independence, their competences and their capacities. This essay covers all those elements, and highlights that courts must guarantee political independence and impartiality; they must be prescribed by law and accessible to every individual; procedures must be credible, and the courts must have the power to implement judgments. These guarantees are particularly endangered in the currently waged war on terrorism, as it is often forgotten that law can provide security only if it is predictable. Finally, Fleiner stresses that the independence of the judiciary depends on the legal education and legal culture of one country. In this regard, he provides an overview of different legal cultures and their distinctive approaches to the power and independence of the judiciary.

As indicated previously, the institutional independence of the European Court of Human Rights is partly illustrated by the so-called 'autonomous concepts' developed in the Court's jurisprudence. Popović tries to define and to explore the main features of these autonomous concepts. Although he notices that it is hard to provide a coherent definition, because a proper approach by legal theory is lacking, he proposes to treat them as terms applied by the ECtHR, which exist in national legal systems of Contracting Parties to the European Convention on Human Rights, but they are to be given special meaning in the Court's jurisprudence. Sometimes, the meaning of these concepts as determined by the Court may differ from almost the universally accepted meaning of legal notions, such as that of *law*, or they can lack support of comparative law, such is the case with the concept of *civil rights and obligations*. The author further explains that autonomous concepts are susceptible to evolution, which means that those being currently in use might be quite opposite to the old ones. Therefore, Popović concludes that a practitioner who deals with jurisprudence of the ECtHR must be aware of the fact that such concepts are typical products of a judge-made law. Moreover, bearing in mind that the ECHR is currently a part of the national law of its member states, national judges and practitioners must be prepared to handle these concepts. To achieve this goal, it is necessary to provide systematic and early legal training and studies on this matter.

The subsequent paper deals with the law and practice of the International Criminal Tribunal for the former Yugoslavia from a human rights' perspective. In particular, Gajić tries to clarify methods by which the Tribunal has sought to protect human rights of parties in the proceedings. In this respect, he criticizes the *Tadic* decision where the Trial Chamber held that it was not bound by universal human rights principles due to its unique structure and the nature of the subject matter it dealt with. In his further analysis of the question of whether the ICTY's jurisprudence is in line with human rights standards, the author explores three sets of questions. First, he investigates certain substantive law issues, in order to determine whether the ICTY is involved in so-called "progressive" development, or this body merely applies the existing rules of International Humanitarian Law. Second, the author explores the equality of the arms principle and concludes that it is one-sided, as there is no real possibility for the accused to properly examine all exculpating and mitigating materials. In addition, the Prosecution is in a much better position in terms of personnel, funds, external support and the obligation of States to cooperate with this body. Third, Gajić argues that, in criminal matters, it is the "beyond a reasonable doubt" standard of proof rather than the "probability standard" that should be preserved. In addition, the standard of the appellate review of uniformity applied by the Appeals Chamber significantly restricts the right of appeal. The author concludes that the ICTY's jurisprudence is, and will be critically evaluated, particularly in attempts to build a solid basis for the imminent jurisprudence of the International Criminal Court.

The third part of the book starts with Thornberry's paper that casts the light on the work of the Committee on the Elimination of Racial Discrimination (CERD), its procedure and the concept of discrimination, focusing primarily on the question of the "victims" of racial discrimination. He attempts to identify the range of persons and communities entitled to bring a communication before the International Convention on the Elimination of all forms of Racial Discrimination. Thornberry argues that challenges faced by CERD are broader than the context of the fight against Apartheid and colonialism that was dominant in 1960s when the Convention emerged. Thus, the Committee practice on victims of racism also includes ethnic and national minorities (with a particular emphasis placed on the Roma), indigenous peoples, caste groups, non-citizens, as well as groups whose identities "intersect" with those identities, such as those based on religion, identity and gender. The identification of groups vulnerable to racism emerged from many contemporary factors, such as economic migration, conflict involving massive displacement, the creation and succession of States, counter-terrorism actions, hate speech, and others. This development was accelerated by developments in relation to the rights of minorities, indigenous peoples, women, and other groups or categories. Thornberry particularly emphasizes that the interpretation of the ICERD has arguably moved beyond the original vision of the drafters, demonstrating that the Convention is a living instrument interpreted in accordance with present-day challenges. However, the problem that still remains is whether the Convention continues to be an instrument 'fit for purpose', which appropriately identifies the victims of racial discrimination, or if it needs to be modified to a certain extent.

One of the obvious present-day challenges to human rights law is their applicability in times of war. This is the topic of Hartwig's contribution. The author argues that human rights norms and humanitarian norms do not exclude each other. In maintaining so, he tries to explicate the applicability of human rights norms in times of war according to the stipulated provisions of human rights treaties. Therefore, Hartwig argues that human rights instruments apply in times of war. He explains his thesis with the fact that these instruments provide for the possibility of derogation of certain human rights in situations of emergency or necessity. Furthermore, the Additional Protocol II to the Geneva Convention recalls in its Preamble that international instruments relating to human rights offer basic protection to individuals. He insists that the logic of human rights guarantees is primarily endangered in emergency situations, and that it would be counterproductive to limit or even eliminate their applicability when they are needed the most. This position is supported by a number of recent judgments which expressly underline the applicability of human rights in times of war. Nevertheless, a particular difficulty in the application of human rights instruments in times of war exists in situations when a State acts under its own jurisdiction beyond its own borders. The author believes that a broader interpretation of jurisdiction is in accordance with the purpose of human rights guarantees. In other words, protection should be granted whenever and wherever a State is acting. This principle also brings the equal treatment of two parties involved in the same armed conflict and fighting in the same territory. Finally, he explains why the generally accepted doctrine of International Humanitarian Law as *lex specialis* to human rights law cannot be upheld, and proposes that, in cases of conflict, the balancing test should be used between military necessity and human rights values. Hartwig concludes his paper with the hope that human rights will prevail over International Humanitarian Law and become a 'gentle civilizer' of States in times of armed conflict.

The next paper deals with another challenge, posed by contemporary terrorism. It investigates international and national initiatives aimed at combating terrorist activities. Barak Erez argues that, from the international perspective, terrorism is considered a threat because it signals that the new world order formed after the World War II is in danger. In this respect, she claims that the Geneva Conventions from 1948 do not represent modern reality and as such are inadequate for current conflicts with terrorist organizations. Also, the Additional Protocol to the Geneva Conventions from 1977 has failed to achieve universal acceptance, especially among those states engaged in terrorist related conflicts. Moreover, many newly adopted conventions on terrorism cover only specific terrorism-related activities and, as such, do not change the basic norms of law applicable in times of armed conflict. At the national level, the specific task concerns balancing human rights with government anti-terrorism actions. However, there is tension between the tradition of punishment based on wrongs that had been carried out, and the need to prevent terrorist attacks. The latter goal opens the room for preventive measures against suspected terrorists, as well as for the introduction of new offences aimed at combating actions considered to contribute to the escalation of terrorism. Barak Erez concludes that there is an urgent need to reconsider the application of both international and national laws, in the light of the new reality, as fundamental human rights would be compromised in any case.

The concluding paper explores the idea of human dignity as a prime constitutional value, concentrating in particular on the case of post-Apartheid South Africa. Botha shows that the Constitutional Court in this country has invoked dignity as a justifiable right, and it has placed dignity at the centre of its constitutional jurisprudence. However, the Court has been criticized not for placing dignity above other values, such as democracy and equality, but rather for claiming that dignity is so open-ended that it could be invoked to justify almost any outcome. In this respect, the author explores five paradoxes which lie at the heart of human dignity. First, human rights demand the absolute commitment to the sphere of personal inviolability, but human dignity is a pervasive value which underlies a variety of rights and cannot escape being subject to balancing. Second, human dignity is inherent to all human beings and transcends cultural differences and national boundaries, but its protection and exact meaning depends on its concretization in a particular legal order. Third, human dignity is inherent to every human being, but it depends on the material conditions and social standing of every person. Forth, dignity demands respect for the cultural and symbolic processes through which every individual becomes a person and makes sense of his or her own world. On the other hand, respect for someone's dignity requires recognition of that person's capacity to transcend the structures of individual socio-economic background and to forge an autonomous identity. Finally, dignity is related to personal autonomy and presupposes the right to freely choose his or her own ends, but respect for dignity requires placing certain limits on freedom particularly in relation to pervasive private power, excessive consumerism and inequality. Botha concludes that despite its paradoxical nature, human dignity can constrain the range of legitimate constitutional interpretations. In this respect, the South African experience provides an interesting case study of the ways in which global legal norms are relied upon, adapted and concretized within a national legal order.

* * *

Christian Tomuschat closes his most recent book *Human Rights – Between Idealism and Realism* with a chapter entitled 'Time for Hope, or Time for Despair?'.[42] As suggested previously, though one may find good reasons to speak of some sort of current crisis of human rights agenda, the situation is certainly far from despair. In fact, this is probably the right time for a new beginning. A human rights program, which was truly born with the adoption of the Universal Declaration on Human Rights, has gone through its phase of adolescence with its numerous ups and downs in the 1960s and the 1970s. After the destruction of a bipolar world, it managed to survive a period of a typical middle-age crisis when, for a moment, it appeared that every goal should and could be achieved and that no barriers existed anymore. Finally, the end of millennium marked a phase of disappointment that came with suddenly rediscovered threats, challenges, and even defeats. At the age of sixty, the maturity of a human rights program should above all reflect in sobriety, consistency and in a sense for what realistic objectives are. It is upon the global community of human rights devotees to make such a program a workable option for future.

42 Tomuschat, *supra* note 24, at 387-389.

Part I

General Issues of Human Rights Theory and Practice

Ian Brownlie

The Politics of Human Rights in Relation to the Rule of Law

First, I must explain the theme of this presentation. In general it is presumed that the Rule of Law and human rights are complementary. In other words, that the development of human rights involves the further implementation of the Rule of Law. However, in the context of international relations as they exist today, the proliferation of human rights instruments, and the erosion of the reserved domain of domestic jurisdiction, have the result that human rights provides a vehicle for hegemonial intervention and the manipulation of political systems within States.

This phenomenon involves human rights having the role of legitimating intervention and promoting unequal relations between states. In these contexts human rights becomes a part of an array of political weapons inimical to the Rule of Law, to the principle of equality of States, and to the practice of genuine democracy.

This political role and the consequent threats to the rule of international law thus constitute my themes. But there is an important proviso. It is not my purpose to suggest that human rights developments tout court are inimical to the Rule of Law. The problem, rather, is the fact that in principle remedial procedures, what in the European Convention is called Just Satisfaction, are neutral and impartial, whereas in the actual conditions of relations between States, some States enjoy a de facto immunity in respect of violations of the law, while others face explicit scrutiny and condemnation, and sanctions.

As I move into my theme it is necessary to record the background elements which are conducive to the appearance of abuses and inequalities in the application of the law.

The first of these background elements is that of political atmosphere and of what is politically fashionable in a given era. A very striking example is the attitude towards the Soviet Union as the World War II was in its final

Miodrag Jovanović & Ivana Krstić (Eds.), Human Rights Today – 60 Years of the Universal Declaration, 21-27.

phase, in the years 1944 and 1945. The Soviet armed forces played a major role in the defeat of the Axis powers. My generation were used to hearing Stalin's Orders of the Day read out on the BBC news. And so in that era there were few references to violations of human rights within the Soviet system. The famous author, George Orwell, found it difficult to get his book Animal Farm published in Britain and the United States. This was because it was assumed to be anti-Soviet. This is a striking case of political orthodoxy. And it must be remembered that the purges of oppositionists and other groups in the period 1936 to 1938 were well-known at this period. Indeed, there was even a locution used in Russian to refer to the phenomenon – the Yezhovschina.

The second of these background elements concerns the determination of critical issues of fact. This element has been especially prominent in the last ten years or so. It is very obvious that in the absence of an effective and objective finding of facts, the abusive application of the law is facilitated. Whilst there are many modern examples of the manipulation of key facts, two recent cases stand out. The first of these is the Kosovo crisis. The situation in Kosovo in 1998 was reported to the Security Council as constituting an humanitarian catastrophe. The NATO states responded in the first place by ordering withdrawal of the 1400 monitors of the Kosovo Verification Mission.

On 19 March 1999 the Chairman of the OSCE wrote to President Milosevic as follows:

> I have today decided to withdraw the OSCE mission (the Kosovo Verification Mission) from Kosovo for the time being. The situation for the unarmed OSCE verifiers has gradually deteriorated and conditions have made it increasingly difficult for the Mission to carry out its tasks.
>
> The OSCE Mission has made an important contribution to stability in Kosovo, and it is with sadness that I have to withdraw the Mission. As OSCE Chairman-in-Office, responsible for the safety of approximately 1400 verifiers from many different countries, I do, however, have no other choice in the present situation.

Five days later NATO began a bombing campaign which covered all of Yugoslavia and included the bridges over the Danube. This extensive use of force was explained by the British representative in the Security Council in these words:

> Mr President,
>
> The action being taken is legal. It is justified as an exceptional measure to prevent an overwhelming humanitarian catastrophe. Under present circumstances in Kosovo there is convincing evidence that such a catastrophe is imminent. Renewed acts of repression by the authorities of the Federal Republic of Yugoslavia would cause further loss of civilian life and would lead to displacement of the civilian population on a large scale and in hostile conditions.
>
> Every means short of force has been tried to avert this situation. In these circumstances, and as an exceptional measure on grounds of overwhelming

> humanitarian necessity, military intervention is legally justifiable. The force now proposed is directed exclusively to averting a humanitarian catastrophe, and is the minimum judged necessary for that purpose.

And so NATO claims that a humanitarian catastrophe exists whilst NATO's associates in the OSCE withdraw 1400 human rights monitors. The facts which emerged subsequently indicate that the real purpose of the bombing campaign was political coercion and regime change. There is also the question of proportionality. Because, if the purpose was to protect human rights, why was it necessary to destroy infrastructure? And why was it necessary to fly 38,000 sorties with NATO bombers?

The second case of manipulation of facts involves the allegation that Iraq possessed weapons of mass destruction. The assertion of non-compliance with disarmament obligations was in fact the exclusive basis of the invasion according to the UK letter to the President of the Security Council on 21 March 2003. In the words of the letter:

> The objective of the action is to secure compliance by Iraq with its disarmament obligations as laid down by the Council. All military action will be limited to the minimum measures necessary to secure this objective. Operations will be conducted in accordance with the international laws of armed conflict. Targets have been carefully chosen to avoid civilian casualties.

It is now reasonably clear that the intelligence data placed before the Security Council had been manipulated and, of course, no weapons of mass destruction were found after the occupation of Iraq.

The third background element consists of the proliferation of forms of international criminal jurisdiction. This process has several aspects. First, the creation of special criminal courts by the Security Council, including the International Tribunal for the Former Yugoslavia and, secondly, the appearance of the Rome Statute of the ICC. Related factors are the reduction of the immunity of heads of state, heads of government, and other ministers, and the blurring of the lines between international criminal law and human rights as such.

The apogee of these developments is the promotion of the criminality of the State as such and the association of the new criminal law with regime change. The treatment of the Balkans by the NATO states combined all these elements. The bombing of Yugoslavia had little to do with humanitarian intervention and much to do with the purpose of regime change proclaimed publicly by Madam Albright.

The last of the background elements which are conducive to the appearance of inequalities is the strong political opportunism controlling the human rights milieu. There are, of course, many examples, and two cases will be sufficient.

The first case relates to the appearance of the UN Charter in 1945. Whilst human rights principles feature in the Charter provisions, they are balanced against the concept of domestic jurisdiction. Moreover, in the practice of member states support for human rights was somewhat qualified. The colonial powers were slow to relate individual rights to the rights of national groups to equal status and self-government. Nonetheless, by the years 1960 to 1966 there was an inevitable flood of decolonisation.

At this stage the colonial powers had become relatively free of pressure from United Nations committees and it was realised that human rights principles were of considerable value in the cold war with the Soviet bloc. There then appeared a process of normative creativity. There was pressure to move on from the normatively weak Universal Declaration to the Covenants on Human Rights of 1966; that is to binding standard-setting multilateral treaties.

But the most striking development was the beginning of the process of negotiation leading to the adoption of the Helsinki Final Act in 1975. The subject-matter of the Final Act was the question of Security and Co-operation in Europe but the instrument included significant sections on respect for human rights and fundamental freedoms.

Thirty-five states subscribed to the Final Act, including the United States and the Soviet Union. In various official statements it was emphasised that the Final Act was not legally binding.

Thus on 18 July 1975, the Journal No. 80/bis of the Coordinating Committee of the CSCE reported the intention of the government of Finland, as depositary of the Final Act, to send a letter to the Secretary-General of the United Nations, reading in part as follows:

> I have [...] been asked to request you, Mr Secretary-General, to arrange for the circulation of this final Act to Member States of the Organization as an official document of the United Nations, and to draw your attention to the fact that this Final Act is not eligible, in whole or in part, for registration with the Secretariat under Article 102 of the Charter of the United Nations, as would be the case were it a matter of a treaty or international agreement, under the aforesaid Article.[1]

This emphasis on the non-binding character of the Final Act made the instrument acceptable to the Soviet Union. In its historical context the Final Act was the equivalent of the Security Treaty which Soviet diplomacy had failed to obtain. Moreover, Soviet international law advisers had not realised that certain sections of the Helsinki Final Act were declaratory in effect.

In the Nicaragua Case, in the decision on the Merits, the International Court took the Final Act into account in evaluating the obligations of the United States.

Thus, the Court observed:

> Also significant is United States acceptance of the principle of the prohibition of the use of force which is contained in the declaration on principles governing the mutual relations of States participating in the Conference on Security and Co-

[1] Digest of US Practice (1975), at 325-327.

> operation in Europe (Helsinki, 1 August 1975), whereby the participating States undertake to 'refrain in their mutual relations, *as well as in their international relations in general*' from the threat or use of force. Acceptance of a text in these terms confirms the existence of an *opinio juris* of the participating States prohibiting the use of force in international relations.

This is a reference to the section of the Final Act on 'Principles Guiding Relations Between Participating States'. The same section included separate headings including the following: VII *Respect for human rights and fundamental freedoms, including the freedom of thought, conscience, religion or belief.*

Of equal importance is the next section of the Final Act entitled: VIII *Equal Rights and Self-Determination of Peoples*:

> The participating States will respect the equal rights of peoples and their right to self-determination, acting at all times in conformity with the purposes and principles of the Charter of the United Nations and with the relevant norms of international law, including those relating to territorial integrity of States.

Thus the principles contained in the Final Act in practice carried more legal weight than was expected by either the United States or the former Soviet Union. And it is probable that the Final Act had a significant role in the ideological war between the Soviet bloc and the NATO states.

I have now reached the stage in this presentation when I can present a series of examples of palpable double standards in relation to human rights and the humanitarian law of armed conflict.

It is useful to start with a very recent case. The insurgency in Darfur has had close attention from the media. Both the media and western Governments have delivered verdicts on the alleged responsibility of the Sudanese Government for human rights violations committed in the course of the civil war, and the ICC Prosecutor has become involved. In parallel with the Darfur crisis the Philippines armed forces have been carrying out major operations against Islamic insurgents in a particular region of Mindanao. Civilians have been badly affected and 300,000 refugees have moved out of the region. The events in the Philippines have not attracted any notice either from Governments, or the Security Council, or the media, or the ICC Prosecutor.

The cynic would be likely to say that humanitarian catastrophes, even when detected, attract very diverse political and legal responses. In the Balkans such situations were used to generate regime change, secessions of parts of Yugoslavia, and criminal trials. The President of Yugoslavia was indicted by a Tribunal created by the Security Council.

With this deluge of legalism and selective criminal process we can compare the outcome of the major conflict between Ethiopia and Eritrea in the 1990s. With the assistance of diplomats from the OAU and the United States the conflict was wound up with a series of fairly complex agreements.

First, there was the Agreement on Cessation of Hostilities of 18 June 2000. In this Agreement the Parties reaffirmed their acceptance of the OAU Framework Agreement of 1999.

Secondly, the Parties concluded a Peace Agreement dated 12 December 2000.[2]

This Agreement established a Boundary Commission and a Claims Commission. For present purposes the Claims Commission is of special interest. Article 5 of the Agreement defines its purposes as follows:

> Consistent with the Framework Agreement, in which the parties commit themselves to addressing the negative socio-economic impact of the crisis on the civilian population, including the impact on those persons who have been deported, a neutral Claims Commission shall be established. The mandate of the Commission is to decide through binding arbitration all claims for loss, damage or injury by one Government against the other, and by nationals (including both natural and juridical persons) of one party against the government of the other party or entities owned or controlled by the other party that are (a) related to the conflict that was the subject of the Framework Agreement, the Modalities for its Implementation and the Cessation of Hostilities Agreement, and (b) result from violations of international humanitarian law, including the 1949 Geneva Conventions, or other violations of international law. The Commission shall not hear claims arising from the cost of military operations, preparing for military operations, or the use of force, except to the extent that such claims involve violations of international humanitarian law.

It is obvious that the claims procedure provides redress for violations of human rights and of humanitarian law. But there is no provision for criminal justice and the claims jurisdiction is precisely based upon claims made. The aim is to address the socio-economic impact of the crisis on the civilian populations.

And, in sharp contrast to the situation in the Balkans, the arrangements were not made under the authority of the Security Council. No state was held to be responsible to any system of criminal justice. No punitive embargoes were applied. No leaders were to be tried.

The arrangements for redress in relation to the conflict between Ethiopia and Eritrea were based on the principles of equality and neutrality. The system created was one of obligation. In some other instances, however, these qualities were absent and opportunities for redress were minimal or lacking.

The approach of the Security Council to the civil strife in Yugoslavia from 1991 onward did not show much adherence to the principles of equality and neutrality. The overall political settlement was the result of coercion. Compromises accepted by the Serbian leadership received neither recognition nor reward. The appalling events in the Krajina in 1995, and acts of intervention by Croatia in Bosnia, did not attract condemnation in Security Council resolutions. One-sided resolutions concerning the civil conflict in

2 ILM (2001), at 260.

Yugoslavia were related to human rights issues, but the political aim of the resolutions was to assist in the plans of Mr Izetbegovic and Mr Tudjman.

Moreover, the pattern of prosecutions before the ICTY has shown unfortunate elements of partiality.

The general performance of United Nations organs in the context of the Balkan crisis was not based upon rule of law principles but upon political favouritism and the use of force. Human rights considerations were used as propaganda. Everyone knows about Srebrenica in a general way but few people know about the role of the 28th Bosnian regiment and the policies of the Muslim leader Naser Oric.

I have now completed this depressing list of examples of double standards in relation to human rights, that is situations in which human rights are invoked as a vehicle for policies inimical to the Rule of Law.

In coming to the close of this presentation, I am not able to offer any ready-made solutions. The abuse of power and the manipulation of evidence are old problems. It is only the scale of the abuse which has changed. The promotion of human rights must involve adherence to the Rule of Law.

Abdullahi Ahmed An-Na'im

Universality of Human Rights: Mediating Paradox to Enhance Practice

1. Introduction

For the purposes of theoretical analysis, the challenges facing the universality of human rights can be seen as conceptual and political. The first set of challenges relates to the theoretical viability of the idea of universal human rights norms in view of the realities of permanent and profound cultural difference among human societies. The basic questions here include: what does universality mean, on whose terms, and how to articulate specific standards? This is what I call the paradox of universality. Political challenges relate to possibilities of consistent and principled application of human rights standards in view of the realities of power relations within and among societies: how to generate and sustain the political will and necessary resources for systematic implementation of human rights norms? This political challenge can be called the paradox of self-regulation by the state, namely, how can states be expected to protect human rights against themselves? In this paper, I will argue that addressing the first set of challenges is in fact necessary for addressing the second. In other words, mediating the paradox of universality will in fact redress the paradox of self-regulation by the state. In particular, I will argue that enhancing the cultural legitimacy of human rights within various societies is necessary for generating the political will to implement these norms.

The role of culture I am discussing here is relevant to all human rights norms, and not limited to specific issues that are often associated with claims of cultural relativism, like female genital cuttings or so-called 'honor killings'. These issues are often cast in terms of a confrontation between chauvinistic assertions of Western perceptions of rights as the established norm of universality of human rights to which all societies have to conform, and non-Western resistance to cultural imperialism. Instead of pursing this

Miodrag Jovanović & Ivana Krstić (Eds.), Human Rights Today – 60 Years of the Universal Declaration, 29-50.

simplistic and unproductive confrontation between 'the West' and 'the Rest', I will attempt to reframe the issue in terms of mediation of paradox in order to enhance the prospects of implementation of human rights norms throughout the world. The proposed mediation, I will argue, is helpful in addressing the underlying concerns of both sides of that confrontation. This approach is necessary, I suggest, in dealing with all human rights issues, whether their association with culture is commonly acknowledged, like female genital cuttings and honor killings, or not so apparent, like the scope of freedom of expression and liberal relativism regarding economic, social and cultural rights, as I will illustrate later.

My working definition of culture is that of the UNESCO Universal Declaration on Cultural Diversity of 2001 (UDCD), namely, that

> culture should be regarded as the set of distinctive spiritual, material, intellectual and emotional features of society or a social group, and that it encompasses, in addition to art and literature, *lifestyles, ways of living together, value systems, traditions and beliefs* (emphasis added).

As the emphasized phrase clearly shows, it is simply not possible to conceive of human rights or expect those norms to command respect and compliance in any society without taking the culture of that society into account. At the same time, I am also in agreement with Article 4 of UDCD, that "[n]o one may invoke cultural diversity to infringe upon human rights guaranteed by international law, nor to limit their scope."

The question then is how to take culture seriously without allowing it to be manipulated to justify or rationalize human rights violations? This is a difficult task because the ruling and other elites who make this claim do so because they find it appealing to their constituencies. We must therefore understand the rationale of that appeal and have an effective response to it if we are to expect the binding authority of human rights to be taken seriously by the people concerned. In terms of the above-quoted UDCD definition of culture, human rights are unlikely to work effectively until they are integrated into the "lifestyles, ways of living together, value systems traditions and beliefs" of all peoples around the world. But that should not mean conceding whatever elites claim in the name of culture because, as I will discuss later, all cultures are dynamics and constantly evolving in response to both external and internal factors and influences.

The premise of my analysis is that the legitimacy of human rights in various cultural traditions is necessary for both the theoretical universality and practical efficacy of these international norms. People must believe the concept of human rights and its normative content to be valid from their own cultural perspective if they are to struggle for the practical implementation of these rights. This view is in fact required by the principle of universality itself; namely, that people cannot be bound by norms they do not freely accept. Respect for the human dignity and collective self-determination as foundations for the concept of universal human rights require the effective participation of all human beings in defining and protecting human rights norms. What I call the paradox of universality is how can universal acceptance be achieved in a world of permanent and profound cultural diversity among and within human societies? As I have argued and tried with colleagues to demonstrate in detail for many years, this paradox can be mediated through the promotion of an 'overlapping consensus' among different cultural traditions through internal discourse within cultures, and cross-cultural dialogue about what is due to human beings by virtue of their humanity.[1]

By overlapping consensus I mean agreement on human rights principles despite our disagreement as to why each of us comes to this common ground. In practice, the process of promoting this necessary overlapping consensus should begin with the UDHR, and build on existing human rights treaties and institutions at the global and regional level. But that should not mean taking any conception or norms as final and conclusive to the exclusion of possibilities of further development and evolution out of the experiences and priorities of peoples in all parts of the world. The Charter of the United Nations initiated the modern human rights paradigm, but it did not eliminate the consequences of colonialism and hegemony of Western powers over the peoples of Africa, Asia and Latin America. With its emphasis on formal sovereignty and territorial integrity, the UN Charter could neither by itself achieve those broader objectives for various countries, nor secure internal self-determination for marginalized communities within national boundaries. When colonized peoples were eventually able to participate in the human rights process as a result of decolonization and subsequent developments, they had to do that on the basis of the assumptions and framework that were already established by Western powers. This is not to deny or underestimate the value of the contributions of the peoples of developing countries to making the UDHR more truly universal now than it was in 1948. On the contrary, my objective is to affirm the value of those developments and build on them to further enhance the effective participation of all peoples in the definition and implementation of human rights.

For this multifaceted participation to be productive, culture must be understood to be dynamic, contestable and constantly evolving in response to internal and external factors and actors. It is critically important, however, that such internal transformation of each culture should be sought through its own frame of reference and institutional resources. In other words, cultures are constantly changing in response to a variety of challenges, but that

1 *See, e.g.*, A. A. An-Na'im (Ed.), Human Rights in Cross-Cultural Perspective: A Quest for Consensus (1992); A. A. An-Na'im (Ed.), Cultural Transformation and Human Rights in Africa (2002); and A. A. An-Na'im (Ed.), Human Rights Under African Constitutions: Realizing the Promise for Ourselves (2003); and *'Area Expressions' and the Universality of Human Rights: Mediating a Contingent Relationship*, *in* D. P. Forsythe & P. C. McMahon (Eds.), Diversity and Human Rights 1 (2003).

happens internally within the culture, and not through external imposition. This approach also rejects the claims of local elites to monopolize cultural authority within their communities because the same principles of human dignity and self-determination that oppose external hegemony also reject internal domination. These processes of transformation operate within the same culture as well as in its relationship with other cultures, but differences in power relations within the same community and in its relations with other communities tend to influence the outcome of contestation initiatives. For example, the ability of women to challenge oppressive gender relations within their communities is proportionate to their economic autonomy, social and political power. To change outcomes in gender relations one must therefore confront the underlying imbalance in power relations, instead of relying on the rhetorical force of international human rights as if that can work on its own. The moral and political force of human rights is indeed useful, but only through the mobilization and action of human beings in their communities, which must take due account of the realities of power relations within the community.

Another aspect of the proposed approach is to de-emphasize the dichotomy between internal and external influence in order to enable those who are contesting oppressive aspects of their own culture to draw on alliances with external actors. Accordingly, all human rights advocates anywhere in the world are entitled and obliged to support these rights in other societies, subjected to two requirements of all participants in these initiatives:

1) To act with sensitivity and respect for the integrity of other cultures because resistance to external pressure on human rights issues is often a reflection of traditional resentments of the missionary zeal and cultural imperialism that were used by European powers earlier to justify colonialism. Taking a patronizing position of moral superiority in telling others what to do is not only counter-productive because people will resist in any way they can when they feel they are being dictated to by others, but also inconsistent with respect for human dignity which is the underlying rationale of the human rights concept itself.

2) To apply the same standards in openly and consistently criticizing their own societies and allies, thereby avoiding the charge of applying 'double standards'. Unfortunately, a lot of hard work in building confidence and trust across cultural boundaries can be seriously undermined by such reckless practices. A most egregious recent example of this is the militaristic response of the United States to the terrorist atrocities of 9/11, especially the invasion of Iraq, practices of secret detention and torture, and illegal transfer of suspects across international borders . These and other travesties of justice and the rule of law on a global scale seriously undermined the standing of international law itself, and diminished

international cooperation in the protection of human rights everywhere. In my view, the consequent mistrust of the motivation of major powers enabled the Government of Sudan to resist international pressure over its atrocities in Dar Fur. It is simply untenable for the international community to condone violations of international law and human rights by the United States and its allies and then attempt to invoke the same principles against the Government of Sudan.

To emphasize in conclusion of this introduction, I am not suggesting that cultural factors are the only source of all difficulties in the application of human rights norms, or that taking culture into account would suddenly resolve all issues, but I do believe that there is always a cultural dimension to both difficulties and solutions. Since the dynamic relationship between culture and human rights is part of the source of some tensions with human rights it must also be a resource for the mediation of those tensions in practice. In order to offer some practical strategies for this mediation, I will begin by discussing the two-fold paradox of universality of human rights and self-regulation by the state to highlight the critical role of culture in the mediation of these tensions. Moreover, I will explain the methodology of internal discourse and cross-cultural dialogue as a practical and realistic approach to mediating serious disagreements about the universality principle or some specific human right norms.

The premise of the proposed approach is that the opponents of universality of human rights have a point that should be *taken seriously but not totally conceded* to the extent of defeating the possibility of the universality of human rights. Those critics are right in observing that the notion of universally valid and applicable norms is paradoxical, but they are wrong in concluding that the effort to establish and implement universal human rights norms should be abandoned for that reason alone. The challenge for the proponents of the universality of human rights is to develop and implement effective strategies for overcoming that difficulty. To respond to this challenge, we should first clarify the following difficulty in order to propose a viable methodology for addressing the issue.

2. The Paradox of Universality and Relativity

The term human rights is often used in popular discourse to refer to notions of freedom and social justice in general, but in fact this concept signifies a particular view of claims of freedom and justice as legal entitlements which are due to all human beings, without distinction on such grounds as race, sex (gender), or religion. While the initial formulation of human rights, as proclaimed in the Universal Declaration of 1948 and developed in subsequent treaties and institutions, was based on the experiences of Western societies that does not necessarily mean that the concept or those formulations are necessarily alien or irrelevant to non-Western societies. The premise of the whole project is that it is about the rights of human beings as such, everywhere, and not only of people of 'the West'. In fact, as clearly confirmed by the frequent endorsement of the Universal Declaration in national constitutions and regional treaties like the 1981 African Charter of Peoples' and Human Rights, the concept of universal human rights has already transcended the limitations of its initial formulations. Nevertheless, this view is by no means universally accepted, even among Western societies as I will highlight later. This issue is often discussed in terms of a binary of universality and relativity, as if one has to either fully accept or completely reject the universality of a presumably a set concept and exhaustive list of human rights. On one side of this purported dichotomy are countries which claim cultural relativity or contextual specificity in rejecting or qualifying certain human rights norms, while those which fully accept the universality of all human rights, are on the other side.

Upon reflection, however, it is clear that this binary view is false and misleading because all countries have a mixed record on the issue, whether in theory or practice. A binary view is false, I believe, in assuming that human rights can either be culturally and contextually neutral, or that a conception of these rights emerging within one culture or context can be imposed on other cultures. It is true that universal rights are necessary for ensuring equal respect for human dignity throughout the world, but these norms can not be imagined or understood in the abstract, without reference to the concrete daily experience of the people who are entitled to them. A binary view is misleading in implying a 'clash of civilizations' between 'the West' that is unanimously supportive of universal human rights versus the rest of humanity who are opposed to those rights. In reality, some people of all societies throughout the world accept the universality of human rights, while others in the same societies reject this view. Nevertheless, there is a need for global consensus on universal human rights because it is not realistic to assume that all societies are able to devise and effectively implement their own conception of rights, freely and with equal participation of all members of each community. The reality of human experience has shown, especially in situations of extreme oppression and violence, that ruling elites often control and manipulate that process to protect their own privilege and power. This reality emphasizes the need for universal rights, but does not resolve the problem of how to come to agreement about those rights.

By the 'paradox of the universality' I mean given the cultural foundation of all normative systems, on the one hand, and the permanent cultural diversity of the world, on the other- how can we determine universally valid human rights standards that are acceptable to all societies regardless of cultural and contextual difference? The basic difficulty here is that any approach to locating the foundation or source of the universality of human rights simply begs the question or postpone it, rather than resolving it for all perspectives.[2] For instance, one can say that all human rights emanate from a particular philosophical or religious premise about human nature, social life, and so forth. But this simply re-frames the question in terms of which premise to select, why, and to what end? To assert that these rights are necessary for protecting human dignity or satisfying certain basic needs presupposes a universally accepted conception of human dignity and its implications, or agreement on basic needs and the manner of their satisfaction. For instance, all human beings need food and shelter, yet liberal culture/ideology tends to assert that these needs should be realized through the political process. That view tends to focus on civil and political rights, like freedom of speech and association, to ensure the fairness and inclusivity of the political process, trusting that the ultimate outcome will provide for other basic human needs. Those who hold the opposite view insist on acknowledging of basic needs like food and shelter, which they rank as matters of higher priority than civil and political rights. Instead of prioritizing one set of human rights over another I hold all human rights to be equal and interdependent. But the point here is that there are, and will continue to be, significant differences about how to identify and define human rights norms. Again, to take a positivistic view of human rights, as whatever states decide them to be through international treaties and national law simply leaves the matter to the culturally and ideologically determined biases, interests and choices of the elite who control the state.

The difficulty of finding a universally accepted foundation of universal rights was clear to some observers even before the United Nations' Human Rights Commission finished the draft of the Universal Declaration of Human Rights. In 1947, the Commission received a long memorandum from the American Anthropological Association (AAA) cautioning against the dangers of ethnocentrism, the tendency to regard one's own culture as superior to those of other cultures.[3] Since standards and values are relative to the culture from which they derive, any attempt to formulate norms that are based on the beliefs or moral code of one culture to that extent detracts from the applicability of the Declaration to humanity as a whole. Even those who accept the idea of the universality of human rights as a legal entitlement of every human being will probably continue to have significant differences about the actual content and implementation of these rights. But if the cultural/contextual sources or foundations of human rights are necessarily multiple and diverse, how can the rights so determined be universal?

[2] For a brief review of controversies over possible justifications for the foundational assertion of Art. 1 of the Universal Declaration that all human beings are born free and equal in dignity and rights, etc., *see* T. Lindholm, *Article 1: A New Beginning*, *in* A. Eide *et al.* (Eds.), The Universal Declaration of Human Rights, A Commentary 31 (1992).

[3] American Anthropological Association, *Statement on Human Rights*, 49 American Anthropologist 539 (1947).

In attempting to address this dilemma, the AAA statement of June 1999 affirmed that cultural or other differences between human societies should not be used as a pretext for justifying human rights violations. But the problem with this view is that it assumes or presupposes the existence of a clearly identified and accepted set of human rights in the first place whose violation cannot be justified by invoking human difference. In an effort to anticipate objections to the circular logic of this view, the 1999 AAA declaration concludes by cautioning against equating or limiting human rights to "the abstract legal uniformity of Western tradition," and emphasizes the need to keep the concept open to additional and new perspectives by asserting that:

> The AAA definition thus reflects a commitment to human rights consistent with international principles but not limited by them. Human rights are not a static concept. Our understanding of human rights is constantly evolving as we come to know more about the human condition. It is therefore incumbent on anthropologists to be involved in the debate on enlarging our understanding of human rights on the basis of anthropological knowledge and research.[4]

I agree with this evolving view of human rights, but do not see how that can resolve the basic tension between ethnocentricity and universality of standards that are now or in the future proclaimed as universal human rights. The phrases 'our understanding' and 'we come to know' in the above quotation may include members of the AAA who supported the adoption of this statement, but not those members who opposed it, and certainly not all Americans. It is good that the training and professional orientation of anthropologists may enable many of them to be sensitive to the risks of ethnocentricity, but that does not necessarily qualify or authorize them to speak for all views on human rights in their own culture, let alone in other cultures.

Another aspect of the universality quandary can be appreciated in relation to what might be called the paradox of state self-regulation in the human rights field. The Charter of the United Nations and the UDHR had to strike a balance between the need for international supervision and respect for national sovereignty and exclusive domestic jurisdiction of nation states. On the one hand, these founding documents sought to universalize certain notions of fundamental rights as binding under international law while, on the other hand, leaving the application of these rights on the ground to the agency of the state. The question here is can we expect state officials to enforce human rights limitations on their own powers, or to hold themselves accountable for violations of these rights? The reality of this paradox of self-regulation by the state means that redressing the underlying causes of violations, as well as providing effective remedy for individual violations, requires the mobilization of the maximum possible degree of political will at the local, national and international level. That political will is unlikely to emerge and be maintained

[4] American Anthropological Association, *Declaration on Anthropology and Human Rights*, available at http://www.aaanet.org/stmts/humanrts.htm, viewed 7 October 2007.

if human rights are perceived to be lacking cultural legitimacy or contextual viability. This is as true of Western countries as it is of non-Western countries, as I will show later.

In this regard, it is important to emphasize the persistence of some Western governments to assert chauvinistic notion of national sovereignty is in fact as relativist as similar claims by non-Western countries like China or Iran. For example, the United States is notorious for seeking to fashion international human rights treaties to fit its own ideological views and social institutions during the drafting process, only to refuse to ratify and incorporate those treaties into its domestic law for application within the country itself. This is true from the 1948 Genocide Convention, which took the United States more than forty years to ratify, and only subject to reservations, to the 1989 Covenant on the Rights of the Child, which is now ratified by every country in the world except the United States and Somalia. Since Somalia has had no government since 1992, the government of the United States stands completely alone in refusing to ratify this Convention. This position is particularly damaging for the universality of human rights because other relativists can cite it as justification for their own positions, at a time when the United States is dominating international relations and exercising excessive influence on the domestic policies of weaker and poorer countries. To say that the United States need not ratify because it already upholds a higher standard than is required by human rights treaties is both incoherent and condescending. If the United States is already in conformity, why not ratify these treaties in order to have the moral standing to challenge other countries when they refuse to ratify or fail to implement? In challenge other countries to do what it is not willing to do itself, the United States is asserting its moral superiority, without being willing to submit to the same standards of verification of compliance that apply to other countries.

3. Mediating the Contingent Universality of Human Rights

In light of the preceding remarks, it is clear that all societies need to engage in constant negotiation about which claims to accept as human rights, and how they can be implemented in practice. In other words, agreement on the concept and normative content of the universality of these rights is to evolve and be constructed overtime, and not proclaimed once and for all. This negotiation should, by definition, include the widest possible range of perspectives and priorities of different human societies for the outcome to be accepted as truly universal. To avoid the appropriation of the collective voice of a culture by its political leaders or some other elite group, such negotiation must take place within each culture, as well as between cultures. The object of this internal discourse within cultures, and cross-dialogue among them, is to promote an overlapping consensus over the meaning and implications of the universality of human rights. While internal discourse seeks to promote consensus within a society or community over human rights norms and their underlying values within a particular society, cross-cultural dialogue attempts to achieve the same among different societies and communities.[5]

To suggest this apparently long-term approach does not mean that the articulation and implementation of all human rights should wait until consensus is achieved on any of them. In fact, the protection of certain rights, like freedom of speech and the right to education is necessary for internal discourse and cross-cultural dialogue to be possible and effective. The point is to work with the existing level of acceptance and implementation of human rights in order to expand and enhance consensus on the validity and practical application of all human rights, including possibilities of evolving new rights in the future.

However, since the proposed discourse and dialogue does not happen in a vacuum, these processes must take into account contextual factors, such as differentials in power relations among different participants in internal discourse within cultures, as well as in dialogue between them. Accordingly, to enhance the ability of cross-cultural dialogue to contribute to the acceptance of the universality of human rights, the impact of persistent and growing global differentials in power relation and material conditions between Western and non-Western societies and cultures must somehow be redressed. As noted earlier with reference to the aftermath of 9/11, the context of discourse and dialogue also include events and developments that affect the rule of law in international relations as the essential pre-request condition for any possibility of acceptance and protection of universal standards of human rights anywhere in the world today.

It is therefore necessary to understand and act upon the profoundly political nature of the whole project. The normative formulation and practical application of the universality of human rights presupposes the political will to allocate the necessary resources and take appropriate administrative or judicial action, including making hard choices in cases of apparent conflict with other national priorities or concerns, and so forth. Therefore, the critical question is how to generate and sustain the necessary political will to respect and protect these rights in different societies, over time. So far, too much emphasis has been placed on a narrow, state-centric, legalistic, and reactive approach to international human rights standards that also presupposes certain institutional and material resources that many not exist in many parts of the world. By 'state-centric and legalistic' I mean the tendency to perceive

---

5 *See, e.g.*, A. A. An-Na'im, *Cultural Transformation and Normative Consensus on the Best Interest of the Child*, 8 International Journal of Law and the Family 62 (1994). Also published *in* P. Alston (Ed.), The Best Interest of the Child: Reconciling Culture and Human Rights 62 (1994).

the legitimacy and authority of human rights standards as founded on the legal obligation of states under international law. Following this approach, advocates of these rights tend to focus on the technical definition of discrete or isolated rights and pursue specific remedies for individual violations through judicial or administrative remedies. Such a reactive, individualized response not only requires developed and settled institutional and human resources, but is also unable to cope with massive violations or addressing underlying causes of human rights violations. Individualized case-by-case remedies should therefore be supplemented by proactive strategies to preempt violations and address the underlying structural and cultural/contextual causes.

For our purposes here, there are two aspects to these two proactive strategies, one internal to the particular community, and the other external, relating to its relationship with other communities or constituencies. On the internal front, advocates of universality must be able to use whatever arguments are likely to be persuasive to the specific community, or able to address their apprehensions and concerns, in relation to whatever frame of reference that is accepted by that community as authoritative or applicable. The objective here is *persuasion*, by showing people how human rights norms 'make sense' in their own daily lives, without being too threatening for them to accept. It is to be expected that oppressive regimes will continue trying to justify human rights violations in the name of law and order, upholding social morality, economic development and other pretexts. The question is therefore whether the arguments human rights advocates can make are capable of overriding such objections by appealing to more fundamental or widely held values, or capable of building alliances to overcome such objections, rather than expecting their view to be acceptable to all.

The external dimension relates to conditions or circumstances that are likely to influence the persuasiveness of the human rights view in the internal debate. For instance, a community's perception of how seriously others take human rights claims will influence their own attitudes and responses. That is why perceptions of 'double standards' in the human rights policies are so damaging to the universality of these rights. In my view, the failure of some countries to consistently respect human rights in their own policies does not justify violations by other countries, but it is unfortunately true that some people tend to draw that conclusion.

The sort of negotiation I am calling for can be seen in recent experiences of European countries with the doctrine of 'margin of appreciation', which permits some discretion in the definition and implementation of human rights due to cultural and contextual factors. The underlying rationale of this doctrine is that universality does not mean total uniformity, without regard to the specificity of the situation where the issue arises.[6] In this way, holding that the same norms should prevail everywhere in the world does not preclude

6 E. Brems, Human Rights: Universality and Diversity 357-422 (2001).

accommodation of diversity in the way these standards are realized in specific situations, through interpretation, balancing and enforcement. The rationale of the 'margin of appreciation' doctrine may apply more strongly in relation to significantly different parts of the world. But even within a relatively homogenous region like Europe, universality cannot mean total uniformity. It may be necessary to devise safeguards against abuse or distortion of the rationale of the doctrine. For instance, Eva Berms has argued that the European Court of Human Rights should reduce the scope of the margin of appreciation when certain core aspects of a right are concerned. In her view, since all rights can be conceived as having a core and a periphery, the further an element is removed from the core, the more room for diversity. From this perspective, the universality of human rights is undermined by contextual diversity of interpretation regarding the core of a right, but not if they pertain only to peripheral elements of the right.[7]

In view of this doctrine and its rationale, it is remarkable that it is not seen as relevant or applicable to minority cultures within a country, like the situation of European Muslims in France, the Netherlands or Denmark. For example, while it is commonly conceded that freedom of expression cannot be absolute, there is little agreement on the appropriate limits of this human right. But such differences exist within cultures as well as between cultures; and tend to change over time, as can be seen in the case of pornography or blasphemy. Moreover, other factors can influence the terms or outcome of debates about freedom of expression. This point may seem to be more obvious in relation to African and Islamic societies,[8] but it is equally true of other parts of the world. Thus, it seems to me, the controversies about the cartoons in Denmark and the headscarf in France, for instance, reflected anxieties about immigration and cultural identity for European societies, and not only among Muslim minorities. Recollections of colonial relations and resentment of post-colonial hegemonies, concerns about terrorism and Turkish membership in the European Unions, and many other factors are relevant and often culturally defined.

Understanding the cultural and contextual dimensions of the debate can help us understand and better respond to these issue. For example, peaceful protest against the Danish cartoons of the Prophet Muhammad should be seen as an effort to define the right and its appropriate limitations, and not denial of freedom of expressions to others. Affirming this view of the situation would help both sides of that issue to come to a mutually acceptable resolution, as

[7] E. Brems, *The Margin of Appreciation Doctrine of the European Court of Human Rights*, *in* D. P. Forsythe & P. C. McMahon (Eds.), Human Rights and Diversity: Area Studies Revisited 81 (2003).

[8] *See, e.g.* A. A. An-Na'im, *The Contingent Universality of Human Rights: The Case of Freedom of Expression in African and Islamic Contexts*, 10 Emory International Law Review 29 (1997).

Muslims would feel that their objections were taken into consideration and the Danish public opinion would not feel threatened by immigrant Muslims dictating to them what to do.

To conclude this theoretical discussion, and turn to some thematic illustrations of my approach, I would emphasize that the universality of human rights and their cultural/contextual expressions can be compatible, and even mutually supportive, but this process should not be assumed to necessarily yield a predetermined or inevitable meaning and content of universality of human rights. These two dimensions can either be mutually supportive or not, depending on how various actors perceive the issue and respond to them in specific situations. In other words, the universality of human rights should be seen as a *product of a process*, rather than an established 'given' concept and specific predetermined normative content to be discovered or proclaimed through international declarations and rendered legally binding through treaties. In fact, the idea of 'discovery' or 'proclamation' itself implies a process, which requires certain actors, context, and other conditions that are conducive to its success. If this is true, understanding the meaning and implications of the universality of human rights calls for an examination of the nature of that process, the role of the actors and context, and other relevant conditions. The proponents of universality need to understand the nature and dynamics of this process in order to develop appropriate strategies for achieving their objectives, instead of expecting affirmation of universality to emerge as simply 'self-evident' or the inevitable outcome of national politics and/or international relations. This approach might be clarified by the following examples.

4. Thematic Illustrations

As emphasized from the start, culture is relevant to the concept of universality of human rights itself, as well as to the definition and practical implementation of every human right norm. Moreover, culture is relevant in these ways to the full range of human rights norms, like freedom of expression, fair trial and rights to education and health, and not only some set or group of rights and not others. To illustrate this point, I will first consider the case of economic, social and cultural rights (ESCR) as human rights. The second illustration will be so-called 'crimes of honor', which are more commonly associated with 'cultural relativism'.

5. Liberal Relativism About Economic, Social and Cultural Rights

In focusing on Western liberal cultural/ideological attitudes regarding ESCR, I am not implying that other parts of the words are better in the protection of human rights in general, or in this field in particular. Rather, the example is chosen to clarify a particular dimension of the relationship between culture and human rights that is not commonly acknowledged in public discourse or examined in scholarly studies of the subject. The factual basis of this illustration is that Western countries have not shown consistent acceptance of the universality of human rights in their own national policies regarding ESCR. The point I am making here is that it is not enough to provide for the services and benefits covered by these rights through the normal political and legal processes of each country because the essence of the universality of human rights is to safeguard such entitlements against the contingencies of politics. To the extent that they do in fact respect and protect ESCR, Western countries have nothing to fear from accepting those rights as human rights. Conversely, such acceptance is necessary whenever those rights are not sufficiently respected in the manner and to the extent required by international human rights standards. Equally important for our purpose here is that Western acceptance of the human rights status of ESCR is necessary for upholding the universality principle regarding all human rights throughout the world.

Regarding the subject of this paper in particular, the main point I am emphasizing is that Western ambivalence about the human rights status of ESCR is in fact as cultural (including ideological in this case) as issues commonly cited as examples of cultural relativism like female genital cuttings or honor killings. Because of its emphasis on individual autonomy and private property, liberal ideology/culture finds it difficult to conceive of ESCR as having the same human rights standing as civil and political rights like freedom of speech or opinion and belief. Liberals may see their views about ESCR as obviously valid to every reasonable person, but that is exactly how ideological or cultural relativism works everywhere. In other words, liberal societies tend to resist accepting ESCR as human rights for the same reason some Islamic societies resist women's rights or so-called 'Asian values' challenge to civil rights in the name of religious or regional ideology or culture. The difference is therefore not in the nature of the cultural/ideological/contextual challenge to the universality of all human rights, but in assumptions about Western 'authorship' of the concept and content of human rights. That is, failure to see the similarity among such Western and non-Western relativists claims contributes to perpetuating the myth that human rights are naturally Western (and therefore fully accepted and implemented by Western countries), while the rest of the world struggles with accepting some of these rights in principle, let alone implementing them. In my view, it is necessary to clearly identify and confront Western cultural relativism about ESCR to emphasize that the human rights challenge faces all societies. I will now briefly clarify and elaborate on this view.[9]

The essential purpose of human rights is to ensure the effective protection of certain fundamental entitlements for all human beings, everywhere, without distinction on such grounds as race, sex, or religion. In other words, the rationale is to ensure the protection of human rights even in countries where they are not provided for as fundamental constitutional rights precisely in order to *safeguard them from the contingencies of the national political and administrative processes*. As global experience has repeatedly shown, states cannot be trusted to respect and protect the inherent human dignity of all those who are subject to their jurisdiction. The United Nations sought to establish a set of *universal standards* in this regard. According to the Preamble of the Universal Declaration of Human Rights (UDHR), these standards are supposed to be "a common standard of achievement for all peoples and all nations." What does this mean, and how is it to be achieved in practice?

The tension between this idea and the principle and practice of national sovereignty require these standards to be acknowledged as the product of international agreement. Moreover, the implied threat of overriding national sovereignty would neither be plausible or acceptable without the promise of international cooperation in the protection of human rights. The claim of the international community to act as arbiter in safeguarding certain minimum standards in this regard is not credible without the corresponding commitment of its members to encourage and support each other in the process. This is particularly critical in view of significant differences in the degree of political will, and gross differentials in institutional capacity and material resources for the implementation of these rights in different parts of the world.

Accordingly, the distinguishing features of human rights for our purpose here are *universal recognition* of the same rights and *international cooperation* in their implementation. From this perspective, I suggest that the term 'human rights' applies to national constitutional and legal protection of these rights, or their implementation as a matter of national policy, only when that is done in furtherance of the international obligations of the state. Otherwise, the concept will lose its essential function of securing these rights against the contingencies of national politics. It is true that human rights cannot be respected and protected in the daily lives of individuals and communities except through the incorporation of international obligations into national law and policy. But if the protection of any entitlement at the national level is separated from international human rights standards, the advantage of international

[9] The following review is based on my article *To Affirm the Full Human Rights Standing of Economic, Social & Cultural Rights*, *in* Y. Ghai & J. Cottrell (Eds.), Economic, Social & Cultural Rights in Practice: The Role of Judges in Implementing Economic, Social & Cultural Rights 7 (2004).

supervision is lost. The national protection of rights without recognition of an international obligation to do so can easily slide back into denial of some of those rights in the name of upholding the democratic principle of majority rule, including effecting constitutional amendments, if necessary.

In this light, even the highest level of provision for education, health care, social security, for instance should not be accepted as compliance with international human rights standards if that state refuses to acknowledge the human rights status of ESCR. This distinction, I suggest, is critical for the coherence and integrity of the human rights idea for two reasons. First, the issue is whether the government of the day should exercise exclusive discretion in deciding which services to provide, for whom, and on which terms, or be bound by some external criteria which apply everywhere regardless of considerations of ideology or political expediency. The *added value* of the human rights idea is to provide an internationally agreed frame of reference to the normal course of ideological, cultural or political struggles over power and resources in domestic politics and foreign policy. Second, a commitment to providing these services as a matter of international human rights obligation should extend beyond a state's commitment to the well-being of its own citizens to all human beings everywhere. Since human rights are for all human beings, not only the citizens of one state or another, the measure of commitment of any state to these rights should be willingness to support their implementation everywhere and not only within its own domestic jurisdiction. I am not at all suggesting that human rights are the only approach to good domestic social policy or humane foreign relations. Indeed, over time it may prove to be an ineffective or counter-productive approach on either or both counts. Rather, my point is to clarify the meaning and implications of a human rights approach as such in order to assess its utility and efficacy.

The formative dominance of liberal perceptions and hierarchy of human rights has been used to support the claim that West European and North American societies fully accept the universality of human rights, while other societies are hampered by cultural, ideological or contextual limitations in this regard. Consequently, the theory and practice of human rights as determined by those societies is taken by some leaders of developing countries as the only model of how these rights are to be defined and implemented everywhere. However, upon taking the full range of human rights as equally universal and indivisible, one can see that West European and North American societies too have their cultural, ideological or contextual problems. Compare, for example, the status of ESCR with that of civil and political rights under the European system. Whereas the latter set of rights has received strong articulation and juridical development within the European system, ESCR have been relegated to non-binding charters and optional protocols.[10] The contrast is

[10] *See, generally*, *e.g.*, D. Harris & J. Darcy, The European Social Charter (2001).

more significant because the members of this system already have the material resources and institutional capacity to implement ESCR.

What is really at issue about ESCR is whether human rights are limited to conservative liberal notions of restraints on the powers of the state, or should also include affirmative obligations to provide for certain vital interests of persons and communities. The principle of non-discrimination, even when viewed in terms of effect or outcome has nothing to say about the affirmative obligation of the state to provide for vital services or resources for the disadvantaged or under-privileged segments of the population. In other words, are human rights only for those who have the material, educational and other resources needed to effectively exercise their rights, or should they also be available to those who are unable to do so? If it is the former, then ESCR are not human rights at all. In that case, one should speak of the 'universalization' of liberal notions of civil and political rights, not of *human* rights that are accepted by all the ideological and cultural traditions of the world. But if human rights are to be genuinely universal they must include ESCR and that cannot be without international supervision of the performance of the normal political and administrative process in this regard. It is true that the set of human rights we now call ESCR need further development, more precise definition and implementation mechanisms, but this will not happen until we accept that these are in fact human rights.

The solution I propose for liberal relativism about ESCR is to affirm the full human rights quality of ESCR by abandoning any classification of human rights, and approach the implementation of each specific right on its own terms, instead of limiting it to what is deemed appropriate for one purported class of rights or another. In particular, I believe that it is critical to challenge the assumption that the implementation of ESCR should be confined to the realm of social policy and administrative processes of governments because these rights do not fit the model of judicial enforcement developed for specific civil and political rights. To leave the matter to the unfettered discretion of governments, however democratic they may be, without any possibility of judicial guidance and supervision, defeats the whole purpose of recognizing ESCR as international human rights.

6. Crimes of Honor

Crimes as such are not human rights violations when committed by private persons and not state actors. However, violence against women in particular can constitute human rights violations when the state fails to protect women against this 'gender-based' violence, or to prosecute offenders or implement other necessary policies because that would constitute discrimination on grounds of sex. The following discussion of so-called 'crimes of honor' is intended to demonstrate the cultural dimension of this phenomenon which affects the response of state officials as well as the perpetrators. In other words, it is the cultural underpinnings of this crime that makes it a human rights violation because it contributes to official failure to protect victims and prosecute offenders.[11]

What distinguishes 'crimes of honor' from other violent crimes is that they are usually perpetrated against women by close relatives for allegations of sexual impropriety in the name of protecting or upholding the honor of the family. As documented in studies of this phenomenon in Turkey,[12] the decision to kill the woman is made in a family meeting that also designates a young man within the family, usually a brother or cousin of the victim, to carry out the crime. By their very nature and alleged rationale, therefore, these crimes arise out of a *collective deliberate decision that is to be executed in public, or at least publicized* for the purported purpose to be achieved. What does this collective, deliberate and public nature of the crime mean for the responsibility of the family and community at large? How can the prosecution and punishment of the immediate perpetrator be appropriate or sufficient where so many others are responsible for instigating or condoning the crime, and perpetuating a social and cultural system that 'demands' the offering of such human sacrifice? Other questions arising out of the nature and context of 'crimes of honor' include whose honor is at issue here, and why are women killed in the name of protecting it? Another set of questions is whether these crimes constitute human rights violations, and what practical difference can such a characterization make? In other words, what distinguishes these crimes from other crimes from a human rights point of view, and what does this mean for strategies for combating them?

Underlying these and related questions is concern about the limitations of an exclusively state-centric approach in this regard. That is, to affirm that the state has the legal obligation to protect the bodily integrity of potential victims and to punish perpetrators of 'crimes of honor', whether as human rights violations or not, does not necessarily mean that the state is willing and able to discharge this obligation. This is particularly true when state actors are not only facing strong and deeply entrenched cultural opposition in this regard, but are themselves sympathetic or indifferent to the moral outrage of these crimes. Another concern relates to the methods and costs/risks of state

[11] The following review is based on my chapter *The Role of 'Community Discourse' in Combating 'Crimes of Honor': Preliminary Assessment and Prospects*, *in* L. Welchman & S. Hossain (Eds.), "Honor': Crimes, Paradigms, and Violence Against Women 64 (2006).

[12] M. Faraç, Töre Kıskacında Kadın (Women Under the Pressure of the Customs) (1998); A. Duzkan & F. Kocali, *An Honor Killing: She Fled, Her Throat Was Cut*, *in* P. Ilkkaracan (Ed.), Women and Sexuality in Muslim Societies 381 (2000); and A. A. An-Na'im, *The Role of 'Community Discourse' in Combating 'Crimes of Honor': Preliminary Assessment and Prospects*, *in* L. Welchman & S. Hossain (Eds.), 'Honor': Crimes, Paradigms, and Violence Against Women 64 (2006).

interventions in the realm of family and community. For example, is it safe to assume that state interventions at that level are going to be effective in combating 'crimes of honor'? How can one ensure that the power to take such intrusive measures will not be abused for other purposes?

The cultural dimension of crimes of honor raise the question of the role of family and community in regulating sexuality. But the discriminatory concern that makes these crimes human rights violations is that this regulatory role of family and community is limited only to women while men are as responsible for any perceived violation of sexual morality, if not more than women. But acknowledging and condemning this discrimination does not address the underlying question whether the family and community have a role in regulating the sexual behavior of their members. If they do, consequent questions would include, for instance, what factors and processes determine or affect the way that role is played in different contexts, and what methods of social control are available to the family and community, especially during periods of transition and crisis. How are such methods to be judged, by whom and for what purposes?

Regardless of one's personal views about the extent and manner it is performed in any given setting or time, families and communities do have a role to play in regulating the sexual behavior of their members in every human society throughout history. While the scope and methods of doing this varies from one community to another, and over time within the same community, I believe that social life itself would not be possible without the regulation of sexuality. Unless one wishes to argue that this is not, or should not be, true anywhere in the world today, the question is one about the scope and manner of regulation, rather than a choice between regulation and no regulation at all.

The basic and most enduring regulation of sexuality happens through the organization of the family and community at the collective level, and through early socialization of children at the individual level. Both aspects are re-enforced in a variety of ways, including action by the state through the legal regulation of marriage and sexual conduct, education, and even taxation and provision of social services. Common experience, I believe, indicates not only that these processes work effectively in the vast majority of cases, but also that families and communities adapt their norms and processes to changing conditions over time. It is also clear to me that both the effective regulation of sexuality and adaptations of its norms and processes occur in subtle, spontaneous and unconscious ways. In this light, 'crimes of honor' are a manifestation of *the failure or inadequacy* of familial and communal regulation of sexuality, rather than an indication that such regulation happens only in societies where these crimes are committed and not in others societies. But as already emphasized, the serious problem with these crimes is that they represent a violent and discriminatory response to the failure or inadequacy of traditional mechanisms for the regulation of sexuality. In other words, these crimes should be combated as excessive and violent methods of regulation of sexuality that usually target women alone, though men are at least as responsible for the transgression as women.

While it is imperative to challenge this state of affairs, I think it is counterproductive to suggest that the family and community have no right to regulate sexuality at all. Even the appearance of suggesting that will undermine the credibility of any effort to combat 'crimes of honor', thereby rendering the women of communities implicated in such practices even more vulnerable to violence in the name of protecting honor than they are at present. The emphasis must therefore be on why violence against women, or men for that matter, is never justified as a response to sexual impropriety, without appearing to imply that abandoning all forms or degrees of regulation of sexuality is the alternative. It is therefore wise to present opposition to 'crimes of honor' explicitly in these terms to avoid any risk of undermining their efforts by allowing supporters of the practice to misrepresent the position of its opponents as promoting sexual promiscuity and license.

A more liberal view of personal autonomy and sexual freedom than that accepted by the communities where 'crimes of honor' occur may be supported by current international standards of human rights. But it is also possible, in my view, to oppose these crimes as human rights violations without necessarily arguing for a more liberal view of a community's approach to the regulation of sexuality as such. That is, one can object to 'crimes of honor' from a human rights point of view because they are excessively violent and discriminatory against women, without necessarily arguing that the community's view of sexual propriety is itself objectionable from a human rights perspective. Although these two positions are not mutually exclusive, I am more concerned here with the view that 'crimes of honor' *can* constitute human rights violations, even if one accepts the community's position on the regulation of sexuality in general.

Generally speaking, human rights are by definition intended to protect people against excess or abuse of the powers of the state, and can therefore be violated only by those who act on behalf of the state or under color of its authority or approval. Consequently, crimes like homicide are not human rights violations unless committed by agents of the state, or with their approval. This point is usually made in relation to acts of violence against women like 'crimes of honor' in terms of the distinction between the public domain of state action and the private domain of the family and community. In my view, however, the state should be held accountable for its failure to act with 'due diligence' in combating violence against women within the private domain of family and community. From this perspective, the state is responsible for its failure to effectively prosecute and punish those who perpetrate violence against women in the private domain, though their crimes cannot be attributed to the state as such. At the same time, this should not mean repudiating the distinction between the public and private domains because once the state is allowed to act within the private domain; it will probably abuse that power to violate human rights instead of protecting them. The question is therefore how can the state and civil society actors combat crimes of honor without abusing that power of intervention in the private domain of family and community?

Another challenge is that exclusive reliance on the state-centric approach tends to be *reactive* to already committed violations by the action or omission of officials of the state, rather than *proactive* to pre-empt their happening in the first place. This approach can also be problematic because it tends to be slow, costly and generally inappropriate for the task at hand. In view of the severe resource limitations of developing countries that might enable state agencies and officials to provide emergency housing, employment or social security for victims, it is more likely that women who are vulnerable to violence from members of their own families will be placed in so-called 'protective custody' to ensure their immediate physical safety. What human quality of life would women in that position have, and who is to protect them from abuse by custodial officials? While appreciating these and other challenges, it is clear to me that certain aspects of crimes of honor do constitute human rights violations. In the more immediate sense, the persistence of these crimes indicates a failure of the state to protect the lives and bodily integrity of women, including the provision of effective remedies against these crimes. More broadly, 'crimes of honor' signify deep-rooted, multifaceted and endemic discrimination against women, which the state is obliged to redress under Article 5 (a) of the International Convention for the Elimination of All Forms of Discrimination Against Women of 1979, which provides:

> States Parties shall take all appropriate measures:
> (a) To modify the social and cultural patterns of conduct of men and women, with a view to achieving the elimination of prejudices and customary and all other practices which are based on the idea of the inferiority or the superiority of either of the sexes or on stereotyped roles for men and women.

However, it is also clear to me that exclusive reliance on a human rights approach may be counterproductive in some situations. In other words, a human rights approach is relevant to combating 'crimes of honor', as a matter of principle as well as for tactical reasons, but should only be seen as one option among others, or as an element of a broader strategy, rather than the only possible and effective approach. I would therefore argue that it is necessary to combat crimes of honor at a cultural/religious level to support the effective application of a human rights approach itself, in addition to implementing other strategies for combating crime of honor. I would therefore conclude that the primary role in combating these crimes is that of local constituencies instead of relying on foreign pressure on the government of the country where these crimes occur. It is also clear to me that local constituencies cannot be developed and supported without a strategic long term engagement in internal discourse within the communities about specific concerns like 'crimes of honor', in its broader context of gender power relations within the family and community. All aspects of this process must necessarily be understood and applied with due regard to local context and all relevant factors and considerations.

In conclusion, the cultural dimension of crimes of honor can best be addressed through an internal discourse within communities as an essential element in a range of possible strategies to combat crimes of honor. By 'discourse' I mean the widest possible range, variety and accessibility of activities and opportunities for discussion and reflection about all aspects of 'crimes of honor' within the community, at every level, public and private. This approach does not in any way condone or seek to justify these heinous crimes, and is not claimed to be the sole or primary means of combating them. Rather, it is simply a matter of exploring every possibility of preempting the occurrence of these crimes in the first place, as well as effectively holding all those responsible accountable for their actions. The premise here is that transforming family and community attitudes towards these crimes through an internal discourse within the community would contribute to eliminating these crimes by addressing their underlying causes, in addition to prompting and supporting state officials and institutions in holding individual perpetrators and their supports accountable for their actions.

This approach is in fact an *essential component* of several complementary strategies for combating crimes of honor. Though it is never sufficient by itself in either preventing these crimes or punishing their perpetrators, community discourse against 'crimes of honor' can be an effective means of denying those who commit or condone such crimes family and community sympathy and support. Such an internal discourse can also play a critical role in the socialization of children into totally rejecting any alleged rationale for these crimes. At another level, community discourse is necessary for generating and sustaining the political will to allocate resources and implement policies for combating 'crimes of honor', punishing perpetrators, and deny them any moral or material benefit from their crimes. It is also necessary for transforming the institutional culture and priorities of policy makers, police, public prosecutors, judges, prison officials and other authorities concerned with the incidence and consequences of these crimes. It is true that the state has the primary responsibility for combating 'crimes of honor'. But t whatever the state can or is expected to do (such as implementing administrative measures to prevent the commission of these crimes, effective investigation and prosecution of perpetrators, rehabilitation of and support for victims) is ultimately dependent on how to motivate and support officials, or pressure them if necessary, to act accordingly. Understanding the basic nature of 'crimes of honor' and their context, the motivation of perpetrators and their supporters, the role of the family and community, and whatever else influences the behavior of state officials and institutions regarding all aspects of this phenomenon, all of this is necessary for implementing viable strategies of prevention, protection of potential victims and accountability of perpetrators.

Anne van Aaken

Balancing of Human Rights – Constitutional Interpretation in International Law

1. Introduction

Human rights are at the normative forefront of public international law (PIL) and in debates about the constitutionalization of international law. Nevertheless, their normative importance is currently not matched by the effectuation of human rights law through international institutions and courts. In spite of the fact that there are only a few specialized adjudicatory mechanisms (not necessarily effective)[1] dealing with human rights explicitly, issues pertaining to human rights are pervasive in international law. Very effective non-human rights adjudicatory mechanisms, such as WTO Dispute Settlement system as well as international investment arbitration also deal with matters touching upon human rights issues.[2] Many regimes in PIL pursue different goals: WTO law pursues free trade, investment law pursues protection of foreign investors as well as development, international human rights law pursues the protection of basic human rights, multilateral environmental agreements pursue the protection of the environment. As the Report of the ILC on Fragmentation convincingly states, a lot of cases cannot be easily

[1] For empirical studies on the effectiveness of human rights treaties, *see* O. A. Hathaway, *Do Human Rights Treaties Make a Difference?*, 111 Yale Law Journal 1935 (2002) and E. Neumayer, *Do International Human Rights Treaties Improve Respect for Human Rights?*, 49 Journal of Conflict Resolution 925 (2005). Effectiveness is different from compliance: it tries to measure causality and asks the questions, whether 'law matters' for a change in behavior of states. Democracy, not the ratification of human rights treaties, is the most important explanatory variable for a good human rights record of a country.

[2] L. E. Peterson & K. R. Gray, *International Human Rights in Bilateral Investment Treaties and in Investment Treaty Arbitration* (April 2003), available at http://www.iisd.org/pdf/2003/investment_int_human_rights_bits.pdf.

Miodrag Jovanović & Ivana Krstić (Eds.), Human Rights Today – 60 Years of the Universal Declaration, 51-76.

classified into those different regimes.[3] dispute before the Appellate Body can easily raise issues of human rights or the environment. Similarly, a property dispute before the European Court of Human Rights[4] can entail investment law issues and conversely investment disputes can raise human rights and environmental concerns.[5] Much depends on the forum chosen and the law under which jurisdiction arose. Both, investment and trade are issue-areas in international law including regulatory matters which would require – were they not transnational – administrative or constitutional adjudication involving human rights. In national law, countervailing values, that is intra-constitutional conflicts, are reconciled through balancing of those values (usually embedded in the application of the proportionality principle). A similar mechanism in PIL is underdeveloped from a methodological point of view.

Fragmentation of PIL is one of the pressing reasons why constitutionalization of PIL is discussed. Interpretative smoothing of the fragmented international law might be a second best solution, its no panacea: it would be more desirable to have international law-makers who think about the fragmentation issues and clarify the relationship between treaties in the codification and/or through more explicit hierachization. Since this is rarely found, the paper proposes to use constitutional interpretational methods, specifically the balancing approach, in order to mitigate the tension between human rights law and other issue-areas of international law. It draws on the Vienna Convention on the Law of Treaties (VCLT),[6] especially Article 31(3)(c) VCLT, as well as a theory of balancing as developed in German legal theory. As was held by the ILC Report on Fragmentation:

> [C]ontrary to what is sometimes suggested, conflict-resolution and interpretation cannot be distinguished from each other. Whether there is a conflict and what can be done with prima facie conflicts depends on the way the relevant rules are interpreted. This cannot be stressed too much.[7]

Thereby de-fragmentation of international law can be achieved through constitutional interpretational means. The potential and the limits of this approach are discussed.

The paper proceeds as follows: First, the fragmentation phenomenon, including the pleas for constitutionalization, in international law is shortly described in order to justify why constitutional interpretation may be applied

[3] International Law Commission, *Fragmentation of International Law: Difficulties Arising From the Diversification and Expansion of International Law. Report of the Study Group of the International Law Commission*, finalized by Martti Koskenniemi. A/CN.4/L.682 of 13 April 2006, para. 21 *et seq*.

[4] U. Kriebaum, Eigentumsschutz im Völkerrecht (2008).

[5] Extensively, A. van Aaken, *Fragmentation of International Law: The Case of International Investment Law*, XVII Finnish Yearbook of International Law 91 (2008).

[6] *Vienna Convention on the Law of Treaties*, Vienna, 23 May 1969, in force 27 January 1980, 1155 UNTS 331; 8 ILM 679 (1969).

[7] International Law Commission, *supra* note 3, para. 412.

(2.), then the interpretational methods are discussed with a special view to Article 31(3)(c) VCLT (3.). Its use will be outlined drawing on the theory of balancing from constitutional law (4.). Some potential applications are meant to illustrate the potential of this interpretational method (5.). The last part concludes (6.).

2. Fragmentation and Constitutionalization

Although not everybody views the fragmentation of PIL as problematic, there is broad consensus, that every legal order, including the international one, strive for unity and coherence. The International Law Commission has considered institutional as well as substantive fragmentation of PIL as a sufficient threat to the international legal order to issue a report. At the forefront of the discussion are issues such as World Trade Organization (WTO) and the relationship between the WTO Agreements[8] and other areas of international law, such as multilateral environmental agreements or international human rights law.[9] More neglected are 'investment and [...]' – issues,[10] although they have become ever more important. Although international human rights law is often viewed at being at the forefront of constitutionalist claims,[11] the role of human rights in non-human rights issue areas on the international level is less developed, certainly from a legal methodology point of view. Thus, I will concentrate here on those potential conflicts.

Legal conflicts can be defined narrowly, thus narrowing the scope of the issues to be looked at, or they can be defined more broadly.[12] Following the

---

8 Marrakesh Agreement establishing the World Trade Organization, Marrakesh, 15 April 1994, entry into force 1 January 1995, 1867 UNTS 154.

9 *See, e.g.*, J. Pauwelyn, Conflict of Norms in Public International Law. How WTO Law Relates to Other Rules of International Law (2003), R. Wolfrum & N. Matz, Conflicts in International Environmental Law (2003), P. Alston, *Resisting the Merger and Acquisition of Human Rights by Trade Law: A Reply to Petersmann*, 13 European Journal of International Law 815 (2002); R. Howse, *Human Rights in the WTO: Whose Rights, What Humanity? Comment on Petersmann*, 13 European Journal of International Law 651 (2002); E.-U. Petersmann, *Time for a United Nations 'Global Compact' for Integrating Human Rights Into the Law of Worldwide Organizations: Lessons From European Integration*, 13 European Journal of International Law 621 (2002), G. Marceau, *WTO Dispute Settlement and Human Rights*, 13 European Journal of International Law 753 (2002).

10 *But see* van Aaken, *supra* note 5; M. Hirsch, *Interactions Between Investment and Non-Investment Obligations in International Investment Law*, *in* C. Schreuer, P. Muchlinski & F. Ortino (Eds.), Oxford Handbook of International Investment Law 154 (2008).

11 S. Gardbaum, *Human Rights and International Constitutionalism*, *in* J. L. Dunoff & J. Trachtman (Eds.), Ruling the World? Constitutionalism, International Law and Global Government (forthcoming).

12 *See* seminal B. Simma, *Self-Contained Regimes*, 16 Netherlands Yearbook of International Law 111 (1985). *See also* C. W. Jenks, *The Conflict of Law Making Treaties*, 30 British Yearbook

International Law Commission's (ILC) Report on the 'Fragmentation of International Law',[13] a wide notion of conflict is adopted as this allows a more encompassing analysis of treaty interaction. A conflict exists not only when "a party to two treaties (can) comply with one rule only by thereby failing to comply with another rule" (incompatibility) but also when a treaty "frustrates the goals of another treaty without there being any strict incompatibility between their provisions."[14] I will follow this wide notion here.

Mostly, the debates on hierarchy, on fragmentation, on de-consensualization in international law, on novel structures such as administrative networks are closely connected to the debate on international constitutionalism. This ever more broad debate cannot be reflected here but will only be alluded to if necessary; I will concentrate on constitutionalism as a means of solving fragmentation problems. The understandings behind the term constitutionalism differ wildly, also due to different ideas hidden behind it, but some basic tenets can be filtered out, although, to speak with Joseph Weiler:

> Constitutionalism is, too (some would say only), but a prism through which one can observe a landscape in a certain way, an academic artefact with which one can organize the milestones and landmarks within the landscape (indeed, determine what is a landmark or milestone), an intellectual construct by which one can assign meaning to, or even constitute that which is observed.[15]

Constitutionalism has to be differentiated from constitution and constitutionalization.[16] *Constitution* is traditionally associated with nation states, even more so among German scholars, where this is even reflected in the notions used (Verfassungs*staat*, Rechts*staat*, *Staats*volk) which makes it more difficult for German scholars to think of a constitution without a state and its demos.[17] This historical understanding of constitution with its

of International Law 401, at 418 (1953); N. Matz, Wege zur Koordinierung völkerrechtlicher Verträge. Völkervertragsrechtliche und institutionelle Ansätze 8-18 (2005) and Wolfrum & Matz, *supra* note 9, at 6-13.

13 International Law Commission, *supra* note 3.

14 *Id.*, para. 24. *See also* Jenks, *supra* note 12, at 426.

15 J. H. H. Weiler, *The Reformation of European Constitutionalism*, 35 Journal of Common Market Studies 97, at 99 (1997). Similar A. Peters, *Compensatory Constitutionalism: The Function and Potential of Fundamental International Norms and Structures*, 19 Leiden Journal of International Law 579, at 605 (2006), who correctly points out that the hermeneutic premise makes reconstruction of (legal) texts not only necessary but is unthinkable without interpretation.

16 For a very good overview on the definitions, *see* Peters, *supra* note 15, at 581 *et seq.*

17 For a critique, *see* B. O. Bryde, *Konstitutionalisierung des Völkerrechts und Internationalisierung des Verfassungsrechts*, 42 Der Staat 61, at 61 *et seq.* (2003) and B. O. Bryde, *infra* note 33. Of course, there are substantive reasons behind this 'thick' notion of constitution which is said to need a demos (Staatsvolk): *see only* D. Grimm, *The Constitution in the Process of Denationalization*, 12 Constellations 447 (2005) and J. Isensee, *Staat und Verfassung*, *in* J. Isensee & P. Kirchhof, I Handbuch des Staatsrechts der Bundesrepublik Deutschland §13 (1987).

restricting terminology (in German) is not used here as a functional approach is taken.[18] Following others, I will understand constitution in a normative sense as a sum of the basic and materially most important legal norms which comprehensively regulate the social and political life of polity and usually have special impediments for changeability.[19] The norms do not have to be written down in one single document.[20] They include the most basic values of a polity as well as its institutional and procedural organization and can be reformulated in decision theory terms as principles to be optimized (see part 4.).

Constitutionalization denotes the process by which constitutional law comes into being; the emergence of constitutional law. There is broad consensus that international law has developed immensely after World War II and increasingly restricts the sovereignty of states, their *domaine reservé* (how one judges that process is another normative question). Whereas most scholars draw a distinction between the old law of co-existence, the interim law of co-operation, and now the process of constitutionalization,[21] *Tomuschat* uses four steps to describe the evolution: first, international law as a law of co-existence; second, international law as a law of co-operation; third, international law as a comprehensive blueprint for social life; and fourth, international law of the international community.[22] This process came about due to de-territorialization of economic, environmental and social problems to be solved and hence contributed to an ever more problematic disability of the nation-state alone to continue to fulfill its traditional functions such as regulating social order and protection of its citizens. Increased global interdependence and transnational actors building up transnational networks called for more dense international norms: not only due to new real world developments which call for international regulation but also in order to compensate for deficits of fulfilling the traditional functions of the state[23] and its

---

[18] For details, *see* A. van Aaken, *A Functional Approach to International Constitutionalism: Methodological Suggestions* (forthcoming, 2009).

[19] *See similarly* Peters, *supra* note 15, at 581 who does not take into account the changeability.

[20] As *e.g.* the British and the Israeli constitutions show which are functioning without a formal, integrated, written constitution. In 1995 the Israeli Supreme Court held that the 11 periodically enacted Basic Laws would function as the nation's constitution, and that the Court would exercise an American-style power of judicial review, *see* M. Edelman, *The New Israeli Constitution*, 36 Middle Eastern Studies 1 (2000) and D. Domer, *Does Israel Have a Constitution?*, 43 St. Louis University Law Journal 1328 (1999).

[21] *See* Peters, *supra* note 15, at 580 and R. MacDonald & D. M. Johnston (Eds.), Towards World Constitutionalism: Issues in the Legal Ordering of the World Community (2005).

[22] C. Tomuschat, *International Law: Ensuring the Survival of Mankind on the Eve of a New Century, General Course on Public International Law*, 281 Recueil des cours / Académie de Droit International de La Haye 13, at 56-88 (1999). *See also* for an analysis of the General course of Tomuschat, A. von Bogdandy, *Constitutionalism in International Law*, 47 Harvard International Law Journal 223 (2006).

[23] Peters, *supra* note 15, who talks about compensatory constitutionalism. *See also* C. Walter,

subsequent disaggregation due to delegated norm generation by International Organizations, transnational cooperation of executive bodies in networks as e.g. in the European comitology or in the Basel Committee for Banking Supervision[24] as well as more prominent private standard setting.[25] Further legal phenomena cited as evidence for the international constitutionalization include growing non-consensual norm generation on the international plane,[26] hierarchization of international law through *ius cogens* and Article 103 UN-Charter, as well as the emergence of individuals as subjects of international law. Nevertheless, some scholars view the possibility of compensation of the loss of constitutional functions on the national plane as too idealistic:

> it is inevitable that, for the time being, a bundling of constitutional functions as it has been achieved by the nation state will remain impossible. It has been lost in the level of the nation state and, at the moment, it cannot be achieved elsewhere.[27]

I will try to show that interpretative methods can at least mitigate the problem.

Constitutionalism is defined in various ways which overlap considerably. In the current discussion, two *foci* can be distinguished,[28] both of them argue for constitutionalism. Whereas some have concentrated on the question whether there are international constitutional dimensions as a legally binding framework for international organizations,[29] states or the international community respectively,[30] others have focused on defining the substratum of constitutionalism, that is, the community for which the constitution is

---

Constitutionalizing (inter)national Governance, 44 German Yearbook of International Law 170, at 173, 188 (2001).

[24] *See* N. Krisch & B. Kingsbury, *Introduction: Global Governance and Global Administrative Law in the International Legal Order*, 17 European Journal of International Law 1 (2006); for e.g. transnational cooperation in standard setting in the financial market sector, A. van Aaken, *Democracy in Times of Transnational Administrative Law: The Case of Financial Markets*, *in* H. Eberhard *et al.* (Eds.), Perspectives and Limits of Democracy 41 (2008).

[25] *See* A. M. Slaughter, A New World Order (2004).

[26] As well described in L. R. Helfer, *Participation, Compliance, and Nonconsensual International Lawmaking*, 2008 Illinois Law Review 71 (2008).

[27] Walter, *supra* note 23, at 188.

[28] Walter, *supra* note 23, at 171.

[29] Often the foundational treaties of international organizations are viewed as partial constitutions, e.g. the WTO Agreement, the WHO, the UN. Those functional constitutions thus embody the "Legal framework within which an autonomous community of a functional (sectoral) nature realizes its respective functional goal, *e.g.* trade liberalization, human rights protection, or the maintenance of international peace and security, *see* E. de Wet, *The International Constitutional Order*, 55 International and Comparative Law Quarterly 51, at 53 (2006) and Walter, *supra* note 23, at 193 *et seq.*

[30] *E.g.* P. M. Dupuy, *The Constitutional Dimension of the Charter of the United Nations Revisited*, 1 Max Planck Yearbook of United Nations Law 1 (1997) and B. Fassbender, *The United Nations Charter as Constitution of the International Community*, 36 Columbia Journal of Transnational Law 529 (1998).

designed. They focus, e.g., on the question whether it is possible to filter out a notional evolution for an international community without the necessary element of the state.[31] They envision – normatively – a world order embedded in constitutionalism and are "striving for a global legal community that frames and directs political power in light of common values and a common good."[32] As Bryde has put it: "a constitutionalist concept of international law tries to bind these actors [states and international organizations] [...] to substantive constitutional principles, especially the rule of law and human rights."[33]

Mainly the authors focus on substantive issue areas which show a tendency to restrict national sovereignty in a yet unknown way. Those are foremost the basic values which constitute a common core of values of the international community (of states), fulfilling certain functions. A focus on the constitutional functions allows to transpose the term constitutionalism to the European Communities as well as to the international sphere. Here therefore, international constitutional law will be defined, following *Peters*, as "the bulk of the most important norms which regulate political activity and relationships in the global polity (consisting of states and other subjects of international law)."[34] There does not exist an exact consensus as to what the constitutional functions in PIL are but some common ground can be filtered out. More abstractly put, a constitution is supposed to limit, guide and legitimize politics.[35] There are different definition of functions to be found – a more minimalist notion suffices with only organizing and institutionalizing a polity, a more specific notion relates to

> rules and principles *fulfilling typical constitutional functions* [...] [that] constitute a political entity as a legal entity, to organize it, to limit political

---

[31] *See* instead of many B. Simma & A. L. Paulus, *The 'International Community': Facing the Challenge of Globalization*, 9 European Journal of International Law 266 (1998); A. L. Paulus, Die internationale Gemeinschaft im Völkerrecht (2001) and Tomuschat, *supra* note 22, at 161 *et seq*. *See also* Walter, *supra* note 23, at 172, citing Art. 42 lit. b and 48 Sec. 1 lit. b ILC Draft Articles on State Responsibility (UN Doc. A/CN.4/L.602/Rev.1.(2001)) which refers only to the 'international community' but not the 'international Community of States' as in Art. 53 VCLT.

[32] Von Bogdandy, *supra* note 22, at 223.

[33] B. O. Bryde, *International Democratic Constitutionalism*, *in* R. St. J. MacDonald & D. M. Johnston (Eds.), Towards World Constitutionalism 103 (2005).

[34] Peters, *supra* note 15, at 582 who does not take into account the changeability as well as de Wet, *supra* note 29, 53:

> This article extends the use of the term constitution [...] to describe a system in which the different national regional and functional (sectoral) constitutional regimes form the building blocks of the international community ('international polity') that is underpinned by a core value system common to all communities and embedded in a variety of legal structures for its enforcement.

[35] Von Bogdandy, *supra* note 22, and Peters, *supra* note 15, at 585.

> power, to offer political and moral guidelines, to justify governance, and, finally, to contribute to integration.[36]

Peters gives also a more normative value-laden definition. Here, substantive functions are added, such as human rights, the separation of powers as necessary elements as well as other functions, such as democracy and a minimum of social security guarantees.[37] More specifically for the international sphere, Tomuschat views this thick constitutional function with respect to international law in

> safeguarding international peace, security and justice in relations between States, and human rights as well as the rule of law domestically inside States for the benefit of human beings, who, in substance, are the ultimate addressees of international law.[38]

Thus, classical functions of the nation state such as safeguarding individual liberty, freedom and safety are transferred to the international sphere. The European Court of Human Rights even declared the European Convention for the Protection of Human Rights and Fundamental Freedoms[39] to be a "constitutional instrument of European public order",[40] having a "peremptory character."[41]

There is no consensus, though, whether constitutionalism is to be viewed as a phenomenon applicable to the entire international community or whether it takes place only in sectoral regimes, such as, *e.g.*, WTO law.[42] It might well be that international organizations, such as the WTO have their own sectoral constitution (as the Marrakesh Agreement). Nevertheless, if we strive for international constitutionalism, unity of PIL is a *desideratum*. Constitutionalism of the international community has to focus on substantive

---

36 Peters, *supra* note 15, at 585 and more extensively A. Peters, Elemente einer Theorie der Verfassung Europas (2001).

37 Peters, *supra* note 15, at 585.

38 Tomuschat, *supra* note 31, at 23.

39 European Convention for the Protection of Human Rights and Fundamental Freedoms, Rome, adopted 4 November 1950, entry into force 3 September 1953, 213 UNTS 222.

40 ECtHR, Case 15318/89, Loizidou *v.* Turkey (preliminary objections), para. 75.

41 ECtHR, Case 45036/98, Bosphorus Hava Yollari Turzim ve Ticaret Anonim Sirketi *v.* Ireland, para. 154.

42 Walter, *supra* note 23, at 195:

> Constitutionalisation only occurs within the various sectoral regimes, but fails to reach the international community as a whole. Given the limited areas in which the Security Council may take legally binding decisions, this statement is also true for the United Nations.

Differently: E. U. Petersmann, *Constitutionalism, International Law and 'We the Peoples of the United Nations'*, *in* H. J. Cremer (Ed.), Tradition und Weltoffenheit des Rechts. Festschrift für Helmut Steinberger 291 (2002). For the constitutionalization of WTO, *see especially* E. U. Petersmann, *Human Rights, Constitutionalism and the World Trade Organization*, 19 Leiden Journal of International Law 633 (2006).

values or the common good which might not to be found in one sectoral regime alone but in the consideration of the different principles found in the different regimes and their reconciliation. In German national constitutional terms, this would be called 'praktische Konkordanz': reconciling different constitutional principles in a most considerate way. Thus, if we think in constitutional functions, it does not matter for our purposes whether there are only sectoral constitutions or one encompassing constitution: "global constitutionalism does not require global constitutional law."[43]

Which are then the 'constitutional principles' to be considered on the international plane? The 'empirical' case to be found for international constitutionalism has to be unearthed in different sectoral developments, filtered out by inductive doctrinal work; the legal phenomena being the 'empirical' material. The issue areas to be cited in the literature are mainly international human rights, which have a tendency to supersede national constitutional law, international humanitarian law, self-determination, international criminal law, the ever more extensive legislating practice of the United Nations Security Council when acting under Chapter VII of the UN Charter, some aspects of international environmental law, and I wish to add international trade law as well as international investment law (as principles of individual property rights and freedom of profession/occupation and free trade). I will concentrate in this paper on substantive legal principles such as human rights on the one hand and trade and investment principles on the other hand. But the constitutional principles to be considered may well be extended, e.g. to environmental protection.

It is submitted that in order to strive for unity of the international legal order, constitutional interpretation is an adequate means,[44] if only a second-best solution in the absence of hierarchy and explicit drafting. This is no new idea,[45] but until now, this has rather been stated as a *desideratum* in the literature on international constitutionalism; no in-depth legal theoretical or methodological analysis has been undertaken, certainly not for horizontal conflicts of 'intra-constitutional' conflicts. It is worth to quote *Bryde* in full:

> Methodologically, the point of reference for classical international law has been private contract law. The commanding inspiration for interpretation is the parties' intent [...]. With a changed structure of international law in which the interests of mankind is paramount and in which lawmaking is subjected to constitutional principles, the methodology, too, can be and must be constitutionalized. Interpretation of international law must be directed towards the attainment of the constitutional principles. These constitutional principles

[43] Gardbaum, *supra* note 11, at 30.

[44] Bryde, *supra* note 33.

[45] *Id.*, at 109; Fassbender, *supra* note 30, at 595 *et seq.*; J. E. Alvarez, *Constitutional Interpretation in International Organizations*, *in* J. M. Coicaud & V. Heiskanen (Eds.), The Legitimacy of International Organizations 104 (2001); G. Ress, *Interpretation*, *in* B. Simma *et al.* (Eds.), The Charter of the United Nations. A Commentary 13 (2002).

> are much more open textured and therefore much more adaptable to new circumstances and to a reception of normative arguments, especially the results of a human rights discourse.[46]

Conflicts of values and principles of different issue areas of PIL can thus be solved through the balancing of those competing principles for solving intra-constitutional conflicts on the international plane.

3. De-Fragmentation Through Interpretation

Constitutionalized legal systems are characterized by rules of conflict, the most important one being the *lex superior* rule, giving constitutional law precedent over other laws. Unless one claims that human rights should *always* 'trump' other international law, a not well sustainable claim, we are still left with a mainly horizontal system with the exception of *ius cogens* (which does contain some human rights) and Article 103 UN Charter.[47]

Clearly, the functions of human rights in the context of international constitutionalism are several. They are seen to fill gaps in the national protection of human rights, either substantially or with a view to territorial limits of the national constitution; they are seen as imposing limits on how a state may treat its own population; they add a new commitment by 'outsourcing' the review of human rights, a "second set of legal limits."[48] All those functions clearly have a vertical implication: they describe the relationship between the international and the national legal order.[49] But there is another, additional function of the international human rights system which can be called a horizontal function: they give guidelines to international courts in interpreting non-human rights law. This is the point I will subsequently focus on, since international human rights are one part of the international value system, but not the only one

---

[46] Bryde, *supra* note 33, at 109.

[47] *See* for details J. H. H. Weiler & A. L. Paulus, *The Structure of Change in International Law or Is There a Hierarchy of Norms in International Law?*, 8 European Journal of International Law 545 (1997). *See* for a cautious change of interpretation of Art. 103 UN Charter now the Kadi/Barakaat Joined Cases C-402/05 P and C-415/05 of 03 Sept. 2008, para. 303:

> Those provisions cannot, however, be understood to authorise any derogation from the principles of liberty, democracy and respect for human rights and fundamental freedoms enshrined in Article 6(1) EU as a foundation of the Union.

It held at para. 307 *et seq*. that the Charter of the United Nations would have primacy over acts of secondary Community law but that primacy at the level of Community law would not, however, extend to primary law, in particular to the general principles of which fundamental rights form part.

[48] Gardbaum, *supra* note 11, at 29.

[49] Generally on this interaction, D. Sloss & D. Jinks (Eds.), The Role of Domestic Courts in Treaty Enforcement (2009).

in the fragmented international system; that is, not the vertical function of human rights but the horizontal function in international adjudication will be analyzed.

Any starting point for the interpretation of treaties are Articles 31 and 32 VCLT.[50] Article 31(1) states as the general rule for interpretation (1) the ordinary meaning of the terms of the treaty, (2) the context and (3) that the treaty has to be interpreted in light of the treaty's object and purpose. It is widely accepted that the aim of treaty interpretation is to give effect to the intention of the parties. There is no consensus of whether there is a hierarchy in the arguments. Whereas common lawyers tend to stress the ordinary meaning,[51] continental lawyers tend to stress the object and purpose as teleological method.[52] Reconsidering the debate on interpretative methods of Article 31(1) VCLT is beyond the scope of this article. Nevertheless, the object and the purpose of a treaty can be of special of interest for defragmenting interpretation. If the object and the purpose[53] of the treaty contains (also) human rights, those may be used in a teleological interpretation of the treaty itself, leading to harmonious interpretation. If, e.g. a Bilateral Investment Treaty (BIT) contains reference to human rights in its preamble, the interpretation of the norms of the treaty should take human rights concerns into account when interpreting the norms of the investment treaty, even if human rights protection is not the main purpose of the treaty.[54] Nevertheless, most non-human rights treaties do not contain such a reference.

---

50 *See* instead of many R. K. Gardiner, Treaty Interpretation (2008); S. Jennings & A. Watts (Eds.), I Oppenheim's International Law, Part 2 to 4 (Peace) (1992/1905), at 1266 *et seq*. Those rules of interpretation are accepted customary international law. For supplementary means of interpretation such as *contra preferentem*, *in dubio mitius* or *expressio unius est exclusio alterus*, *see id*., at 1277 *et seq*.

51 Although it is well known from legal theory that in order to construct the ordinary meaning of a term, exactly those other interpretational methods are needed. As stated early on in Jennings & Watts, *supra* note 50, at 1267: "The finding whether a treaty is clear or not is not the starting point but the result of the process of interpretation."

52 For different schools of thought in treaty interpretation *see* G. Fitzmaurice, *Law and Procedure of the International Court of Justice 1951-4: Treaty Interpretation and Other Treaty Points*, 33 British Yearbook of International Law 203 (1957); T. Wälde, *Interpreting Investment Treaties. Considerations and Examples Highlighting Confusion Arising and Clarity Desired*, *in* Festschrift Christoph Schreuer (forthcoming).

53 Especially treaties with a constitutional character, such as the Treaty of the European Communities, the object and purpose becomes more important. Generally, the purpose of a treaty can be found in its preamble and annexes. *See* Fitzmaurice, *supra* note 52, at 227-229 with references to court decisions.

54 *See e.g.* the draft Norwegien Model BIT (now abandoned) in its preamble:

> Reaffirming their commitment to democracy, the rule of law, human rights and fundamental freedoms in accordance with their obligations under international law, including the principles set out in the United Nations Charter and the Universal Declaration of Human Rights [...].

Another opening window for considering human rights treaties in the application of non-human rights treaties is Article 31 (3) (c) VCLT. Its explicit use has only recently become more frequent; it has just awoken to its potential significance and literature on its operationalization is scarce.[55] The possibility of using Article 31(3)(c) VCLT has been discussed for the WTO, but not for investment law, although ICSID tribunals[56] have heavily relied on the application of the VCLT,[57] especially Article 31(1) VCLT. But they do not resort explicitly to Article 31(3)(c) VCLT for interpreting clauses of BITs, even if they used other special PIL for interpretation. But the correct means of integration of human rights law, that is, non-investment or non-trade law in investment and trade disputes is the applicability of Article 31(3)(c) VCLT under which an interpretation should take into account "any relevant rules of international law applicable in the relations between the parties."[58]

Commentators have viewed Article 31(3)(c) VCLT as a "general principle of treaty interpretation, namely that of systemic integration within the international legal system," having the "status of a constitutional norm within the international legal system. In this role, it serves a function analogous to that of a master-key in a large building."[59] No international law norm can be considered in isolation, it has to be interpreted in the light of other international law, be it general international law, customary international law or even other treaty norms which might be conflicting.

Gardiner views the different functions of Article 31(3)(c) VCLT as following:

> (a) resolving time issues (including application of the intertemporal law); (b) completing the legal picture, or filling gaps, in a treaty by reference to general international law; (c) deriving guidance from parallel treaty provisions; (d) resolving conflicting obligations arising under different treaties; (e) taking account of international law developments.[60]

---

55 International Law Commission, *supra* note 3, para. 433.

56 Convention on the Settlement of Investment Disputes Between States and the Nationals of Other States (ICSID Convention), Washington D.C., 18 March 1965, in force 14 October 1966, 575 UNTS 159. Most investment disputes are conducted under this convention.

57 *See* C. Schreuer, *Diversity and Harmonization of Treaty Interpretation in Investment Arbitration*, 3 Transnational Dispute Management (online journal) (2006) for the application of the VCLT by investment tribunals and Hirsch, *supra* note 10. *See e.g.*, for NAFTA, Pope & Talbot, Inc. *v.* Canada (26 June 2000), Interim Award – Unreported (UNCITRAL), paras. 65-66 and Mondev Int'l, Ltd. *v.* United States, NAFTA, ICSID Case No. ARB(AF)/99/2, Second Submission of Canada, para. 5.

58 That is the commonly held view, *see* J. Pauwelyn *The Role of Public International Law in the WTO: How Far Can We Go?*, 95 American Journal of International Law 554, at 554-566 (2001); Marceau, *supra* note 9.

59 C. MacLachlan, *The Principle of Systematic Integration and Article 31(3)(c) of the Vienna Convention*, 54 International & Comparative Law Quarterly 279, at 280 *et seq*. (2005) as well as the International Law Commission, *supra* note 3, para. 413 *et seq*.

60 Gardiner, *supra* note 50, at 260.

The latter two are of special relevance to this article as will be illustrated later on.

Several issues are discussed in conjunction with the interpretation of Article 31(3)(c) VCLT: first, which sources of international law may be used – customary norms, general principles and/or treaty law. Here, a consensus is emerging, also due to the *traveaux préparatoire* of the VCLT,[61] that all sources of international law, including treaties are meant to be included.[62] Also human rights law which has acquired the status of customary international law can thus be considered in the application of non-human rights treaties under Article 31(3)(c) VCLT.

Second, as concerns treaties, it remains an open question whether, in cases of multilateral treaties, all parties to the treaty have also to be party to the other treaties relied upon (identical membership requirement) or whether Article 31(3)(c) VCLT allows already for the application of PIL relevant only to the parties in the dispute at hand – greatly enhancing its significance.[63] Generally, the literature takes the latter, broader view. One, in my view, convincing argument *ad absurdum* against the identical membership argument was made by Gabrielle Marceau. If a multilateral treaty is to be applied, the more encompassing its membership, the less could other treaty law be taken into account. If, *e.g.*, 153 WTO members are party to a human rights treaties, allowing to take the human rights treaty into account, then a new acceding member to the WTO which is not party to the human rights treaty would, under this understanding, then prohibit the reference to this human rights treaty later on. In other words: the more successful a multilateral treaty, the more it would have to be read in isolation.[64] Nevertheless, in the Biotech case, the WTO panel took this narrow view. Here, the European Community had argued that its ban on the importation of genetically modified organisms (GMOs) could be justified, *inter alia*, by non-WTO rules. In particular, it was argued that account should be taken of the 1992 Convention on Biological Diversity and the related Biosafety Protocol of 2000. The panel held that all the parties to the treaty to be interpreted needed to have become parties to that other treaty:

> we note that Article 31(3)(c) does not refer to 'one or more parties'. Nor does it refer to 'the parties to a dispute'. We further note that Article 2.1(g) of the Vienna Convention defines the meaning of the term 'party' for the purposes of the Vienna Convention. Thus, 'party' means 'a State which has consented to be bound by the treaty and for which the treaty is in force'. It may be inferred from these elements that the rules of international law applicable in the relations between 'the parties' are the rules of international law applicable in the relations

[61] *Id.*, at 256 *et seq.*; International Law Commission, *supra* note 3, para. 429 *et seq.*

[62] Marceau, *supra* note 9, at 780; Gardiner, *supra* note 50, at 261 *et seq.*; International Law Commission, *supra* note 3.

[63] *See* for discussions Marceau, *supra* note 9, at 781 *et seq.* and MacLachlan, *supra* note 59, at 314 *et seq.* and Gardiner, *supra* note 50, at 269-275.

[64] Marceau, *supra* note 9, at 781.

> between the States which have consented to be bound by the treaty which is being interpreted, and for which that treaty is in force. This understanding of the term 'the parties' leads logically to the view that the rules of international law to be taken into account in interpreting the WTO agreements at issue in this dispute are those which are applicable in the relations between the WTO Members.[65]

Since the US is not a member of the Biosafety Protocol, it was not applicable. The panel also held that the precautionary principle has not acquired the status of customary law nor has it become a general principle of PIL and was thus not applicable.[66]

Third, there is the problem that the relevant rules to be taken into account may operate on different levels of generality: they can thus be rules or principles in legal theoretical terms. This is not the same distinction as is drawn in Article 38 ICJ statute, which includes as a source "general principles of law recognized by civilized nations," but the theoretical character of the principles is similar to the principles as understood in legal theoretical terms. Rules are undisputedly relevant. But are principles relevant? As the Biotech Panel held, yes. Also in the case of the Iron Rhine,[67] the Tribunal held that

> [t]here is considerable debate as to what, within the field of environmental law, constitutes 'rules' or 'principles'; what is 'soft law'; and which environmental treaty law or principles have contributed to the development of customary international law. Without entering further into those controversies, the Tribunal notes that in all of these categories 'environment' is broadly referred to as including air, water, land, flora and fauna, natural ecosystems and sites, human health and safety, and climate. The emerging principles, whatever their current status, make reference to conservation, management, notions of prevention and of sustainable development, and protection for future generations [...][68]

Those general principles would also fulfill the definition of principles as understood by legal theory: they can be fulfilled more or less and are to be optimized.

The European Court of Human Rights refers also to principles as being relevant under Article 31(3)(c) VCLT:

> Article 31 para. 3 (c) of the Vienna Convention indicates that account is to be taken, together with the context, of 'any relevant rules of international law applicable in the relations between the parties'. Among those rules are general principles of law and especially 'general principles of law recognized by civilized nations' (Article 38 para. 1 (c) of the Statute of the International Court of Justice)[...].The principle whereby a civil claim must be capable of being

[65] *European Communities – Measures Affecting the Approval and Marketing of Biotech Products*, Reports of the Panel, 29 September 2006, WT/DS291-3/R at 333, para. 7.68.

[66] *Id.*, para. 7.89.

[67] *Arbitration Regarding the Iron Rhine ('IJzeren Rijn') Railway* (Belgium/Netherlands), Award of 24 May 2005.

[68] *Id.*, para. 58.

> submitted to a judge ranks as one of the universally 'recognised' fundamental principles of law; the same is true of the principle of international law which forbids the denial of justice. Article 6 para. 1 must be read in the light of these principles.[69]

Fourth, there are different opening windows for including other special law into the regime at hand, each giving different interpretational leeway to international courts and tribunals. They can thus be only discussed with a view on the treaty norm to be applied. In WTO law, the general exceptions in Article XX GATT[70] or Article XIV and Article XIVbis GATS are relevant opening provisions. Also, there might be an explicit provision in one treaty calling for the application of other treaties, as e.g. in Article 104 NAFTA and clarifying precedence.[71] Furthermore, a treaty rule may be unclear and other PIL may be used to clarify the meaning with interpretational means of Article 31(1) VCLT. In this latter case, not balancing is the issue, but rather the clarification of the content by definitional means. But choosing interpretation under Article 31(1) or interpretation under Article 31(3)(c) VCLT can be a difficult task. Although a distinction has to be drawn conceptually between the *application* of other (general or special) norms of international law in non-human rights disputes directly on the one hand and the *interpretation* of non-human rights law by considering human rights law, indirectly, through Article 31(1) or Article 31(3)(c) VCLT on the other hand, there might nevertheless be only a fine line between applying human rights law directly or importing it through interpretation:

> In practice [...] there is a good chance that the two (application and interpretation) might lapse into each other – such would seem well-nigh inevitable, if only because it would be difficult to apply something without at the same time interpreting it, and to interpret a term without a context in which to apply it.[72]

---

69 Golder *v.* the United Kingdom, Series A, vol. 18 (Judgement of 21 February 1975), para. 35.

70 As e.g. the Appellate Body has done in *United States – Import Prohibition of Certain Shrimp and Shrimp Products* (6 November 1998) WT/DS58/AB/R, DSR 1998:VII, at 2794-2797, paras. 127-131 when applying Art. XX GATT.

71 Art. 104:

> Relation to Environmental and Conservation Agreements: 1. In the event of any inconsistency between this Agreement and the specific trade obligations set out in: a) the Convention on International Trade in Endangered Species [...]; b) the Montreal Protocol on Substances that Deplete the Ozone Layer [...]; c) the Basel Convention on the Control of Transboundary Movements of Hazardous Wastes and Their Disposal [...] such obligations shall prevail to the extent of the inconsistency, provided that where a Party has a choice among equally effective and reasonably available means of complying with such obligations, the Party chooses the alternative that is the least inconsistent with the other provisions of this Agreement.

72 J. Klabbers, *Reluctant Grundnormen: Articles 31(3)(c) and 42 of the Vienna Convention on*

Article 31(3)(c) VCLT does not state *how* potentially conflicting norms have to be integrated systemically, it just states that they have to integrated. It is worth quoting the ILC in full:

> None of this predetermines what it means to 'confront' a norm with another or how they might enter into 'concurrence'. These matters must be left to the interpreter to decide in view of the situation. The point is only – but it is a key point – that the normative environment cannot be ignored and that when interpreting the treaties, the principle of integration should be borne in mind. This points to the need to carry out the interpretation so as to see the rules in view of some comprehensible and coherent objective, to prioritize concerns that are more important at the cost of less important objectives. This is all that article 31 (3) (c) requires; the integration into the process of legal reasoning – including reasoning by courts and tribunals – of a sense of coherence and meaningfulness. Success or failure here is measured by how the legal world will view the outcome.[73]

It is submitted that Article 31(3)(c) VCLT allows for what German constitutional lawyers call 'praktische Konkordanz':[74] reconciling different and competing principles of a constitutional order in cases when Article 31(3)(c) VCLT allows for the taking into account of other rules and principles of PIL.[75] Tribunals may thus deal with the underlying conflicts of human rights law with other special areas of PIL through interpretational means such as balancing and the principle of proportionality by using human rights law in the interpretation of non-human rights law through Article 31(3)(c) VCLT. The question of *how* other rules of PIL are to be incorporated by interpretation is not dealt with by Article 31(3)(c) VCLT. I would therefore suggest using a functional approach similar to national constitutional law, based on a rational theory of balancing following Robert Alexy.[76]

---

the Law of Treaties and the Fragmentation of International Law, *in* M. Craven, M. Fitzmaurice & M. Vogiatzi (Eds.), Time, History and International Law 141, at 144 (2007).

[73] International Law Commission, *supra* note 3, para. 419.

[74] K. Hesse, Grundzüge der Verfassungsrechts der Bundesrepublik Deutschland (1995), para. 72:

> Verfassungsrechtlich geschützte Rechtsgüter müssen in der Problemlösung einander so zugeordnet werden, daß jedes von ihnen Wirklichkeit gewinnt. [...] beiden Gütern müssen Grenzen gesetzt werden, damit beide zu optimaler Wirksamkeit gelangen können.

This was followed by the German Constitutional Court as well as e.g. the *Court Constitutionel* in France.

[75] Similarly, Gardiner, *supra* note 50, at 288 *et seq*.

[76] R. Alexy, *On Balancing and Subsumption. A Structural Comparison*, 16 Ratio Juris 433 (2003); van Aaken, *supra* note 18.

4. A Rational Theory of Balancing

The method of balancing is mostly used in constitutional law and finds its most prominent form in the principle of proportionality. Starting from German law, it diffused around most legal systems of the world and deeply into international law.[77] As the Israeli Supreme Court has held, "[p]roportionality is recognized today as a general principle of international law."[78] Although it may be named differently, it is widely applied in all countries with constitutional review as well as in international law (*e.g.* by the European Court of Human Rights as well as in Appellate Body Decisions in the WTO).[79]

The legal theoretical elaboration of the principle of proportionality has been delivered by Robert Alexy. Alexy's work is being cited as "one of the most penetrating, analytically refined, and influential general accounts of constitutional rights available,"[80] and "arguably the most important and influential work of constitutional theory written in the last fifty years."[81] Two main propositions are central to Alexy's theory: first, the distinction between rules and principles and second that principles are optimization programs, that is, they have to be realized to the greatest extent possible, given factual and legal constraints. Rules may or may not be applicable but principles are more or less fulfilled and command optimization under consideration of the factual and legal possibilities, thus giving also more space to social science considerations.[82]

Conventionally, legal methodology distinguishes between subsumption on the one hand and balancing or weighing on the other hand. Whereas the first is used if one deals with rules, the latter is used if one deals with

[77] Extensively for a description of the diffusion, *see* A. Stone Sweet & J. Mathews, *Proportionality Balancing and Global Constitutionalism* (2008), available at http://works.bepress.com/cgi/viewcontent.cgi?article=1010&context=alec_stone_sweet.

[78] Beit Sourik Village Council *v.* The Government of Israel, HCJ 2056/04 (30 June 2004), para. 37. This is widely confirmed, *see* R. Higgins, Problems and Process. International Law and How We Use It 219 (1994); T. Meron, Human Rights and Humanitarian Norms as Customary Law 65 (1989); J. Delbrück, *Proportionality*, *in* R. Bernhardt (Ed.), III Encyclopedia of Public International Law 1140 (1997).

[79] For the necessity test in WTO law, *see* P. A. Delimatsis, *Determining the Necessity of Domestic Regulations in Services: The Best is Yet to Come*, 19 European Journal of International Law 365 (2008).

[80] M. Kumm, *Constitutional Rights as Principles: On the Structure and Domain of Constitutional Justice*, 2 International Journal of Constitutional Law 574, at 596 (2004).

[81] Stone Sweet & Mathews, *supra* note 77, at 14, referring to R. Alexy, Theorie der Grundrechte (1996), English translation "A Theory of Constitutional Rights", J. Rivers (trans.), (2002). Here, the German version will be used.

[82] For the difference between rules and principle as applied here, *see* Alexy, *supra* note 81, at 72 *et seq*. and R. Alexy, *Zum Begriff des Rechtsprinzips*, *in* R. Alexy (Ed.), Recht, Vernunft, Diskurs: Studien zur Rechtsphilosophie 177 (1995), discussing also Dworkin's way of understanding this distinction.

principles. Rights as well as to collective goods or goals formulated in the constitution (Staatszielbestimmungen), such as environmental protection are seen as principles.[83] Proportionality is thus not confined to individual rights balancing. This is to be kept in mind, since the original and still most common application of the principle of proportionality is in human rights adjudication, where a legitimate state or public interest might be used to limit human rights or where the human right of one person is balanced against the one of another person. But the principle of proportionality may also be used if two competing public purposes or state interests are at stake, such as trade and environment.

Principles are thus applicable even if they are not 'fully' satisfied: they are norms which can be more or less realized, *e.g.* the democratic principle, the right to freedom of opinion or the principle of free trade. One may also call them concepts which have to be concretized in the discourse of legal application to find (common) conceptions.[84] Concepts such as justice, fairness, human rights, peace and security as values are concretized in PIL, be it through treaties, custom or general principles, but they have to be further concretized in the discourse of law application to find (common) conceptions as they are sometimes competing. One realization of this imperative is the proportionality principle.

I will argue here in line with Alexy that balancing is a rational procedure in its main part and very close to the reasoning of optimization (or cost-benefit analysis). Formulated in normative decision theory terms,[85] this means the optimality of measures generally and regulations, laws and legal acts specifically with a view on a defined system of goals (the international constitutional principles) and under consideration of (legal) constraints. A 'constitution' is viewed as a multicriterial or multidimensional decision system. Thus, different decision-alternatives can be compared with regard to their contribution to the constitutional objectives. The optimal decision is the alternative that maximizes the net-surplus, defined as benefits minus the cost of a measure. Benefits and costs are defined in constitutional terms and include the positive effects of the measure in question on all relevant constitutional principles as benefits and the negative effects as costs. In order to evaluate different decision alternatives, the proportionality principle of balancing is used.

The proportionality principle comprises three sub-principles: the principle of suitability, the principle of necessity and the principle of proportionality in a narrow sense. The first two sub-principles lend themselves easily to

[83] Alexy, *supra* note 81, Ch. 3, esp. at 98.

[84] Seminar, W. N. Hohfeld, *Some Fundamental Legal Conceptions as Applied in Judicial Reasoning*, *in* W. W. Cook (Ed.), Fundamental Legal Conceptions as Applied in Judicial Reasoning and Other Essays (1923) and W. B. Gallie, *Essentially Contested Concepts*, 56 Proceedings of the Aristotelian Society 167 (1956).

[85] *See* extensively A. van Aaken, Rational-Choice in der Rechtswissenschaft. Zum Stellenwert der ökonomischen Theorie im Recht 288 *et seq.* (2003).

consequentialist and instrumental reasoning as they require comparative institutional analysis regarding the impact on the constitutional principle in question. The principle of suitability covers the question whether the measure or the law is in principle suitable to achieve its goal. The principle of necessity covers the question of whether there are other, less intrusive means with regard to the constitutional principle in question which are equally able to achieve the stated goal of the measure. Applying the principle of proportionality, as it has been done by the investment tribunals, human rights courts as well as the Appellate Body, thus necessarily includes consequentionalist reasoning. This method of reasoning in turn requires social science analysis if one does not want to resort to every day intuitions of a judge. The third principle, proportionality *strictu sensu*, is more open to value judgements and does not lend itself easily to social science approaches but rather to rational justification in law application. Alexy develops a complicated formula, developing scales on the intensity of interference with rights ('light', 'moderate', 'serious') and the importance of the right (*e.g.* right to life has a more abstract weight than freedom of expression, though the concrete weight has to be elaborated on a case-by-case basis). These scales are not arbitrary but to be justified by giving reasons in order to be contestable.[86] It is unnecessary to introduce higher criteria for decision-making, but it is necessary to use decision rules and make those transparent. Normative decision theory has developed many of these, *e.g.* the rules on the desired level of satisfaction ('Theorie des erwünschten Niveaus'; in legal speak: the essential content of a principle which may not be violated; 'Wesensgehalt'). A decision rule like that provides for a setting of a required level of satisfaction.[87] The decision of the German Federal Constitutional Court on the Air-Transport Security Act, e.g., set the required level of satisfaction for human dignity so high that any balancing is excluded (following the traditional doctrine in German constitutional law).[88]

But how do the principle of proportionality and Article 31(3)(c) VCLT connect? As the ILC has stated and as has already been cited:

> First is the effort to harmonize the apparently conflicting norms by interpreting them so as to render them compatible. Second is the technique whereby the question of validity has been replaced by a question of priority. The norm that

---

[86] Alexy, *supra* note 76.

[87] Graphically, one may clarify that by drawing a utility curve in a coordinate plane which allows weighing *strictu sensu* only in a range above a certain ordinal number. *See also* Alexy, *supra* note 81, at 147 *et seq*. In substance, that is similar to the proposal by E. Zamir & B. Medina, *Law, Morality, and Economics: Integrating Moral Constraints With Economic Analysis of Law*, Paper presented at the Annual Conference of the European Association of Law and Economics, Copenhagen 2007.

[88] BVerfG 1 BvR 357/05 (First Senat) – Decision of 15 Feb. 2006. *See also* O. Lepsius, *Human Dignity and the Downing of Aircraft: The German Federal Constitutional Court Strikes Down a Prominent Anti-terrorism Provision in the New Air-Transport Security Act*, 7 German Law Journal (online journal) (2006).

> will be set aside will remain as it were "in the background", continuing to influence the interpretation and application of the norm to which priority has been given. It follows that, contrary to what is sometimes suggested, conflict-resolution and interpretation cannot be distinguished from each other. Whether there is a conflict and what can be done with prima facie conflicts depends on the way the relevant rules are interpreted. This cannot be stressed too much.[89]

For conflicts in international law between non-human rights law and human rights law, this means that first, the judge has to consider whether human rights law informs the interpretation of the non-human rights treaty under Article 31(1) VCLT. Second, she has to consider whether human rights law is applicable between the parties under Article 31(3)(c) VCLT. This can either be the case if the human rights norm in question has acquired the status of customary international law or if both states to the dispute are parties to the human rights treaty in question. The judge then has to balance the principle of the treaty to be interpreted and in presumed conflict with human rights law with the human rights principle in question. In order to illuminate this technique, some examples of investment law and trade law will be given below.

5. Some Possible Applications

I will concentrate on here on the interaction of human rights law and international investment law as an example for the more general problems, since in international investment law those conflicts come to the fore quite obviously.[90] Investment law, as codified in Bilateral Investment Treaties (BITs) is being increasingly criticized, mainly because other areas of special international law are viewed as not being sufficiently taken into account. BITs are public international law treaties, giving foreign investors substantive protection against political risks and thus certain behavior of their host states as well as mostly direct access to international arbitral tribunals.[91]

First, states may explicitly take human rights inspired general measures in order to fulfill their international or constitutional human rights obligations but those measures may have a negative impact on foreign investors. Here, arbitral tribunals have considerable scope to interpret the BIT provisions in a way to balance human rights and investor protection, especially if the state has taken a non-discriminatory measure. The most prominent and mostly used protective provisions are indirect expropriation and 'fair and equitable treatment'. Those norms, as very indeterminate legal terms, also constitute opening windows

[89] International Law Commission, *supra* note 3, para. 411 *et seq*.

[90] *See* more extensively van Aaken, *supra* note 5.

[91] For overviews on investment law, *see* R. Dolzer & C. Schreuer, Principles of International Investment Law (2008) and Muchlinski, Ortino & Schreuer (Eds.), *supra* note 10.

for the consideration of human rights norms under Article 31(3)(c) VCLT. They require investment tribunals to identify the proper reference points for assessing the fairness and equity of measures adopted or maintained by host states. In the case of indirect expropriation, tribunals may not apply the 'sole effects' doctrine but may also include the purpose of the regulatory measure. Hereby, they may include e.g. potential environmental obligations or human rights obligations of a state as a reasonable purpose for the national measure in question.[92] The interpretation of 'indirect' expropriation has been meandering between the so-called 'sole effects doctrine', i.e. only the effect of the measure on the property is looked at, and the inclusion of the regulatory purpose. The inclusion of the latter allows for the application of the proportionality principle as e.g. the European Court of Human Rights (ECtHR) practices it for the European Convention for the Protection of Human Rights and Fundamental Freedoms (Article 1 of Protocol No. 1 for the right to property[93]).[94] The literature has taken up this idea from the Tecmed case, where the tribunal explicitly referred to the ECtHR jurisprudence.[95] Using the balancing of the proportionality principle greatly enhances the possibility of defragmentation in those cases. The new US Model BIT of 2004 mandates that when it states in its Annex B on expropriation that

> [e]xcept in rare circumstances, nondiscriminatory regulatory actions by a Party that are designed and applied to protect legitimate public welfare objectives, such as public health, safety, and the environment, do not constitute indirect expropriations.

The defendant state may then not only invoke its own law (if chosen), but also international non-investment law either indirectly through the national law or directly. Furthermore, in the context of fair and equitable treatment, the reference points for judging the fairness and equitableness of a measure could include special areas of PIL. If, *e.g.*, a country chooses to introduce protective

---

92 As *e.g.* the Appellate Body has done in *United States – Import Prohibition of Certain Shrimp and Shrimp Products* (6 November 1998) WT/DS58/AB/R, DSR 1998:VII, at 2794-2797, paras. 127-131 when applying Art. XX GATT.

93 Protocol to the Convention for the Protection of Human Rights and Fundamental Freedoms, Paris, adopted 20 March 1952, entry into force 18 May 1954, ETS 009.

94 *See e.g.* James and Others *v.* the United Kingdom (judgment of 21 February 1986, Series A no. 98), Lithgow and Others *v.* the United Kingdom (judgment of 8 July 1986, Series A no. 102), Matos e Silva, Lda., and Others *v.* Portugal, Judgment of 16 September 1996, Reports of Judgments and Decisions 1996-IV, at 1114, §86. *See more generally* U. Kriebaum, *Privatizing Human Rights: The Interface Between International Investment Protection and Human Rights*, 3 Transnational Dispute Management (online journal) (2006).

95 Tecnicas Medioambientales SA *v.* Mexico, (ICSID Arbitration Nr. ARB (AF)/00/2) (29 May 2003) (Tecmed), para. 122:

> There must be a reasonable relationship of proportionality between the charge or weight imposed to the foreign investor and the aim sought to be realized by any expropriatory measure.

measures for indigenous tribes and restricts the investment, the application of the ILO conventions on Indigenous People could enter the interpretation of fair and equitable treatment as well as expropriation.[96] Thus a balancing of conflicting values – investor protection and human rights – would take place on the international plane and by international tribunals.

Second, the state may use human rights as a defense for taking action against a foreign investor violating human rights under its duty to protect. Another possibility is that the investor and the state are complicit in human rights abuses. A case like this is unlikely to come to an international investment tribunal as tribunals do not have jurisdiction to hear human rights complaints by third (affected) parties. Clearly, in the first case, if a measure is taken in order not to violate a norm of *ius cogens*, *e.g.* prohibitions on forced, compulsory, indentured labor or other forms of slave-like labor, an investment tribunal would be bound to consider Article 53 of the VCLT as applicable law. Furthermore, a state may defend itself by taking recourse to its duty to respect, protect and fulfill its human rights obligations.[97] That may involve taking measures against a foreign investor or imposing regulations on foreign investors.[98] Nevertheless, states have rarely invoked their human rights obligations[99] and therefore, they have not yet been considered extensively by tribunals although there are some interesting cases pending.

One such case concerns issues of international human rights law in the field of discrimination. In this case Italian investors challenged the South African Black Economic Empowerment program as partially contained in the

---

[96] *See* Non-Party Submission, Glamis Gold Ltd. *v.* United States of America, Submission of the Quechan Indian Nation, Nature of the Cultural Resources and Sacred Places at Issue in Claim, at 8 *et seq.*, at http://www.naftaclaims.com/Disputes/USA/Glamis/Glamis-Amicus-Quechan-01--19-08-05.pdf. Here, the potentially affected people by the investment project in question, a mine, assert that they are protected by *inter alia*, the 1966 International Covenant on Civil and Political Rights, the 1972 UNESCO Convention on World Cultural Heritage, the ILO Convention on Indigenous and Tribal Peoples, and the Inter-American Convention on Human Rights.

[97] On those duties first Asbjørn Eide in his capacity as then Special Rapporteur on the Right to Food of the UN Sub-Commission on the Prevention of Discrimination and the Protection of Minorities. *See* A. Eide, *Right to Adequate Food as a Human Right* (1989) and *id.*, Final Report 'The Right to Adequate Food as a Human Right', UN Doc. E/CN.4/Sub.2/1987/23.

[98] The European Court of Human Rights, *e.g.* stated that states have the positive obligation to impose certain informational duties on firms which emit emissions dangerous to health under Art. 8 of the ECHR, *see* Case of López Ostra *v.* Spain (Application No. 16798/90), Judgment of 9 December 1994, Series A (1995) No. 303, at 41, Case of Guerra and others *v.* Italy (Application No. 14967/89), Judgment of 19 February 1998, ECtHR 1998-I, No. 64, at 210.

[99] To my knowledge, the only cases which have been decided until now, concern the Argentinian crisis where Argentina invoked human rights obligations of its constitution, based on international human rights instruments. *See* CMS Gas Transmission Company *v.* Argentine Republic, (ICSID Case No. Arb/01/8), (12 May 2005), para. 114. The tribunal found that there was no collision between investment protection and the constitution of Argentina, para. 115 *et seq.*

2004 Mineral and Petroleum Resources Development Act (MPRDA).[100] They alleged that this affirmative action program of South Africa for 'historically disadvantaged individuals' infringes on their rights under the Italian-South African BIT, including national treatment. This pending case will certainly give rise to principal issues of conflict not only between the BIT and Article 9 of the South-African Constitution but also under international human rights norms such as those contained in the Convention on the Elimination of All Forms of Racial Discrimination[101] and other provisions on discrimination in international human rights law.[102]

Other potential conflicts may arise in the area of privatized public services such as water.[103] Does international human rights law such as the right to water need to be taken into account when adjudicating upon the measures of the host state? What if, *e.g.* a price cap or price differentiation is demanded for by governmental measures *ex post*? What if there is a dispute on the contractual fulfillment by the investor and/or water 'black outs' or contaminated water delivery? Similar issues were at stake in some cases already and more are expected to come up.[104] Depending on how the contract is (not) performed in a public service concession, the state's duty to protect might be at stake, i.e. it may be that it has to take certain regulatory measures in order to fulfill its international (and probably also constitutional) obligations. It may be required to do so by acting based on the precautionary principle, even if *ex post* there was no danger to health.[105] Clearly, tribunals are aware that human rights issues are at stake[106] and they have the interpretational freedom to take the

[100] Piero Foresti, Laura De Carli and others *v.* Republic of South Africa, ICSID Case No. ARB(AF)/07/1 (31 August 2007).

[101] Adopted by G.A. Res. 2106A (XX), U.N. GAOR, XX, Supp. No. 14, at 47, UN Doc A/6014, adopted 21 December 1965, entry into force 4 January 1969.

[102] *See* for details M. Coleman & K. Williams, *South Africa's Bilateral Investment Treaties, Black Economic Empowerment and Mining: A Fragmented Meeting?*, 9 Business Law International 56 (2008).

[103] The right to water is spelled out in CESCR General Comment No. 15 (2003), The right to water (Arts. 11 and 12 of the CESCR), E/C.12/2002/11, 20 January 2003.

[104] Several cases involving water distribution and sewage services have been brought: Compañía de Aguas del Aconquija S.A. and Vivendi Universal *v.* Argentine Republic, ICSID Case No. ARB/97/3 (20 August 2007); Azurix Corp. *v.* Argentine Republic, ICSID Case No. ARB/01/12, (14 July 2006); BiwaterGauff (Tanzania) LTD. *v.* Tanzania, ICSID Case No. ARB/05/22 (24 July 2008); Aguas del Tunari *v.* Boliva, ICSID Case No. Arb/02/3, Decision on Jurisdiction of 21 October 2005. More than 10 cases are pending in water services, not all of them known, *see* Investment Treaty News of 26 July 2006.

[105] That was at issue in the *Vivendi* Case, where the water showed turbidity during approximately three month (paras. 4.13 *et seq.*) but posed no danger to human health. Nevertheless, the facts are such that for a government acting on precaution, some of the measures taken seem appropriate and even requested.

[106] *See* Biwater *v.* Tanzania, Procedural Order No. 5, at http://icsid.worldbank.org/ICSID/FrontServlet?requestType=CasesRH&actionVal=showDoc&docId=DC532_En&caseId=C67 (visited 2 February 2007); Order in Response to a Petition for Participation as Amicus Curiae,

human rights obligations of host states into account when adjudicating upon indirect expropriation as well as fair and equitable treatment.

A further problem may arise in cases where indigenous rights are at stake, e.g. in natural resources extraction.[107] One pending NAFTA case illustrates that quite well. A California law[108] requires the complete backfilling of open-pit mines near Native American sacred sites, including the site of a planned project by Glamis Gold, a Canadian investor who claims indirect expropriation. The Quechan Indian Nation, who claim that their religious sites are affected by the mining project, filed an amicus curiae brief,[109] alleging *i.a.* the relevance of Article 27 of the International Covenant on Civil and Political Rights.[110] They as well as the defendant mention the relevance of several other international law instruments concerning cultural heritage.[111] Here again, the question is

---

in the proceedings between Aguas Provinciales de Santa Fe S.A., Suez, Sociedad General de Aguas de Barcelona S.A., and InterAguas Servicios Integrales del Agua S.A. .*v*. The Argentine Republic, ICSID Case No. ARB/03/17 (17 March 2006), para. 18:

> The factor that gives this case particular public interest is that the investment dispute centers around the water distribution and sewage systems of urban areas in the province of Santa Fe. Those systems provide basic public services to hundreds of thousands of people and as a result may raise a variety of complex public and international law questions, including human rights considerations. Any decision rendered in this case, whether in favor of the Claimants or the Respondent, has the potential to affect the operation of those systems and thereby the public they serve.

[107] A case which could have been a potential investment dispute concerns a known case of the Inter-American Court of Human Rights: The Mayagna (Sumo) Awas Tingni Community *v*. Nicaragua, Judgment of 31 August 2001, Inter-Am. Ct. H.R., (Ser. C) No. 79 (2001), where the government of Nicaragua granted logging concessions to logging firms on the territory of an indigenous tribe. If the government had been revoking those licences (as it had to after the judgment) and the firms would have been foreign investors protected by a BIT, the issue before an investment tribunal would have been clearly conflicting. *See* for that decision S. J. Anaya & C. Grossman, *The Case of Awas Tingni v. Nicaragua: A New Step in the International Law of Indigenous People*, 19 Arizona Journal of International and Comparative Law 1 (2002).

[108] California State Mining and Geology Board (SMGB) regulations and California Senate Bill (SB 22).

[109] Submission of Non-Disputing Party Quechan Indian Nation, Glamis Gold Ltd *v*. The United States of America, *supra* note 96, at 6 *et seq*.

[110] International Covenant on Civil and Political Rights, adopted 16 December 1966, entry into force 23 March 1976, 999 UNTS 171.

[111] Also the counter-memorial by the defendant, the USA, of 19 September 2006, at 33 *et seq*. cites various international law instruments concerning cultural heritage. UNESCO, Recommendation concerning the Safeguarding of Beauty and Character of Landscapes and Sites, 11 December 1962 (Adopting a principal that preventative measures should protect sites from the dangers posed by mines and the disposal of their waste products); UNESCO, Recommendation concerning the Preservation of Cultural Property Endangered by Public or Private Works, 19 November 1968 (Member States should give due priority to measures required for the preservation in situ of cultural property endangered by private works to preserve historical associations and continuity); and UNESCO, Convention concerning the Protection of

whether the tribunal will interpret the indirect expropriation also in the light of the international human rights instruments, especially norms protecting minorities and indigenous people[112] as well as the freedom of religion, thereby taking the purpose of the measure into account.

Nevertheless, investment tribunals have been hitherto rather reluctant to include other special areas of PIL in the protective provisions of investment law. The Tribunal in *St. Elena v. Costa Rica*[113] held in a dispute concerning the damages for expropriation for the purpose of erecting an environmental conservation area that

> [w]hile an expropriation or taking for environmental reasons may be classified as a taking for a public purpose, and thus may be legitimate, the fact that the property was taken for this reason does not affect either the nature or the measure of compensation to be paid for the taking. That is, *the purpose of protecting the environment for which the property was taken does not alter the legal character of the taking* for which adequate compensation must be paid. *The international source of the obligation to protect the environment makes no difference.*[114]

In *SPP v. Egypt*,[115] a dispute on expropriation for cancellation of a tourism development project near the pyramids, the tribunal held that the 1972 UNESCO Convention for the Protection of the World Cultural and Natural Heritage was, though in principle relevant,[116] not applicable in the case as the international obligation entered only into force for Egypt after the investment had been concluded. Here, the tribunal follows clearly a timeline argument of *lex posterior*, but, as a principle, held that other international law obligations might be relevant. This example could be followed by other tribunals as well.

6. Conclusion and Outlook

Fragmentation of international law is, presumably, here to stay with us for quite while. An international legal system nevertheless strives for unity and coherence. Unless states mitigate the fragmentation problem in drafting treaties

---

the World Cultural and Natural Heritage, Paris, adopted 16 November 1972, entry into force 17 December 1975, 1037 UNTS 151 (to ensure effective and active measures to protect and conserve cultural and natural heritage, party states shall take legal, technical and administrative measures to protect this heritage).

112 Also relevant to those kind of cases would be Arts. 4, 5, and 7 ILO Convention (No. 169) concerning Indigenous and Tribal Peoples in Independent Countries, adopted on 27 June 1989 by the General Conference of the International Labour Organisation at its seventy-sixth session, entry into force 5 September 1991, 28 ILM 1382 (1989). But it has been ratified by only 17 countries and not by the United States. It could become relevant in other cases though.

113 Santa Elena *v*. Costa Rica ILR 153 (2000).

114 Santa Elena *v*. Costa Rica, para. 71 (emphasis added).

115 SPP (ME) *v*. Egypt, 19 Yearbook Commercial Arbitration 51 (1994).

116 *Id.*, para. 78.

accordingly and unless there is hierarchy in PIL, the problem of how to achieve unity stays. Thus, defragmentation through the means of interpretation comes to the fore. Systemic integration can be achieved through interpretation mainly through Article 31(3)(c) VCLT. But the Vienna Convention tells us only which other international law can be considered when adjudicating on a non-human rights treaty. It does not tell us how to do it. The principle of proportionality, as a principle of international law is the most probable candidate for integration. It considers conflicting principles and harmonizes them through balancing. The legal theoretical background of doing so has been elaborated by Robert Alexy. This allows for the consideration of human rights in other areas of PIL and thus helps to defragment PIL. Since human rights are one important principle and value in a constitutionalized international order, they should be respected also in the other areas of international law. International adjudication can help this by interpreting PIL in an adequate way.

Jasminka Hasanbegović

Human Rights Culture and/or Human Rights Ideology – Rhetorics and Realities

"The tragedy of great ideas is that they are interpreted by fools and implemented by bullies."

1. Introduction

Human rights are, beyond any doubt, one of the greatest legal and sociopolitical ideas in the history of ideas and probably the greatest legal and sociopolitical modern invention and practical *novum*.[1] Without human rights, there is no citizen – only *Untertan* (referred to by the more precise German word rather than the English word '*subject*'). Without human rights, there is neither modern democracy nor modern constitution or constitutionalism, nor *Rechtsstaat* in the sense of the rule of law.[2] This is why – from a historical perspective, finally in modern times – the modern idea, concept or notion of *justice* can both be relatively precisely and legal-positivistically operable, deconstructed and (re) constructed only as an achieved level of real enjoyed human rights.[3] Human rights are, thus, the backbone of life in a modern community, as well as the

1 J. Hasanbegović, *Universalität der Menschenrechte und Kant*, *in* P. Wolf & D. N. Basta (Eds.), Wider die Beliebigkeit: Kant's Metaphysische Anfangsgründe der Rechtslehre nach zwei Jahrhunderten 77 (1997).

2 J. Hasanbegović, *Rhetorizität des Rechts und Rechtlichkeit des Staates – Über die Unvereinbarkeit von Souveränität und Rechtsstaat*, *in* D. Basta & W. Krawietz & D. Müller, Rechtsstaat: Ursprung und Zukunft einer Idee 63 (1993).

3 More in a forthcoming paper: J. Hasanbegović, *Jedna filozofija prava kao filozofija ljudskih prava: (Post)moderna (de)konstrukcija pravde* [*A Philosophy of Law as Philosophy of Human Rights: (Post)modern (De)construction of Justice*].

Miodrag Jovanović & Ivana Krstić (Eds.), Human Rights Today – 60 Years of the Universal Declaration, 77-86.

object of permanent rethinking and an inexhaustible literary topic. And – just as it is with sex – human rights are written about so much because they exist to be practiced and enjoyed, not merely to be described and explained.

The conceptual pair of human rights culture – human rights ideology are most often positioned as opposites. However, independently of this pair of phenomena and concepts, human rights culture is most often understood ideally, as a type of legal culture that can be marked as a civic legal culture, which is confronted with an *Untertan* legal culture, *i.e.* a submissive legal culture, and which presupposes not just the normative proclamation of specific (initially only civil and political) human rights for all people – more precisely: for all citizens or nationals – but also for their effective guarantee, namely the possibility of their realization in practice.

The concept of human rights culture defined in this way, which is additionally a criterion for the assessment of whether such a culture exists in a particular legal order or not, represents a crossbar raised so high that only a few contemporary legal orders can jump over it. This is why the phenomenon of human rights culture must be approached differently, with having a feeling for nuances, in order to cognitionally obtain more worthy results.

Such an approach presupposes the existence of different human rights cultures, not just one sole ideal-type (understood in the sense of Max Weber) of human rights culture, where the realization of the standards set by the Universal Declaration on Human Rights (1948) appears as the criterion, both universal and minimal, for the assessment of whether in a specific legal order a civic or submissive legal culture exists, and if the civic one does exist, to what extent it has been developed, which means whether and to what extent an advancement from minimal standards has been made within it regarding the matter of human rights set by the Universal Declaration.

On the other hand, it appears that a nuanced approach to different legal cultures and the assessment of the state of human rights culture in different contemporary legal orders should cover at least two types of analysis: on one hand, the differentiation between normative and factual state of affairs, and on another, the influence of tradition, including legal tradition, on the state in the matter of human rights in specific contemporary legal orders.

2. Different Aspects of the Human Rights Culture Debate

Let us first consider the necessity of differentiating between normative and factual aspects of the analysis. Why is it important? In general, it is safe to say that the differentiation between the normative and the factual in a legal order, namely the differentiation between the normative and factual state of affairs within it, is characteristic of the continental-European understanding of law and legal order (both for the theoretical, scientific, philosophical, jurisprudential understanding, and the practical, legal-dogmatic, lay one), but it is not characteristic of the Anglo-Saxon, that is, Anglo-American understanding of law and legal order – quite the opposite. However, a pretty sharp differentiation, even a separation of the normative and factual appears in other legal orders as well, specifically in certain segments where modernization processes dominate, meaning where a constitution, laws and international contracts, as sources of law appear as the main tools of these modernization endeavors. Thus, it appears that the differentiation between a normative and factual state of affairs in a specific legal order is not important solely to the analysis of continental-European and similar legal orders that belong to the same legal tradition.

Presently, human rights culture, beyond a doubt, encompasses minority rights culture, as human rights (at least the way in which they are considered in this paper) include certain minority rights. Human rights culture depends on the legal, political and general culture of a specific society, on the fundamental values that society actually resides on. This is why it is important to stress that the normative legal framework of human (as well as minority) rights, contained in constitutions and laws, as well as in formally passed or ratified international instruments, may be, but does not necessarily have to be, an authentic expression of these cultures.[4]

In societies transitioning towards democracy, as in societies with modernizing endeavors and tendencies in general, this normative legal framework, as a rule, is not an authentic expression of these cultures, but rather an expression of the strivings of only one part in the minority of the society, namely, the expression of the strivings of the predominant part of the political elite in that society. If these societies were to be judged only on the basis of the existing normative legal framework (constitution, laws and ratified international agreements), the inevitable conclusion would be that human rights culture exists in them. However, even if understood in this normative way, such a human rights culture, as we have already mentioned, most often does not represent an authentic expression of either general, or political, or even legal culture in these societies, because it does not represent an expression of the needs of these societies in their entirety, or at least of their majority parts. The normative legal framework of human rights in these societies has an entirely different function: not to satisfy the existing social need of individuals and social groups which represent the majority, but to direct each of these global societies, namely, each of these legal orders, towards

4 J. Hasanbegović, *Cultura dei diritti umani e cultura dei diritti delle minoranze – Il caso della Serbia (traduzione di Claudio Tommasi)*, *in* G. Gozzi & F. Martelli (Eds.), Guerre e minoranze: Diritti delle minoranze, conflitti interetnici e giustizia internazionale nella transizione alla democrazia dell'Europa Centro-orientale 181 (2004).

a particular system of values for which – willingly or unwillingly, sincerely or deceitfully – the predominant part of political elite in those societies is committed to.

If we ask ourselves why a part of the political elite in transitional and/or modernizing societies unwillingly and deceitfully advocates the acceptance of universal standards in the matter of human rights, as well as some basic minority rights, which in essence have the same function, the answer is not hard to give. A normative commitment to human rights by one part of the political elite in these societies is only unwilling and deceitful because, at the beginning of the 21st century especially in Europe, it is practically impossible to be a part of the political elite, and at the same time deny, namely to refuse to accept such social, political and legal values as modern democracy (which by definition is not just the rule of majority, but – in the modern times – the rule of majority with needful real legal protection of the minority, which in the beginning was solely the protection of the *political* minority, and then, afterwards, of some other minorities in the society as well), or value of the modern nation state (which by definition rests on civic, namely the citizenship principle, and not on the ethnic principle), or values like a modern constitution, constitutionalism, the rule of law, and the like. All these social, political and legal values: a (modern) democracy, a (modern) nation state, a (modern) constitution, constitutionalism, the rule of law, etc. would be nothing but hollow legal forms, or – essentially reduced and thus – just pre-modern, outdated phenomena and concepts without human and minority rights, which represent their essence and main content. To be openly against universally or regionally (on the European level) accepted human and minority rights – as well as against democracy, constitutionalism and the rule of law – is not in fashion, not "in", and it is not just politically incorrect (especially in terms of international policy), but may also be risky. This explains why such a small number of those belonging to the political elite are openly against these values, and this is also why international standards in the matter of human rights are relatively easily accepted, but are hard to adopt and realize. This explains as well, why relatively decent constitutions are passed, but not followed by appropriate laws, or even if they are followed by completely acceptable laws, court practice, and, especially, reality is far from adopted normative standards.

The great discrepancy between the normative and the real should particularly be taken into consideration, for specific reasons, for societies in transition. Firstly, this great discrepancy between the normative and the real, between the political and the legal proclamations and real life is a lasting characteristic of pre-transitional – socialist and communist – societies. Secondly, it is still an important feature of transitional post-communist societies, especially in the domain of human rights. In this sense it is safe to say that this discrepancy between the normative and the real is inherited from the preceding political and legal culture as something accepted, and if not entirely normal, then almost inevitable. This, of course, does not contribute to the cause of human rights itself, nor to the transition towards democracy in general. However, it has to be specifically pointed out here that all post-communist societies are transition societies, but not all of them are in transition towards democracy. Some of them showed pronounced characteristics of transition from one type of authoritarian system to another type of authoritarian system. Until the fall of 2000, Serbia certainly belonged to this group.

Due to this discrepancy between the normative and the real, the state of affairs not only in human and minority rights culture, but also in legal culture in general, can be marked as normative optimism: normative legal framework, namely normative solutions are not that bad, yet since they are not the expression of the authentic need of the majority of individuals and social groups and their commitment to specific legal values and are rather imposed from outside by the policy of the international community, and from above by a predominating part of the political elite, these normative solutions do not have, as their natural complement, a corresponding legal and social reality. Normative legal framework with its legal solutions is thus followed, not by a corresponding reality, but by *hope* that slowly, in time, normative solutions themselves will create an appropriate legal culture, and a corresponding legal or social reality. This hope is only sometimes well-founded, but, due to the situation in the judiciary and the judicial system in general, it is often totally unfounded. This is why one can speak about (un)founded normative optimism. Another very important factor that influences legal culture, and especially human rights culture is, as we have already mentioned, tradition. Taking tradition into consideration demands and enables a more nuanced approach to the assessment of the existence of human rights culture, both understood as the normative one, and one which really exists in social and legal practice. In addition, by taking tradition into consideration as a factor that influences the type of human rights culture, the Euro-centric approach to this culture is avoided, an approach otherwise inevitable if a Universal Declaration is taken as both the universal and the minimal criterion for the assessment of the existence of this culture. Tradition is an extremely complex phenomenon and thus, it seems that when its influence on human rights culture is concerned, one should firstly single out two of its aspects: political tradition, and within spiritual tradition – religion.

Political tradition, namely the tradition of a particular political culture essentially determines legal culture and human rights culture as well. From a simplified point of view, there are two basic types of modern political culture: democratic and authoritarian political culture, of course, with different sub-variants and mixed forms. They are followed by two basic types of modern legal culture: human rights culture or civic legal culture, and *Untertan* or submissive legal culture, again with different sub-variants and mixed forms. There is no doubt that Serbia, judged by its tradition – in more than two centuries of minor and unsuccessful attempts to become a modern democratic state – nevertheless belonged, almost in its entire tradition, to an authoritarian type of political culture, and a submissive type of legal culture, which occasionally, and only normatively, gained the appearance of civic legal culture.[5] This very uncommon claim should be justified by at least a short review of the Serbian political and legal tradition.

3. Human Rights Culture in Context – The Case of Serbia

The history of the modern Serbian state begins with the First Serbian Uprising in 1804 which can, on one hand, be labeled as the onset of a relatively successful struggle for liberation from Ottoman rule and, on the other hand, as the embryo of the modern, nation state of the Serbs on another. It was little more than a hundred years over which an independent and modern Serbian state had been shaped (until the 1 December 1918, when the Kingdom of Serbs, Croats and Slovenians was proclaimed, which in 1929 was renamed the Kingdom of Yugoslavia). These years were marked by uprisings, revolts, wars, changes of dynasties, a struggle for international recognition, territorial aspirations and efforts to make the state an organized and functioning one. It can hardly be said that the constitutions and regimes that changed during this period were democratically judged by the criteria of the time. And yet, romantic historiography treats the brief period from 1903 to 1912/14 (until the outbreak of the Balkan Wars and World War I, respectively) as a golden age of Serbian democracy and parliamentarianism. This is a romantic exaggeration, though not utterly unfounded. In any case, this first stage of the Serbian state's formation and independence was hardly one marked by a respect for human rights. As for minorities and their status, apart from religious ones (Islamic in particular and a small Jewish community), there were almost no other, ethnic

[5] For the explanation why it is so, *see* O. Popović-Obradović, *Koreni antimoderne političke kulture u Srbiji [Roots of Anti-Modern Political Culture in Serbia]*, *in* S. Lilić (Ed.), Pravni kapacitet Srbije za evropske integracije [Legal Capacity of Serbia for European Integrations] 151 (2006). And more detailed in O. Popović-Obradović, Parlamentarizam u Srbiji 1903-1914 [Parliamentarianism in Serbia 1903-1914] (1998), soon to be published in English, and *also* O. Popović-Obradović, *The Idea and Practice of Constitutionality in Serbia 1869-1914: Between a Liberal and "Popular" State*, *in* J. Kurjak, O. Popović-Obradović & M. Šuković, Russia, Serbia, Montenegro 25 (2000); as well as O. Popović-Obradović, *Development of Modern Legal Institutions in the 19th and 20th Century Serbia (up to 1914)*, The First Workshop on the Modernization of East European Law, Max-Planck-Institut fuer europaeische Rechtsgeschichte in Frankfurt am Main, November 2002. *See also* other essays by O. Popović-Obradović, Kakva ili kolika država: Ogledi o političkoj i društvenoj istoriji Srbije XIX-XXI veka [What Type of Sate or How Large State: Essays on Political and Social History of the 19th to the 21th Century Serbia], (edited by L. Perović), (2008).

or linguistic. For, it was only in 1912 that Kosovo was incorporated into Serbia (and partially into Montenegro), while Vojvodina (the northern part of Serbia) was incorporated in 1918.

From 1918 to 1941 Serbia made up a part of the Kingdom of Serbs, Croats and Slovenians, and, later on, of the Kingdom of Yugoslavia. Neither this, so-called first Yugoslavia can be considered to be a model democratic state in the modern sense. Its first constitution, declared as late as 1921, defined the state as a unitary, centralized parliamentary monarchy with the monarch maintaining large prerogatives. Moreover, laws and regulations passed before and after the 1921 Constitution either restricted or negated political rights (e.g., the celebration of May Day was prohibited, the Communist Party was banned, the authoritarian Law to Protect the State was passed, the Croatian Popular Agricultural Party was outlawed, etc.). In 1929 the King annulled the existing Constitution, dismissed the Parliament and banned political parties – in brief, he imposed a personal, absolutistic regime, a dictatorship, which, in 1931 he actually legalized by proclaiming the so-called Constitution *Octroyée* ('The Donated Constitution'). Even after the King was assassinated in 1934 and regardless of some democratic electoral forms, the regime did not acquire any democratic substance. On the contrary, its rule was marked by forged elections, terror, bans on strikes and trade unions, fascist decrees and laws (such as those on setting up concentration camps or, later on, so-called labor battalions for communists). This unitary state refused to recognize the Macedonian language, as well as Macedonians and Montenegrins as ethnicities. Minority rights were severely restricted and especially the situation of the Albanian minority community was extremely difficult.

The so-called second Yugoslavia (1945-1990/92) was also an authoritarian state, though of a different type. Immediately after World War II (1944-1950) this authoritarianism had even some totalitarian traits. Still, Yugoslavia differed from other socialist, i.e. Communist states, especially from the 1960s onwards, with its "milder" communist regime. Unlike its predecessor, this "second" Yugoslavia was a federation. All ethnicities were officially recognized, and territorially and politically organized within federal units, while all ethnic minorities (except for the Roma) enjoyed full recognition and exercised considerable rights that were even beyond international and comparative law standards. However, the situation of human rights was not wholly adequate. The so-called second generation of human rights – economic, social and cultural rights – was normatively and factually protected in a proper way, but the exercise of so-called "classic" human rights, first generation ones – civil and political – was both normatively and factually limited. Some human rights, such as the freedom of association (this particularly refers to political parties) or the freedom of expression, were essentially denied. This serious failure in the actual exercise of civil and political rights marked the regime as authoritarian. This is why the actual and positive impact of all the regime's accomplishments (that included economic, social and cultural rights, minority rights, developed federalism, etc.) can be perceived from the angle of this deficiency only: a deficiency characteristic of all communist regimes, where, in a nutshell, "all people are equal, though some (i.e. the nomenklatura) are *more equal* than others."[6]

The so-called third Yugoslavia (1990/92-2000/02) was actually a "remainder", left over after dissolution of the former, and was made up of two federal units: Serbia and Montenegro. While assessing the situation of its human and minority rights, one should bear in mind the following: Firstly, one collectivistic ideology, the class ideology of a socialist, i.e. a communist type had been replaced by another collectivistic ideology, the ideology of ethno-nationalism – at the beginning the two had been combined into a dangerous amalgam of ethno-socialism.[7] Secondly, there were wars in which Serbia, or more exactly the third Yugoslavia, had not officially participated, neither had its territory been a battlefield (except for the NATO bombing of 1999). However, Serbia had actually waged these wars, supported and channeled them in a variety of ways under the pretext of protecting the interests of Serbian ethnicity. Thirdly, normative solutions and standards that had been incorporated into the Constitutions (of Serbia in 1990, and of Yugoslavia in 1992) with much delay and reluctance, corresponded more or less to internationally recognized normative solutions and standards in the domain of human and minority rights, but later on they were systematically tacitly abrogated: either through new laws and by the very fact that power was entirely in the hands of one man, one party and one group of satellite parties, or through consistent destruction of the judiciary, courts and prosecution offices in particular, which to this very day have not managed to recuperate and become highly professional, independent and incorruptible. Fourth, one should have in mind the years-long state of emergency in Kosovo, and the accompanying developments in the province, including low intensity armed conflicts. Replacing one type of authoritarianism (of the second Yugoslavia) with another (of the third Yugoslavia) in a country that has persistently tried to present itself as a regime of transition towards democracy has had to have a bad effect on the situation of human and minority rights: not only when it comes to non-Serbs, but also to those, the regime has perceived as 'bad' Serbs who opposed its ideology and ethno-nationalistic program.

Finally, still concerning tradition as an important factor that influences legal culture, and especially human rights culture, just a few words should be said about religion as a main influencing part within the spiritual tradition

[6] J. Hasanbegović, *Retorika ljudskih prava u (ne)pravnoj državi* [*Rhetoric of the Human Rights in a Rule of Law(lessness)*], XLIII Naša zakonitost 1306 (1989).

[7] J. Hasanbegović, *Unreasonable Law – The Case of Post-Communist Societies (Perelman's theory as a frame for analysis – critically reviewed and developed), in* G. Haarscher (Ed.), Chaïm Perelman et la pensée contemporaine 451 (1993).

of every society. Here again one should single out two aspects: the influence of religion(s) and that of church(es). The impact of religions on human (and minority) rights cultures may be regarded as a hermeneutical problem as to what interpretation and to what extent a certain system of religious beliefs and teachings is compatible with human (and minority) rights normative solutions and standards. Here one can distinguish not just different impacts of different religions, such as Buddhism, Judaism, Islam, Christianity (Catholicism, Orthodox Christianity, Protestantism…) etc., and different answers – according to time and place – to the same question or problem in teachings of one and the same religion, but also to zealotry and bigotry within different religions, as well as within different kinds of atheism, and within the post-communist turn from atheism to a specific religion too. The impact of churches, as organizations and institutions, on human (and minority) rights culture must always to be regarded not just as a hermeneutical problem, but also as a practical problem that has repercussions on the everyday life of individuals and social groups.[8] Therein, among an infinite number of illustrations, one may prove to be sufficient: the last two articles, namely Articles 24 and 25, of the Cairo Declaration on Human Rights in Islam (1990) are as follows:

> All rights and freedoms stipulated in this Declaration are subject to the Islamic Shari'ah. The Islamic Shari'ah is the only source of reference for the explanation or clarification to any of the articles of this Declaration.

4. Conclusion

Now, in the conclusion, it turns out clearly how difficult it is to differentiate human rights cultures and human rights ideologies, as well as human rights rhetoric and human rights realities. As when it comes to human rights – culture, ideology, rhetoric and reality are so intertwined that they cannot be singled out. And it does not matter how ideology is conceived: either as a system of political ideas, or as a source of manipulation, or as a distortion of reality and an inverted explanation for social relations, or as an action-oriented system of beliefs and ideas whose purpose is not epistemic, but political, and whose role is not to render reality transparent, but to motivate people to do or not do certain things, requiring sometimes the obfuscation of reality.

[8] E. Karić (Ed.), Ljudska prava u kontekstu islamsko-zapadne debate [Human Rights in the Context of Islamic-Western Debate] (1996); E. Papo (Ed.), Judaizam i ljudska prava [Judaism and Human Rights] (1998); V. Blažević (Ed.), Ljudska prava i Katolička crkva [Human Rights and Catholic Church] (2000); the editor in chief of the whole project, professor Zdravko Grebo announced also a book on Othodox Faith and Human Rights, the manuscript has not been published yet. For something on this topic relating to Serbia *see* O. Popović-Obradović, *The Church, the Nation, the State: The Serbian Orthodox Church and Transition in Serbia*, *in* D. Vujadinović *et al.* (Eds), Between Autoritarianism and Democracy: Serbia, Montenegro, Croatia – Civil Society and Political Culture 145 (2004).

Like the normative and real aspects of human rights culture, human rights ideologies have also their characteristic value and reality aspects that make an amalgam. If a law is the legal expression of a political ideology, the presence of the ideological in a law does not necessarily have to compromise the law's integrity. As, when it is about human rights laws, some ideologies are seen as friendly and some as hostile to human rights (*e.g.* liberal, conservative, etc., and fascist, communist, and so on). This can be nothing but meta-ideology, i.e. ideology on ideology, equally like the position that in a liberal democracy there is no necessary connection between the law and a particular ideology. If it were so, in liberal democracy there would be neither a paradox of liberty (for the enemies of liberty), nor that of democracy, *i.e.* the obligation to dialogue (with everyone, including abusers of discussion). Another great difficulty is to differentiate real concern for human rights, *i.e.* human rights policy, and mere human rights rhetoric, as well as the to assess their respective consistency – which makes human rights issues just even more complex. If it is true that no power in the world, especially no great power has ever followed a human rights policy, so that the only way in which a more humane policy can be imposed on a state power is by the popular movements of its citizens,[9] then the following starting position should be taken very seriously: Human rights are to be practiced, enjoyed, and not to be described and explained. Then again, who and how is to assess and judge critically those human rights practices and enjoyment without their descriptions and explanations.

9 N. Chomsky, *On Human Rights and Ideology*, Forerunner, 13 October 1979.

Part II

Courts and the Human Rights Protection

Thomas Fleiner

The Independence of the Judiciary

Public attitude towards judges, courts, tribunals and to justice in general is often very ambiguous. Judges receive respect but are also objects of mistrust. People admire the splendour of justice but they fear its strictness; they believe in its independence but are outraged by its temptations; they trust it yet wish to control it. One would prefer justice to be near, but the closer it gets the more frightening it becomes. One wants to reform the judicial system of ensuring justice but at the same time wants to avoid distorting it.

An important factor in ensuring the proper functioning of the judicial system is an independent judiciary. Judges as human beings are constantly subject to external influences, therefore one has to look for institutional guarantees that shield the judges from these external influences and provide the greatest possible framework that allows judges to reach a verdict that is based only on the relevant facts presented in the court according to law and influenced only by their personal interpretation of the legal texts. The essential elements for guaranteeing the independence of the judiciary are:

1) the fact-finding procedures,
2) the institutional organisation of the court,
3) the procedure for the election of the judges,
4) the protection and guarantee of judges' independence,
5) their competence and
6) their capacities

This paper provides an insight into all these elements. But before examining these elements, we need to take a look at why an independent judiciary is necessary.

* I thank Dr. Rekha Oleschak for her help in editing this paper in particular for improving the English language.

Miodrag Jovanović & Ivana Krstić (Eds.), Human Rights Today – 60 Years of the Universal Declaration, 89-112.

1. Why an Independent Judiciary?

1.1. The Judge as Mediator

1.1.1. Two Children Dispute Over a Cake: the Judge as Mediator

Franz and Martin, two first-graders, have a dispute over a cake in the hand of Franz. Martin claims the whole cake is his, and that he was given it by his uncle, who gave it him unconditionally. Franz insists that this is not true, he was given the cake by Martin's uncle, who told him that the cake is his, and that, if he wishes, he may give a piece to Martin. As they are not able to solve their dispute, they ask Alice to be their mediator. Alice is the mother of their friend Felix. She now intervenes in order to solve the dispute. First she asks the children which of them has been given the cake and under what conditions. The children might tell her two different stories. If neither of the 'parties' is able to give her convincing evidence that he has been given the entire cake in order to distribute pieces at his whim, she may conclude that she will have to decide the dispute along the general presumption that the cake be divided into two halves. She may propose this to the children and, with their approval, settle the matter by distributing it equally among the two.

1.1.2. Legitimacy of Alice?

Would both the children have accepted Alice's verdict, if it was decided by either Martin's or by Franz's mother? Or would a third person unknown to the children have been able to mediate with the same result as the mother of a common friend did? Would they have accepted the deal, if it would have been proposed by a one of their classmates? It seems that an independent broker, who is known and respected by both children, was the best possible person to solve the dispute. Alice, the mother of Felix, had legitimacy to solve the dispute, because Franz and Martin knew her, because both accepted her as an impartial umpire and because the verdict was not one which made one of them a total loser and the other a total winner.

1.1.3. Lessons Learned

This story highlights a few important reasons for the principle of independence of the judiciary. In this case, the judge is a mediator and his or her verdict is based firstly on some major moral standards such as: 'treat children equally and fairly', and, secondly, on some experiences adults have with regard to quarrelling children. One additional interesting element of this little story should be addressed: The mother solving the dispute among the children does not examine the facts. She does not ask them whether the story of Franz or of

Martin is true. Without decisive evidence, she comes to the conclusion that she cannot find the real facts and nevertheless she is asked to give a verdict. Alice acts like the famous judge Solomon. Knowing that she probably never will know what really has happened between the children, and knowing that both the children will insist on their view of the facts, she tries to solve the problem without fact-finding, *i.e.* by cutting the cake in two pieces, hoping that this might definitely solve the problem. Indeed, it does solve the problem if the parties agree to the verdict. If they disagree, the conflict might go on at a higher instance of a new mediator. The assumption that when children quarrel, usually both of them are partly right and partly wrong, and therefore careful fact-finding would not produce any result, can only be made by someone who is close to the children, and who comes from the same culture as the children, knowing how children usually are educated. This means that the credibility of the mediator also depends on the fact that people accept him or her as someone belonging to the same culture.

1.2. The Judge as an Independent Fact-Finder

1.2.1. Fact Finding Problems

Fact finding of the past: The students in my class on administrative law recently told me the story of one of their colleagues who had failed his exam. The reasoning given by professor evaluating the exam was that the student had written such an excellent exam that he obviously could not have written it by himself, but that he must have copied a text from a book. The professor was neither successful in finding such a book nor did he have evidence to support his position. This dispute is quite different from the dispute of children and their cake. Here the student, as the weaker party, is in dispute with a university professor. We can assume that the university is run by public authority and that the relationship between the university and its students is regulated by public law.

1.2.1.1. Fact Finding of the Future

However the risks at stake are much higher as this case. Take the example of an injunction filed in Hawaii against the experiments with the Large Hadron Collider (LHC), carried out at the European Organization for Nuclear Research (CERN) in Geneva. These experiments might put the entire world at risk. How should a judge decide in a case of uncertain but high risks?[1]

[1] Opponents of the project had hoped to obtain an injunction from the European Court of Human Rights that would block the collider from being turned on at all, but the court rejected the application. However, the court will rule on allegations that the experiment violates the right to life under the European Convention of Human Rights.

1.2.1.2. An Issue of Credibility?

If in the cake dispute, it was clear beyond any reasonable doubt that the cake belonged either to Franz or to Martin, the mediator would have had no credibility if she distributed the cake equally among the quarrelling children. But how should a mediator decide in the exam case? He could, for instance, decide in favour of the professor, giving him more credibility due to his function as an official and representative of the state authority. In the old authoritarian administrative law of the civil law countries, the administration, and in this case the professor, is responsible for establishing the facts and thus decides on the truth. How should a mediator decide? Obviously he or she can not decide simply in favour of the student in case the truth remains open. But can he or she then decide in favour of the professor and give him or her higher credibility? The school has the responsibility to train and educate young students. On the one hand it is responsible and accountable to the public to grant degrees and diplomas to those students who deserve it. On the other hand, students who have studied for their exam and who expect equal treatment by their teachers, consider that if they can prove in the exams their knowledge and their capacities with regard to the subject, they have a vested right to pass the exam. Their evaluation should not be at the whim of the professors.

1.2.1.3. Public Administration and Private Citizens

In the cake case both quarrelling children were on an equal level. Now the issue is how should a dispute be decided between unequal parties, for example, between a student and teacher? In the cake case the mediator did not do any fact finding. The children accepted the verdict based on the authority and credibility of the mother. In the case involving the student and the professor, fact finding is crucial. If the student can prove that he has not cheated, he will pass the exam with very high grades. If the teacher finds the text he has copied, the student will fail. However, the main problem is that most probably neither can the student nor his teacher provide reasonable evidence for their arguments. How can an excellent student prove that he did not copy the text from an already existing textbook? How can the professor find the text that he has unsuccessfully been looking for? Thus the question is what kind of decision can be made in a dispute where the facts cannot be established based on evidence that would prove the facts beyond any reasonable doubt?

1.2.1.4. Credibility of the Administration

An independent mediator would require that teachers evaluate the texts written by the students and that they can only refuse the evaluation if they can reasonably prove that the student has copied the text. Without any proof they cannot claim that the students have cheated. This might be a reasonable solution. Yet, turning to the administrative procedure in Switzerland, one finds that administrative authorities are given the unquestioned power to decide on the truth after the administered have had the opportunity to present their view of the facts.

In 1987, the European Court of Human Rights decided in the famous Belilos case that Article 6 of the European Convention on Human Rights applies without reservation to Switzerland. Thus, in administrative cases under Article 6, an independent court and not a purely administrative tribunal should decide on the facts.[2] In the Belilos case, the defendant was sentenced to a fine by the administrative police tribunal as she was found guilty of having participated in an illegal demonstration. She claimed that she had not participated in this demonstration, but was in a restaurant to get an alimony payment from her ex-husband. She offered the testimony of her ex-husband. The tribunal decided that it was not necessary to ask her ex-husband, because one of the policemen recognized her as one of the participants in the demonstration.

1.2.1.5. Traditional Public Law Concept

According to the traditional conception of administrative law in civil law countries, administrative authorities not only have the power to reach a final decision on the facts, but also have the power to refuse proposed evidence, if considered unnecessary. Accordingly, in civil law countries, administrative authorities were seen as having a high degree of credibility as they were considered to be the institutions defending and promoting the public interest. Thus it was assumed that civil servants in the service of the public interest could never be considered as a private party in a dispute with the citizens. Only under the jurisdiction of the European Court on Human Rights, was Switzerland forced to change its position and procedure with regard to administrative cases. Accordingly, a constitutional amendment influenced by art. 6 of the ECHR, provides every the right to access to a independent court, whenever he or she has a legal dispute with the administration. Under these circumstances, it is now important that the court, which, instead of the administration, has to decide on the facts, is fully independent from the administration.

1.3. Institutional Requirements for Independent Fact-Finding

Alice, the mediator in the cake dispute, is not a sustainable institution. She is a private person who was able to establish a general credibility as an unbiased mediator among quarrelling children on her personal initiative and on her

2 Belilos *v.* Switzerland, 132 ECtHR (ser. A) (1987).

personal capacities. In order to become an institution, the children would have to accept that for all quarrels there is a person belonging to an institution installed by another institution, for instance the school, with the competence to mediate. Now the question has to be answered, how such institution could gain credibility among the children. This credibility depends on various factors like:

- The legitimacy of the institution (constitution maker, legislator) setting up the mediation office;
- The legitimacy of the concept of the institution, its function and its jurisdiction;
- The legitimacy of the fact finding procedure and the legitimacy of the position of the parties in this procedure;
- The legitimacy of the electorate and the election procedure to elect or appoint the institution and;
- The legitimacy of the person elected or appointed to the institution.

1.3.1.1. Adversary Versus Inquisitory Fact finding

One of the most important elements in ensuring the credibility of justice is to have the guarantee of independent fact-finding. With regard to this task, the first question to be asked is which institution is better suited to decide on facts: an independent judge, a jury or the administration? In common law countries the adversary system based on the equal opportunities of the parties to convince the independent jury of their view of the facts was developed under the auspices of habeas corpus. In civil law countries, the adversary system was allowed only in civil cases, whereas in administrative and criminal cases the administration, or the prosecutor, is in charge of finding the truth. The judge could only intervene exceptionally if the truth is obviously distorted by the administration. The development of administrative procedure and the guarantee of equal opportunities of the parties in the European Human Rights Convention have finally influenced both systems to merge. Yet, some important differences remain with regard to fact-finding.

1.3.1.2. Assumptions

Let us take a look at the famous judgement of Solomon: the judge who had to decide in the conflict of two women fighting for a child. Solomon had to find out which one was the natural mother with the right to keep the child, as both women claimed to be the child's natural mother. Solomon proposed to cut the child in two pieces and to give each of the women a part. As everyone would assume, one of the women protested heavily and wanted to give in for the sake of the child and to leave it to the opposite party. This reaction was clear evidence for Judge Solomon that she was the real, that is, the natural, mother of the child. The proposal of Solomon is considered a wise, just and efficient way of fact finding.

But of course, this fact finding is based on essential assumptions. First of all Solomon is considered to be an impartial umpire without any relationship to the parties or to the child as its possible father. Solomon moreover assumed that the biological mother would oppose harm being done to her child, which can be taken as a generally shared assumption. For 90% this might be true; what about the other 10%? If it was the 'wrong' mother who opposed the murder of the child, it might still be in the best interests of the child to be given to the mother opposing the murder because, although not the biological mother, she might be a better mother than the mother not opposing the proposal to cut the child. Thus, the fact finding is based on assumptions which might turn out to be wrong.

With regard to all these examples, the independence of the judge and his impartiality with regard to the parties turns out to be fundamental and crucial. It is the *conditio sine qua non*. But this leaves us still open with the unsolved problem of the procedure with regard to fact finding.

1.3.1.3. Independent Fact Finding and Political Pressure

If the administration is in charge of fact finding in concrete cases, it may be confronted with conflicting interests, such as in cases of asylum seekers. Here the political interest, for instance in Switzerland is to limit the number of asylum seekers and to grant fewer asylum seekers a refugee status. This is in clear contradiction to the interest of the asylum seeker, fearing persecution, torture or death when returned to his home country. In the process of fact finding, the administrative authorities have to answer the question, to what extent the asylum seeker is in danger in his country of origin and they also have to look into the concrete facts of the general situation in the country concerned and the danger of the asylum seeker with regard to the authorities of this country. Such fact-finding and evaluation of the concrete danger gives the administration wide discretionary powers. In many cases, the administration is overloaded with the task of finding the truth. For this reason, the Swiss legislation now only requires the administration to evaluate the credibility of the asylum seekers and to make a final decision only based on their credibility. Thus, even though an asylum seeker may in fact be in danger in their country, they might be refused asylum based only on their lack of credibility.

1.3.1.4. Jury as Fact Finder

In countries with a common law legal tradition, the procedure based on the fair trial principle most often entrusts fact-finding duties to the parties asked to convince an independent jury by means of the evidence available. This jury is to be chosen randomly. The parties have to present the facts and the necessary evidence to the jury and the jury will have to decide which facts it considers relevant and true. In this so called 'adversary procedure' the parties are on equal footing and fight for their view of the facts before the independent jury. Thus, the jury will consider as relevant only those presentations of facts supported by convincing evidence. Each party has to defend its own interests and thus no party has any privileges or special trust with regard to fact-finding.

1.3.1.5. Judge as Fact Finder

In countries with a civil law tradition, it is the judge who decides on the facts, and only rarely the jury. In criminal cases the prosecutor is often given a special position as one assumes that the prosecutor produces not only the facts as an adversary of the defendant but also as a public officer defending public interests, including the interests of the defendant. Consequently, the public prosecutor has more credibility with regard to the defendant, who in criminal cases, however, has the benefit of the doubt. While in common law countries these principles were developed by court cases, in civil law countries they were implemented by the legislation.

1.3.1.6. The Truth to Be Found by the Administration

Within the system of adversarial proceedings, both parties are on equal footing. Within such a system the independence and impartiality of the court as a non-committed broker is much more credible than in a system which gives the power to decide on the fact into the hand of the administration, which is the case according its investigation method in the civil law system. In order to assess the independence of the judiciary, it is important to also examine the procedures. In inquisitorial systems based on investigation by the administration, the possibilities for the courts are limited with regard to independent fact finding. Often they have to take facts produced by the administration for granted. Only in cases with reasonable doubt on the objectivity of the facts, can the courts require additional fact finding. Therefore, some additional due process guarantees, such as Article 6 of the European Convention of Human Rights, are indispensable. These rights require courts in criminal cases to grant important rights to the defendant in order to guarantee a fair and due process, and in particular the possibility of an effective defence within the court.

1.3.1.7. Avoiding Lynch-Justice

Actually several political tendencies in different countries tend to support a judiciary more accountable and dependable on politics. Such new political developments should remember the famous Mississippi cases which took place in the United States and which obliged Congress to enact the civil rights legislation. In these cases, defendants belonging to the African-American community, in spite of being innocent had no chance of getting an acquittal for murder charges as the judges and the jury were all under the pressure of the racist mobs. As soon as courts are subject to the influence of politics and ethnicity, they are induced to decide according to the prejudices of the public opinion than in accordance with the law. If, what already has been decided in the famous Bonham case in 1610,[3] the aim of the judiciary is to ensure that men are ruled by law and not by men, the judiciary must achieve as much as possible independence from political pressure.

2. Independent Courts

2.1. Pre-Condition for Human Rights International Obligation

All international legal documents providing for the basic elements of the rule of law give a clear priority to the principle of independent, impartial and competent courts provided by law. Thus Article 14 of the International Convent on Civil and Political Rights states that:

> All persons shall be equal before the courts and tribunals. In the determination of any criminal charge against him, or of his rights and obligations in a suit at law, everyone shall be entitled to a fair and public hearing by a competent, independent and impartial tribunal established by law.

Courts thus no longer are the personal possessions of a ruler, a priest or a high ranking politician. Men should be ruled by law and not by men!

2.1.1. Human Failure

Courts and tribunals are institutions that are established by law. Therefore, one must know in advance the jurisdiction, the powers and, of course, the jurisprudence of the court he or she will be dealing with. By knowing the jurisprudence of the court, the parties can better defend their cause by basing their arguments on decisive precedents. Also, judges are to be known in advance. Although judges have different legal traditions, and may belong to different parties, they should only be influenced by the law. However, they can not avoid interpreting legal texts without to some extent taking into account their own personal beliefs, education and personal experiences.

[3] 8 Co. Rep. 114 (Court of Common Pleas [1610]). Read more: http://law.jrank.org/pages/6484/English-Law-DR-BONHAM-S-CASE.html.

The main idea is not to nominate a big ruler in order to be able to believe in his or her integrity and to hand over the entire justice system to a most moral, honourable and legitimate person. Rather, what matters is the legitimacy of the institution, which is the court, the legitimacy of the procedure and the legitimacy of the procedure for electing the judges. These elements are basic in order to guarantee impartiality and independence of the court.

2.1.2. Powerful Courts With Regard to Authorities

First and foremost, the court must be competent. This requirement may be looked at from two different points of view. The court is competent if its jurisdiction is ruled by law and if the court has the power to decide independently on its competence. Moreover, the competence of the court also includes its power to rule over the parties in order to manage the procedure in an impartial way. Here we find clear and important differences between the common law system and the civil law system, in particular in cases where the administration is involved in the procedure as one party. First of all, in the civil law system the complaint against the administration is always addressed against an anonymous authority representing the hierarchy of the administration involved in the case. Within the common law system, the claim against the administration is often personalized *e.g. Marbury v. Madison*[4] in order to have a concrete person who has to defend the administration's interest as a party. As a consequence, the person who takes part in the procedure on behalf of the administration can be held responsible for its attitude before the judge within the trial. In particular, the judge, using the power of contempt of court, can oblige the member of the administration to, for example, hand in the relevant documents necessary for fact finding. If they refuse the judge has the power to condemn the party to a fine or even to prison. When the judge finally decides the case, he/she can provide for any measure necessary to reinstall the rule of law.

In case of refusal, the person is responsible for the execution of the judgement and can be fined or also imprisoned. In the civil law system the abstract authority as such can never be fined or imprisoned. Thus the judge has very limited power with regard to the administration because there is no possible sanction possible against an abstract authority in case the authority refuses an order from the judge. This may be one important reason why, in the civil law system, the judge has no power to enforce its decisions, require concrete measures or prohibit certain action and to implement its verdicts with regard to the administration.

For this reason, the only claim possible within civil administrative law is the request to quash an administrative decision. The traditional common law remedy of injunction does not exist in the civil law system.

4 Marbury *v.* Madison, 5 U.S. 137 (1803).

2.2. Why the Administration Cannot Function as an Independent Judge

2.2.1. Acting on Behalf of the Public Interest

In the Swiss administrative law system, which has been influenced by the French and German systems, the administration has had, for a very long time, significant powers to function as an independent judge. The main idea behind this power is the conviction that the administration acts in the public interest. It is asked to fulfil the will of the legislature and thus needs independent powers in order to implement the existing positive law. Acting on behalf of the executive, the administration needs to have at its disposal the same enforcement means with regard to ordinary citizens as a judge has. Thus, the administration has the power to enforce legal obligations through administrative acts and then to enforce these acts with coercive means of execution. These administrative decisions may also contain concrete threats to fine those subjects who do not obey administrative orders.

2.2.2. Administrative Hierarchy Has no Credibility

Based on this conviction, many complaints against illegal acts of the administration could only be addressed to administrative bodies at the next level of the hierarchy. In many instances the administration could not be sued before an independent judge. Instead, the administration, as institution acting in the public interest, had full credibility as an independent legal actor.

2.2.3. Independence According to Article 6 of the ECHR

This concept radically changed with the adoption of the European Convention on Human Rights (ECHR), and in particular with Article 6 of this Convention. The landmark case for Switzerland was the Belilos case, which clearly illustrates the problem of the independence and the credibility of the administration. The case started with a fine that was imposed on Marlène Belilos for having participated in an illegal demonstration in Lausanne, the capital of the Swiss Canton of Vaud. Belilos denied having participated in this demonstration, and claimed that at the time she had been meeting with her former husband in a restaurant to receive her alimony payment.

According to the legal system in the Canton of Vaud, if a fine based on cantonal criminal law is rejected by a subject, a so-called police court is responsible for reviewing the case. This police court is composed of former police officers who, for a limited time, sit in the court. As members of this police court, they were granted a degree of independence. In particular, the government of the Canton was not allowed to give any directives to this court, or to any of its members.

In particular, Ms. Belilos claimed that an administrative body such as the police court can not be considered as an independent court according to Article 6 of the ECHR. A police court is not credibly unbiased when it is asked to decide on facts that are claimed by the police on one side and by a private citizen as witness on the other side. According to Article 6 of the ECHR, criminal judgements as well as decisions of the administration infringing civil rights, can only be decided upon by an impartial and independent court provided by legislation and having full jurisdiction in the case which has to be decided in a public hearing. Moreover, with regard to police matters, a police court cannot be seen as impartial.

The Court looked into the merits of Article 6 with regard to this concrete case. The Court had to decide whether the Cantonal administration's police court could be considered as an independent court in the sense of Article 6 of the ECHR. This the court denied for the following reasons: The police court or municipal court is composed of individual members who are, with regard to their concrete function, more or less independent. However, as the members of the court belonging to the police service can again be nominated by the executive for administrative functions within the police, this court could not be considered really independent. The judges could be influenced in their decision by their interest in continuing their career within the administration. Thus, the executive deciding on the possibility of such a later function had de facto an important influence on the decision making of the municipal court.

2.2.4. Political and Administrative Dependencies

Because members of this municipal court could have an interest for their own professional future in being appointed by the executive for new administrative functions, they cannot be considered functionally as independent. The credibility of the independence of the court is not to be questioned because the members are appointed by the executive. The election procedure is not questioned, but the fact that the members are interested in being promoted within their function jeopardizes the credibility of the municipal court.

Indeed, if one analyzes the concrete case one has to admit that a court composed of former police officers who may again carry out this function has a very low credibility when it is asked to assess the credibility of a private witness and former husband of Ms. Belilos against the formal declaration of a police officer pretending that he has seen her participating in the demonstration. How can a court composed of police officers who have an interest in working again within the same administration claim to be an independent court when it has to decide on facts contested among police officers and private subjects?

2.2.5. Lessons Learned

This case is interesting also with regard to another issue. Ms. Belilos had been fined because the court had decided that she had been at the demonstration, a fact which Ms. Belilos denied. The court did not believe her declaration or the testimony of her former husband. It only believed its own police officer and colleague who confirmed during the trial that he had seen her at the demonstration. Here we witness the problem of unbiased fact finding by a court that is composed of former police officers. Even though these former police officers would consider themselves not to be influenced by their former activity, and would maintain that they have no positive prejudices with regard to their colleague being a witness, people outside of the administration would always doubt the truth of such a confirmation. Although the municipal court may have done justice, this justice was not seen to be done.

2.3. Checks and Balances

When we analyze the principle of separation of powers, we are reminded of the well known sentence of Montesquieu in his spirit of the Laws in Chapter XI:

> But constant experience shows us that every man invested with power is apt to abuse it, and to carry his authority as far as it will go. Is it not strange, though true, to say that virtue itself has need of limits? To prevent this abuse, it is necessary from the very nature of things that power should be a check to power. A government may be so constituted, as no man shall be compelled to do things to which the law does not oblige him, nor forced to abstain from things which the law permits.[5]

This basic wisdom that "power corrupts and absolute power corrupts absolutely" (Lord Acton)[6] is at the very root of the principle of separation of powers.

2.3.1. That Men Are Ruled by Law

All philosophers who were in favour of the rule of law required in particular that the judiciary should be independent from the executive and legislative powers. This does not mean that judges cannot be nominated by the executive. Neither does it mean that the executive may have some disciplinary control over the behaviour of judges. The minimal standard required is that judges can never be removed from their office because of their judgments handed down and argumentation in the court, that no decision of a court can be quashed by

[5] Montesquieu, Spritit of Laws (1748), Ch. XI.

[6] John Emerich Edward Dalberg Acton, first Baron Acton (1834–1902) in a letter to Bishop Mandell Creighton in 1887.

the executive and that the executive has no power to issue any directive with regard to the very function and jurisprudence of the court. If, for instance, judges are nominated by the executive, as in the US, but the Constitution provides that they remain in office for life and that their salary can never be reduced during their stay in office, such guarantees counterbalance the influence of the executive when it appoints the judges. Therefore one has always to look into all aspects of checks and balances between the two branches in order to evaluate the independence of judges in a concrete case. The same is the case with the legislature and its power of impeachment or its power to repeal immunity in the case of a criminal warrant against a judge.

2.3.2. The Case of Mohammed Caricature

Recently the entire world was in turmoil because of a caricature first published in a Danish newspaper and later in many other European newspapers. This caricature showed the Prophet Mohammed with a turban hiding a bomb on his head. For the great bulk of Muslims this was an unacceptably racist publication as it suggested that the religion as such is terroristic and thus all believers to be either terrorists or supporting terrorists.

Let us assume that in this concrete case the legislature would have to apply the constitutional guarantee of freedom of the press and the criminal law prohibiting any racist publication. It would thus have to balance between the constitutionally guaranteed freedom of press and of opinion on one side, and the right of religious people not to be offended for their religious beliefs and to be protected against any racist activity on the other side. Would it be credible that the legislature would decide on this issue in an unbiased manner and not take into account the political interests of either those defending the liberty of the press or those defending Islam?

Indeed, the legislature would have all means to convince the public that, as it created the law, it knows best the goals to be achieved and thus that the law has to be interpreted in the way the legislature decides. However, such decisions can only credibly be made by a court which has jurisdiction over human rights. It is only a court which credibly can evaluate all the different contradictory interests in such a case.

2.3.3. Thomas More's Conviction

Thomas More's conviction by the 16th century English Parliament under King Henry VIII is well known in this context. In this case the parliament had to decide whether the refusal of Thomas More to accept that the King was the supreme head of the church should be considered as high treason. As this law was made by the parliament, the parliament, in applying this law, was its own judge for deciding this concrete case. But those who have enacted a law can never decide on its content, interpretation and application in a concrete case. They would always consider the law according to the most appropriate political circumstances and interpret it not in the way everybody would understand it, but only in the way they understand at the moment, taking into account the current majority and its concrete interest.

For the same reason, the executive power cannot be asked both to apply and implement the law, and to be the final legal instance in case its interpretation is disputed. When the executive implements laws approved by the parliament, it is up to the court to decide whether it executes the will of the parliament correctly and according to a common understanding. If there is a dispute on speed limits, for instance, on the question whether 5 kilometers or only 3 kilometers over the speed limit are to be tolerated according to the law, the final decision on such issues should be made by the independent court. Moreover, with regard to fact finding, the power to decide on the facts finally should not be within the administration but it should be given to the court. How could one imagine, for example, that the police officer regulating the traffic could at the same time implement the traffic rules and fine a car driver for violating traffic regulations? The police officer may have overseen some basic facts that an independent court would recognize, mainly because there is an adversary party which can formulate other views of the facts or other arguments with regard to the law. But the police officer cannot possibly be his/her own judge when deciding on rules that have to be implemented and the power to impose sanctions and decide finally on fines or even imprisonment of a driver violating the law. Such a power can only be exercised by an independent court.

2.4. Independent Judges

2.4.1. Election and Nomination of Judges

In some countries, such as Germany and Spain, constitutional courts are composed of judges elected for a limited time period and are not to be re-elected for a second term. In both countries the constitutional court is a special judicial branch whose jurisdiction is limited to the constitutional review of any legislation or any other state activity. Thus only the constitutional court has jurisdiction over the constitution. All other ordinary courts are requested to refer to this constitutional court with regard to all issues involving the constitution.

In other cases, the highest court, such as the Supreme Court in the US and the House of Lords in Britain, is composed of judges nominated for a lifetime. However, only the American Supreme court has established (in 1803) its own jurisdiction over the constitution based on the famous case *Marbury v. Madison*. In this case Chief Justice Marshall followed the principle that the judicial branch is sovereign in each case and when it is asked to adjudicate a legal dispute it is also required to look into the highest legal act: the

Constitution. When it comes to the conclusion that the legislature has violated the constitution, it must have the power to review the statute established by the legislature. There can be no limit to the judicial branch when it is asked to decide a case on the principle of justice because America, as Chief Justice Marshall said, has to be ruled by law and not by men.

2.4.2. Fixed Term or Appointment for Life

If judges are appointed for a life time or for a fixed period they are of course always embedded in the current spirit of the time and of the society. They might exceptionally be a bit progressive with regard to the mainstream of the actual thinking of the society, but they cannot be expected to make decisions which are not comprehensible at all by the leading intellectuals of the society.

If judges are appointed by the executive, as in the United States, the executive could easily misuse this power in order to appoint judges whose views are in line with that of the president. The scale between the two parties can be kept in equilibrium if the position of president alternates regularly between the parties. However, if, one party gets to nominate a larger part of the judges of the Supreme Court, the Court will lose its credibility. This would be even more so the case if presidents, as they are now, are inclined to nominate judges closer to the extreme edge of party ideology than to the moderates.

2.4.3. No Unlimited Independence

In fact, a constitutional court, or a supreme court with the power to review the constitutionality of legislative acts is never totally politically independent. Judges are part of social and political reality. However they are expected to decide cases with arguments comprehensible to the legal profession. Such arguments may always be weighed and influenced by political ideology. But they can never be influenced only by the political interests of the judges, as these are not subject to any renewal procedure.

The Chief Justice of the Indian Supreme Court once told us a shocking story about one of his cases. In a case in which he had to decide on a criminal charge brought against the son of the head of one of the federal states (Chief Minister), the Chief Minister told the judge that if he decided against his son he would be taken straight to prison upon leaving the court. Notwithstanding these terrible threats, he decided against the son of the Chief Minister.

There are certainly not many judges who would have behaved the same way. The case shows how difficult a dilemma the state system presents to the judiciary. The existence of political power controlling the judiciary often results in abuse. For example, we could mention the terrible decisions taken by almost all courts during the Nazi Regime. The loyalty of the judges, their fear of being arrested and the absolute power of the Führer had no limit with regard to the judges and the entire judiciary.

Another example comes from Switzerland, where there is a famous case of a court that condemned a police commander who falsified documents for Jewish refugees who wanted to enter Switzerland against the official rules. This judgement was reversed only more than 40 years later, in the 1980s, with the argument being that the police commander Grüninger was not guilty because he helped human beings under clear threat for death in a concentration camp.[7]

Judges are not immune from the political and social mainstream of a state and society. The scandalous decisions of the American Supreme Court against Japanese-Americans during the World War II are well known. Today, the justice system, or better the lack of the judicial control, over the camp of the so called illegal combatants in Guantanamo is very much disputed. Prisoners in Guantanamo are called illegal combatants in order to exclude them from the protection of the Geneva Conventions and, for several years, have had no access to justice. In addition, military committees are in charge of the trials. Although in *Hamdan v. Rumsfield* the Supreme Court decided that military committees installed by the decree of the President are illegal, Congress has now enacted a new bill providing such committees based on congressional authority.[8] How can a military tribunal be credibly independent with regard to the prisoners?

2.4.4. Controlling Judges

The elements of control mentioned above constrain the behaviour of judges, the management of the court, and its social competence as far as it does not contain its decisions in the court. Decisions in the court are often subject to be controlled by the possibility of the parties to have an appeal to the higher court. Decisions of the court are often public and can be criticized in the media or in the public discourse of the law profession. In the United States the judges may become subject of an impeachment procedure on the state or on the federal level. This impeachment tradition has been taken over from the old British system. In Britain, however, there has not been any impeachment decision of the Parliament since 1806. In the United States, on the other hand, the impeachment of judges has taken place in recent years.

---

7 See http://www.hagalil.com/schweiz/gruening.htm.

8 Hamdan *v.* Rumsfeld, 548 U.S. 557 (2006).

3. Unbiased Justice: Nemo Judex in Causa Sua (No Person Can Judge a Case in Which He or She is a Party)

3.1. How Independent Can Judges Be?

The principle that nobody can be the judge in their own cause is probably one of the most important and oldest legal principles, its roots going back as far as the Roman law of ancient times. Indeed, as soon as a judge's private interests become involved in the case on which they are to rule, justice can never be seen.

Let us consider one of the most striking cases in recent history: lynch justice carried out in the southern United States, particularly in Mississippi, until the late 1960s. In this region, where segregation still functions on a social level, thousands of African-Americans have been killed by lynch justice. Lynching is the practice whereby a mob, usually several dozen or several hundred persons, takes the law into its own hands in order to injure and kill a person accused of some wrongdoing. The alleged offence can range from a serious crime like theft or murder to a mere violation of local customs and sensibilities. The issue of the victim's guilt is usually secondary, since the mob serves as prosecutor, judge, jury, and executioner. Due process yields to momentary passions and expedient objectives.

The mob functioning as a 'judge' is serving its own emotions and interests. In all those cases the main interest for lynching the African-Americans was to uphold the illegal segregation and to prohibit African-Americans from entering into a society based on equal rights. Sheriffs did not take action on many of those crimes, neither did the prosecutors prosecute the crimes, nor were the judge or jury impartial in cases which for one reason or another came to court. Indeed, the judiciary of the state was totally on the side of the white majority. Thus, there was no impartial justice with regard to the crimes of lynching, and also not with regard to the African-Americans if they had been brought to the court for other crimes. Capital punishment was regular with regard to crimes committed by the discriminated races and was the big exception – if it took place at all – with regard to whites.

These cases of racial discrimination reveal a very special and modern problem of the implementation of the principle of unbiased judges and jurors. In countries that are ethnically divided, the personal interest of the case is often not personal wealth or personal advantages, it is much more the interest of the racial or ethnic majority to uphold its privileges and to subdue the minorities as second class citizens in order to serve the interest of the majority.

Moreover, the cases reveal that, although the principle that nobody can be judge in their own cause is undisputed, it is most difficult to implement in reality. This reality may even not be affected by divided ethnicity; it can very often also be seen in the division among educated and non educated people or among rich and poor people. Just because of their education or their economic wealth, defendants may profit from a judge with positive prejudices based on their social standing, or they may feel discriminated because of their social standing. In the United States, the issue of unbiased judges has been extended to the choice of the members of a jury. Trial lawyers get special training in assessing jury candidates to be chosen by the specific party of the trial. The people who have to be available for the jury are randomly chosen. Thus, unlike for a political election, everybody really must be and is available to become a member of the jury. To become a member of the jury every citizen is indeed a candidate. This candidacy is not dependent on wealth, on any political party or on adherence to a religion. The choice thus is really democratic. However, there are still some doubts with regard to the independence of the jury. With regard to capital punishment, the percentage of African-Americans who have been executed is far higher than their percentage of the population is. Indeed, 40% of those executed by the state are African-Americans, who make up only 12% of the entire American population. With regard to the death penalty, those who oppose the death penalty are excluded from sitting in the jury in a trial with the possibility of the death penalty.

3.2. Independence From Whom?

From whom should a judge be independent? It is obvious that a judge who is a weak personality and who is dependent either on his or her partner, or on their children or parents, can not be dismissed from their position. There is also no legal possibility to prevent such a kind of dependence. One might even ask whether such independence is needed. Here we have got to go back to the roots of the value of judge independence. In his Spirit of the Laws, Montesquieu postulates the separation of powers for the sake of individual liberty. For him, the goal of the principal of separation of powers is better protection of individual liberty. If this is the main goal of judicial independence, social or family dependence should not even bother the most suspicious theoreticians of judicial independence.[9]

However, the principle of judicial independence does not only have political roots, it also has roots in the concept of justice. A court decision can be considered as just if all parties have had the same opportunities to argue their case before the court. This, however, can only lead to a just decision if the judge or the jury hearing the case is not influenced by any opinion outside of the court. Any opinion outside the court may be to the detriment of one party, and it could therefore discriminate against the party.

However, here we have to distinguish between fact-finding and 'law-finding'. With regard to fact-finding, only the parties represented in the trial

9 Montesquieu, *supra* note 5, Ch. XI.

and the judge should have an influence on fact-finding. External influence from media or persons other than witnesses should not have any impact on the outcome of the facts relevant to the jury. It is for this reason that within the American tradition the members sitting in the jury are kept isolated from the public during the trial in order to exclude external influence on the case. With regard to law-finding the judge has to obey and apply the law, but only the law. Thus any argument for a certain interpretation of the law should be made available for the judge who has the responsibility to decide which way of argumentation with regard to a specific interpretation is the most convincing. Arguments coming from the outside should never force or put pressure on the judge. He/she needs to have the proper understanding and argumentation which he/she considers to be most convincing and thus successful. Whatever legal reasoning comes from the outside can be helpful if it enables the judge to follow and apply the law and only the law.

3.3. Access to Justice

Even the most independent courts can not improve the rule of law within a country in which citizens do not have access to justice. This general access has to be provided especially for cases of possible human rights violations by state officials and state administration. Thus the most challenging issue with regard to access to justice is the possibility of citizens to sue the administration for violation of human rights.

With regard to this challenge of access to justice, we have first to be aware of the fact that for historical reasons the two major legal systems, common and civil law, have a very different concept of access to justice. The civil legal system restricts access to justice for claims against the administration because it prevents any jurisdiction of the traditional courts in the field of public law. In the common law system, access to justice against the administration was considered as access to justice against the servants of the Crown. As the Crown could not be sued in court, and as judges were also servants of the Crown, this access was only possible with the traditional common law remedy of injunction, in most cases excluded against a civil servant of the Crown. However, the institution of the Lord Chancellor, who could provide for additional remedies for access to justice in cases of claims against the administration, was already possible with the beginning of the habeas corpus, demanding a legal basis for the arrest of individuals, and later on with the traditional public law remedies.

For this reason we shall first describe the different concepts of access to justice according to the different legal systems and then we shall look at the importance of a broad access to justice in the field of human rights.

4. The Different Legal Systems With Regards to Public Law and Private Law

4.1. Human Rights Guarantees

In the famous case of *Brown versus Board of Education*, the Supreme Court of the United States decided to oblige public schools to admit children of African-American parents.[10] The fact that this case could be brought to court was due to the availability of the remedy of injunction. The parents were able to ask the court through an injunction to oblige the school to admit the children. The court itself was able to enforce its judgement, as with its general power of contempt of court, it could oblige the school to admit the children.

In the civil law system it would have been much more difficult to provide for a remedy in order to let the children be admitted. The ordinary remedy is the claim of citizens to quash a decision. However, in Brown there was no decision to be quashed: the parents asked for a positive action from the school. Thus, in the civil system, the parents would have had to wait until they got a negative decision from the school. But even if the decision was quashed, the court would have no power to enforce a positive decision. The lack of remedies in civil law systems is even more shocking in cases where human rights are severely violated, such as in cases where prisoners are tortured. The famous case of the Israeli Supreme Court, which decided in September 1999 that the torture of prisoners based on administrative rules was prohibited, might have never reached a court in a civil law system. The current claims against European states for having allowed the CIA to use their airspace in order to transport prisoners for the aim of torturing them in a foreign country will probably never reach the courts because of lack of remedies.

These examples clearly show the relationship between the guarantee of human rights and the remedies providing for access to justice. There may be wonderful formulations with regard to human rights within the constitution of a country, but if the administrative law and the remedies provided for access to justice are restricted, even the best human rights catalogue can not really improve the human rights situation in a country.

The same is to be said with regard to international treaties protecting human rights. The effect of these treaties within the different states depends first of all on the applicability of those ratified treaties by domestic courts. The question of applicability depends on whether the state has a monistic or dualistic concept of international law. According to the monistic concept, international treaties are internally applicable without additional legislative acts. Most civil law countries more or less follow the monistic system. In the dualistic system, which is the rule in common law countries except the

[10] Brown *v.* Board of Education of Topeka, 347 U.S. 483 (1954).

United States, international law is only to be applied by the national court if, in addition to having been ratified by the state, it has also been incorporated by the legislature within the domestic legal system. So, for example, in the UK the European Convention on Human Rights could not be applied by the courts for a long time. It was only after the enactment of the Human Rights Act in 1998 that British courts could apply the provisions of the European Convention.

With regard to the human rights guarantees, we also have to be aware of the different approaches of the two legal systems. The focus of the common law tradition with regard to human rights is on procedure and remedies. Thus, a fair procedure, and natural justice, including independent courts, is the real focus of the common law tradition. The civil law tradition is focused much more on substantive guarantees such as human dignity, liberties and freedoms. Thus, the most important human right is considered to be human dignity, while in common law country the most important right is clearly the habeas corpus, which guarantees any person deprived of their liberties access to an independent court.

4.2. The War on Terrorism, or, No One Can Be a Judge in Their Own Case

In 2005, the US and some European states were accused by many human rights organizations of having transported persons suspected of terrorism to countries outside of their jurisdiction for interrogation, in order to avoid the use of the rights of habeas corpus and due process guaranteed within the state jurisdiction. Such practice has been defended with the argument that terrorists are enemies of the rule of law and thus have no right to be privileged according to the rights granted to the citizens of those countries. Of course, the independence of the judiciary is not guaranteed in such cases. First, by using the terms of war, the authorities consider terrorists to be enemies to be defeated with all means. They consider that their civilization has all possible rights in order to defend itself and its survival.

In such a situation of war, is it possible for any kind of judicial independence to exist? With regard to traditional wars, the law of armed conflict provides some fundamental guarantees with regard to prisoners of war. It prohibits the enemy state from treating its prisoners as criminals and indicting them as criminals, although they may have killed the enemy state's own soldiers during the war. In case they are accused of war crimes, however, even the enemy state can indict them. Here we are at the edge of the possibilities of the rule of law and we come to the fundamental question of whether those who wage war in a way that violates the rule of law can require that the rule of law applies also to them. It is important to consider that the independence of the judiciary not only has the aim of guaranteeing a fair trial for the indicted, but also to provide for the best possible standards that the real facts are known. If a secret service which is under pressure to provide the most possible information on possible terrorist activities can interrogate potential suspects without any accountability, there is no guarantee at all that such a service will provide the full truth. Rather one can assume that information would be filtered in order to be covered for any possible political pressure.

Moreover, these suspects will be under the total whim of the persons in charge of the secret service. These persons will use all possible means to give information to their superiors and to use all possible means to get this information. As they have total and uncontrolled power over their prisoners, they are also easily prepared to make the prisoners to feel all their personal frustration. The famous saying of Lord Acton that power corrupts and absolute power corrupts absolutely is also applicable in situations where only one person, as a prisoner, is under the total and unaccountable control of another person having all possible physical and psychological power over the victim.

Let me conclude this dilemma by quoting from the decision of the Israeli Supreme Court against the rules of torture established by the administration. This court is an outstanding example of a judicial institution within a most tense and controversial political environment. One may not endorse Israeli politics, but one has still to admire the judges ruling within this most sensitive context. Thus, I think that there is no more convincing evidence to be found of the dignity of an independent court than in these words written by a Supreme Court of a country always in fear of its future existence:

> Deciding these applications weighed heavy on this Court. True, from the legal perspective, the road before us is smooth. We are, however, part of Israeli society. Its problems are known to us and we live its history. We are not isolated in an ivory tower. We live the life of this country. We are aware of the harsh reality of terrorism in which we are, at times, immersed. Our apprehension is that this decision will hamper the ability to properly deal with terrorists and terrorism, disturbs us. We are, however, judges. Our brethren require us to act according to the law. This is equally the standard that we set for ourselves. When we sit to judge, we are being judged. Therefore, we must act according to our purest conscience when we decide the law. The words of the Deputy President of the Supreme Court, Justice Landau, speak well to our purposes: 'We possess proper sources upon which to construct our judgments and have no need, and while judging, are forbidden from, involving our personal views as citizens of this country in our decisions. Still, great is the fear that the Court shall be perceived as though it had abandoned its proper place and descended to the midst of public debate, and that its decision making will be obstructed by one side of the population's uproar and by the other side's absolute and emotional rejection. In that sense, I see myself here as someone whose duty is to decide according to the law in all cases legally brought before the Court. I am strictly bound by this duty. As I am well aware in advance that the public at large will not pay attention to the legal reasoning, but to the end result alone.

> And that the Court's proper status, as an institution above partisan debates, risks being harmed. What can we do, as this is our function and role as judges.'[11]

5. Conclusions

What are the main conclusions we can draw from these reflections on judicial independence? In principle we have seen that justice depends not only on good legislation and good legal principles but also on the procedures, the legal system and the legal culture as well as the position of the court and of the judges. Justice must not only been done, it must be seen to be done. Even the best substantial legal principles cannot guarantee justice without the corresponding procedure and the respective guarantee of the independence of justice.

The question we need still need to answer is: would the open democratic assembly or the parliament be a much better judge and just as independent as the court and the judiciary? Law can only provide security if it is predictable. However, the very notion of the parliament and legislature is not to be predictable with regard to the past but to foresee the future and provide creative regulations for future developments. Human beings, on the other hand, need to know which prescriptions are valid and have to be complied with. Law must be predictable. This principle can only be guaranteed by a system of courts that have full knowledge of the law to be applied in a certain case and which are able to establish the facts in close cooperation with the adversarial parties. Judges have to look into the past, while the politician needs to look into the future. This is the main reason why the judiciary, which at best complies with the principle of predictability of the application of the law, needs to be independent.

[11] H.C. 390/79 Dawikat *v*. The State of Israel, 34(1) P.D. 1, at 4.

Dragoljub Popović

Autonomous Concepts of the European Human Rights Law

1. What Are Autonomous Concepts?

Although often mentioned and discussed, the autonomous concepts of the European Human Rights Law are not easily defined. They are products of a judge-made law, or, more precisely, the achievements of the case-law of the European Court of Human Rights (hereinafter – Court). The autonomous concepts themselves emerged as a result of the application of the provisions of the European Convention on Human Rights (hereinafter – Convention) before the Court.

There is no unanimity among scholars with regard to a possible definition of the notion of autonomous concepts as such. Major manuals on European Human Rights Law usually mention them, but hardly ever offer proper definitions.[1] The Court's case-law does not always provide sufficient grounds for legal definitions and scholars often reproach the Court that its case-law actually lacks 'general and abstract' notions.[2] This being true, scholars did not miss out on the opportunity to try and create these very notions. Their search for a definition shows two basic approaches. One such method is to provide a simple denomination of the notion of autonomous concept, whereas the other one is more complex.

Examples of the first approach can be found in Mahoney and Leach, among others. The latter is of opinion that autonomous concepts are such "terms used in the Convention" for which "the classification under national

1 F. Sudre, Droit européen et international des droits de l'homme 232-233 (2005); C. Ovey *et al.*, European Convention on Human Rights 31-32 (2002); C. Grabenwarter, Europäische Menschenrechtskonvention 48-49 (2003).

2 E. Kastanas, Unité et diversité: notions autonomes et marge d'appréciation des Etats dans la jurisprudence de la Cour européenne des droits de l'homme 374 (1996).

Miodrag Jovanović & Ivana Krstić (Eds.), Human Rights Today – 60 Years of the Universal Declaration, 113-126.

law will be a factor in the Court's determination as to whether the Convention is applicable, but it will not be decisive."[3] Mahoney, for his part, insists on the fact that an autonomous concept ensures "the universality of the international standard," and also underlines that the legislations of Contracting States to the Convention provide "sources for deducing the common core of the concept."[4]

More complex approaches to the problem of defining autonomous concepts of the European Human Rights Law basically lead to similar results. Letsas has recently made an effort to make a profound analysis. One of his conclusions is that autonomous concepts are "technical terms that are employed in national legal sources and are invested with a special, non- ordinary meaning." He therefore underlines the existence of a phenomenon he calls "law's eccentric vocabulary."[5] However, the author also admits that the problem of classification at national level is essential in cases before the Court in which autonomous concepts find application.[6] In such cases, the Court inevitably has to provide reasons in its judgments as to why, in its view, certain classifications at national level are mistaken.[7]

In short, it should be pointed out that autonomous concepts are terms applied by the Court that exist in national legal systems of Contracting States to the Convention, but which are given a special meaning in the Court's case law. Whoever wants to apply the provisions of the Convention must deal with these concepts and understand them properly.

2. Main Features of Autonomous Concepts

Autonomous concepts, typical products of a judge-made law, usually escape precise definitions (2.1). Some of them even contradict the mainstreams of legal theory (2.2). Despite the fact that such concepts have connections to comparative law, they sometimes lack its support (2.3). And last but not least, autonomous concepts are susceptible of evolution (2.4).

2.1. Escaping Definition

An illustration of how an autonomous concept escapes a clear-cut definition can be found in the notion of *possessions* in Article 1 of Protocol 1 to the

[3] P. Leach, Taking a Case to the European Court of Human Rights 165 (2005).

[4] P. Mahoney, *The Comparative Method in Judgments of the European Court of Human Rights: Reference Back to National Law*, *in* G. Canivet, M. Andenas & D. Fairgrieve (Eds.), Comparative Law Before the Courts 135, at 145-146 (2004).

[5] G. Letsas, A Theory of Interpretation of the European Convention on Human Rights 48 (2007).

[6] *Id.*, at 51.

[7] *Id.*, at 53.

Convention (hereafter – Article 1 First Protocol). The provision's title announces protection of property. Its text in its English version, however, speaks of *possessions*.

It is not only the ambiguity of the term 'property' in the English language which causes the problem in this text. The concept of *possessions*, as developed in the case-law of the Court certainly goes beyond the reality covered by the notion of ownership as traditionally inspired by Roman Law.

Thus, one Dutch scholar will tell us that the concept "does not refer to the technical, legal concept of property," and a bit further that "the concept of *possessions* within the meaning of Article 1 First Protocol is much broader than the Dutch private law concept of *eigendom*."[8]

It is quite clear today that, irrespective of what the drafters' original ideas may have been, owners of rights *in rem* other than proprietors sometimes do enjoy protection under Article 1 First Protocol.[9] The case-law of the Court has gone rather far in its development of the autonomous concept of *possessions*. At the beginning of its evolution the Court ruled in *Marcks* that the term had an autonomous meaning in respect of Article 1 First Protocol.[10] The concept applies to a wide range of terms and objects. A brief survey of the Court's case-law on the subject provides an idea of its scope.

Among the objects that benefit from protection as *possessions* under Article 1 are company shares.[11] This also goes for assets belonging to what in French is known as *propriété industrielle*, such as patents, for instance.[12]

A claim before domestic courts of law can also be considered to fall within the scope of protection as in Article 1 First Protocol. Such a claim represents *possessions* in the sense of the provision, as just mentioned.[13] Last but not least, the idea of *possessions* includes a concept that could hardly be denominated as an asset, known in the European Human Rights Law as *legitimate expectation*.[14]

The examples that have been mentioned here stand among others of a similar kind and well illustrate the difficulty of posing a definition of the autonomous concept of *possessions* in terms of Article 1 First Protocol. It is hard to imagine a comprehensive approach, which would include all species belonging to the class of *possessions*, as presently existing in the Court's

---

[8] T. Hartlief, *The Right to Own Property Under the ECHR*, *in* J. P. Loof, H. Ploeger & A. van der Steur (Eds.), The Right to Property – The Influence of Article 1 Protocol No. 1 ECHR on Several Fields of Domestic Law 29, at 31-32 (2000).

[9] E. A. Alkema, *The Concept of Property – In Particular in the European Convention on Human Rights*, *in* J. P. Loof, H. Ploeger & A. van der Steur (Eds.), The Right to Property – The Influence of Article 1 Protocol No. 1 ECHR on Several Fields of Domestic Law 20 (2000).

[10] Marcks *v*. Belgium, Judgments and Decisions 31, para. 63 (1979).

[11] Bramelid and Malström *v*. Sweden, Decisions and Reports 29, 82 (1982).

[12] Smith Kline and French Laboratories *v*. The Netherlands, app. no. 12633/87.

[13] Pressos Compania Naviera *v*. Belgium, Judgments and Decisions A332 (1995).

[14] Pine Valley Developments Ltd *v*. Ireland, Judgments and Decisions A222 (1991).

case-law.[15] Such a task would be even more difficult if notions and definitions of domestic legal systems were taken into account, but this problem will be addressed below. Suffice it to mention that some scholars have come up with proposals to constitute a specific concept at national level in order to meet the one developed in the European Law of Human Rights. This idea should be referred to as constitutional property and should include all patrimonial, but not personality rights. These proposals, however, have not yet found many supporters.[16]

2.2. Contradicting Mainstreams of Theory

Autonomous concepts of the European Human Rights Law may, on certain occasions, run counter to the established and long lasting conclusions of almost universally accepted legal theory. One of the best-known and most outstanding examples of this kind is the notion of *law* as developed by the Court.

The English term again gives rise to ambiguity especially from a continental point of view. What the English refer to as *law* can be perceived as either *droit* or *loi* in French, the Convention's other official language. The French text of several provisions is quite clear, however, and does not raise any misunderstanding or ambiguity, as the term *loi* is used. It might be concluded that the English term *law* should be understood as an *act of Parliament*. But then, could this term also include sources of law that do not find their origins in written law? Is, due to the ambiguity in English, the formula of the French text of the Convention '*prévue par la loi*' to be understood as referring to domestic case-law or customary law of a member-state to the Convention?[17]

The question occurred for the first time in a case as early as in the seventies of the last century. The case was *The Sunday Times v. United Kingdom*[18] and concerned press reporting on the consequences of the use of thalidomide. Taken by expectant mothers, it often resulted in serious deformities affecting their children. The Court found that the injunction against the newspaper that had reported on the issue at domestic level was not necessary in a democratic society. The injunction at domestic level was not issued according to the provisions of an act of Parliament, whereas Article 10 of the Convention provides that a measure should be 'prescribed by law', or in the French version 'prévue par la loi'.

---

15 *Cf.* A. van Rijn, Right to Peaceful Enjoyment of One's Possessions, *in* P. van Dijk *et al.* (Eds.), Theory and Practice of the European Convention on Human Rights 865 (2006).

16 A. R. Çoban, Protection of Property Rights Within the European Convention on Human Rights 34 (2004).

17 Kastanas, *supra* note 2, at 38.

18 The Sunday Times *v.* The United Kingdom, Judgments and Decisions A30 (1979).

The Court's conclusion, of interest for the purposes set out above, was that the concept of *law*, or *loi* in French, should, in terms of the Convention cover both written and unwritten law.[19] An attitude like this, however, hardly fits the standpoints of legal theory on the European continent.

A few examples will clarify this. Ardent states that the *law (la loi)* is a decision taken by Parliament or by the people in a procedure provided by the Constitution. He adds that only the legislator can modify or abrogate such an act.[20] This is almost the same stance as the one expressed by Marie-Anne Cohendet, who defines *la loi* as a general and impersonal rule adopted in democracy by the people or its representatives, freely and regularly elected.[21]

Pactet, for his part, invokes the authority of Carré de Malberg and his monograph consecrated to the notion of *loi*, more or less following the path traced by Rousseau. Pactet thus defines *law* in the French sense of the term as an act voted in Parliament according to legislative procedure, and promulgated by the head of state.[22] A last French example is Mathieu's study entitled *La loi*, in which he starts at the traditional organic and formal definition of *law*, as an act voted by Parliament. A brief analysis of the French evolution, of institutions as well as legal theory, leads Mathieu to understand *law* in the Fifth French Republic as an act of what he calls 'a superior power'. To this day, the latter description can still be found in French legal theory, which regards *law* as a written document, deliberated upon and voted by assemblies or adopted by the people.[23]

Haller and Költz define their "material notion of legislative Power" as the one posing general and abstract legal rules. The power to legislate, i.e. produce those rules is vested with Parliament as the legislative body.[24] Fleiner makes a synthesis of the classical German doctrine on the subject, by recognizing the difference between a substantial and formal notion of law (Gesetz). In that respect, he follows Laband, and agrees with the wide-spread conclusion of the German scholarship, that demands all laws which, in the substantial sense of the notion, pose limits to either liberty or property be formal laws, *i.e.* acts of Parliament.[25] It should be added that the Serbian doctrine has always been in line with the approach of classical German scholars. Its most outstanding author of all times, Slobodan Jovanović, was also inspired by Laband.[26]

19 Kastanas, *supra* note 2, at 37.
20 P. Ardent, Institutions politiques et droit constitutionnel 44 (2003).
21 M. A. Cohendet, Droit constitutionnel 231 (2006).
22 P. Pactet, Institutions politiques – Droit constitutionnel 594 (2002).
23 B. Mathieu, La loi 11-14 (2004).
24 W. Haller & A. Költz, Allgemeines Staatsrecht 249 (1999).
25 T. Fleiner & L. Basta-Fleiner, Allgemeine Staatslehre 415-416 (2004).
26 S. Jovanović, O državi [On the State] 196 (1922).

The Court for its part did not want to attach itself to the continental legal theory. It abandoned the organic and formal approach to the definition of a legal term, which had been almost universally accepted on the European continent.

The Court went deeper into the social reality in order to create an autonomous concept for the purposes of the Convention. Therefore it accepted the unwritten law of falling within the scope of the French expression *loi*. The Court demanded, nonetheless, that an unwritten rule might fall within the scope covered by the notion of *law* if it could fulfil certain conditions. As far as the case-law at domestic level was concerned such a rule should be constantly followed by domestic courts of law, it should be made public, abundant, and accessible.[27]

The approach that emerged in *The Sunday Times* has been followed by the Court ever since. One of the cases illustrating this was *Kruslin v. France*. It concerned interference by public authority in the exercise of applicant's rights to respect of correspondence and to private life under Article 8 of the Convention.[28] The term 'law' was understood by the Court in its substantive Sense, and not in the formal one. It included both the enactments that were of lower rank than statutes and even 'unwritten law'.

In *Kruslin,* the Court went a step further than in *The Sunday Times*. In paragraph 48 of the judgment in *the latter,* the Court tried to reconcile the standpoints of the two great legal systems of the world "in order to realize the aim and achieve the object" of the Convention. In *Kruslin,* the Court somehow denied the difference between great legal systems, by finding, in paragraph 29 of the judgment, that written and unwritten law can be separated in neither of the two.[29] This leads to the question on relations existing between autonomous concepts on the one hand and comparative law on the other.

2.3. Lacking Support of Comparative Law

Although the autonomous concepts are to a great extent related to comparative law, and are even considered by many to be products of a comparative approach to legal terms, they sometimes lack support of comparative law. In other words, there are autonomous concepts of the European Human Rights Law that neither represent a common core of similar terms existing in the member-states' legal systems, nor exactly fit any of their terms.

An example of the latter is the concept of the earlier mentioned *possessions*, created for the purposes of Article 1 First Protocol. There is no national legal system that could be considered to have the same notion. This has already been

27 Kastanas, *supra* note 2, at 43.

28 Kruslin *v*. France, Judgments and Decisions A176 (1990).

29 D. Popović, Uvod u uporedno pravo [An Introduction to Comparative Law] 45 (2007).

mentioned in relation to Dutch law.[30] The same applies to French, Austrian, German and Swiss laws and their respective civil codes.[31] None of these national legal systems possess a full equivalent to the concept of *possessions*, as it exists in the European Law of Human Rights.

Going deeper into the problem and beyond national level, so as to take into consideration the great legal systems or legal families that member-states of the Convention belong to, one finds that the situation remains the same. Neither the Anglo-Saxon legal system, nor the one based on the Roman Law tradition, has developed a concept identical with the one created by the Court's case-law. Neither the complex network of estates, tenancies and leases of various kinds in England and Wales, nor the continental idea of a simple ownership, easily defined by the presence of *usus, fructus* and *abusus* among owner's entitlements, can fully correspond with the autonomous concept of *possessions*, as developed by the Court.[32]

Other examples of this kind can be found in two autonomous concepts that will be dealt with more profoundly below. The meaning of *civil rights and obligations* may be clear for any law student. However, the problem of understanding such terms will arise when application of Article 6 of the Convention is sought, for the simple reason that its provision does not contain a definition of the above mentioned term.

What *civil rights and obligations* are in respect of Article 6 of the Convention should be determined only with reference to the case-law of the Court. This autonomous concept has a relatively close connection with the terms of national legal systems, but they are not exactly the same.

Civil rights and obligations are usually opposed to public duties and rights.[33] Yet it is impossible to learn the exact meaning of the autonomous concept, unless the Court's case-law is taken into account, although the concept is such that, at first glance, it does not seem to call for a broader explanation. It will become clear that there was a line of development in the Court's case-law that shaped the concept to its present perception. Its pattern changed, or, in other words, the concept was susceptible of evolution.

---

30 For the Dutch law *see* Hartlief, *supra* note 8.

31 *Cf.* Popović, *supra* note 29, at 98, 113, 118, 122.

32 *Cf.* S. van Erp, *Comparative Property Law*, *in* M. Reinmann & R. Zimmermann (Eds.), The Oxford Handbook of Comparative Law 1051 (2006); J. Gordley, Foundations of Private Law 49-53 (2007); D. Popović, Evropski sud za ljudska prava [European Court of Human Rights] 114-115 (2008).

33 Kastanas, *supra* note 2, at 375.

2.4. Susceptibility of Evolution

Susceptibility of evolution of autonomous concepts of the European Human Rights Law can well be exposed if we take the example of the concept I have just mentioned – *civil rights and obligations* in respect of Article 6 of the Convention.

The earliest precedent of relevance for the determination of *civil rights and obligations* within the scope of Article 6 of the Convention was the *Ringeisen case*,[34] concerning an applicant who had speculated with land in Austria. Even though he had purchased some plots of land from private persons, he had to address some administrative bodies in the course of the domestic proceedings. Thus the question arose before the Court of whether or not the application concerned *civil rights and obligations* and, consequently, whether or not Article 6 of the Convention would apply to the case. The Court ruled, in paragraph 94 of the judgment, that "the French expression 'contestations sur (des) droits et obligations de caractère civil' covers all proceedings the result of which is decisive for private rights and obligations." The Court stated at the same time that the English text of the provision confirmed that interpretation. The rule in *Ringeisen* seemed to limit the possibility of creating an autonomous concept. Basically, as scholars have remarked, the term 'civil' in the judgment was understood as the equivalent of 'private'.[35] The approach therefore corresponded with the conclusions of legal theory. Nonetheless, the rule posed in *Ringeisen* was abandoned in *Pelegrin v. France*,[36] the facts of which were, in brief, the following. The French Ministry of Cooperation and Development recruited the applicant as a technical advisor to governments of Western African states. Yet a medical report stating that he was permanently unfit to serve overseas prevented him from being eligible for the post.

The Court ruled in paragraph 64 of the judgment that "in order to determine applicability of Article 6.1 to public servants [...] it should adopt a functional criterion based on the nature of the employee's duties and responsibilities." This being so, the Court felt obliged to conclude in the same paragraph that "it must adopt a restrictive interpretation, in accordance with the object and purpose of the Convention, of the exceptions to the safeguards afforded by Article 6.1." The Court held that Article 6 of the Convention did not apply to the case.

The idea behind the rule in *Pellegrin*, as stated by the Court, was that in public service sector "certain posts involve responsibilities in the general interest or participation in the exercise of powers conferred by public law." The Court estimated that holders of such posts exercise "a portion of sovereign power." The State has a legitimate interest when it requires servants, holding

[34] Ringeisen *v*. Austria, Judgments and Decisions A13 (1971).

[35] Kastanas, *supra* note 2, at 375-376.

[36] Pelegrin *v*. France, Reports of Judgments and Decisions,1999-VIII.

such posts to possess "a special bond of trust and loyalty." This was, in fact, what prevented the Court from applying Article 6 of the Convention to the case: the matter at issue concerned "special bonds of loyalty" rather than *civil rights and obligations*. It is worth mentioning that there was a parallel between this attitude of the Court and the position of the UN Committee of Human Rights, when the latter applied Article 14 of the International Covenant of Civil and Political Rights.[37]

The rule in *Pelegrin* had been followed by the Court for years. A deviation of the case-law appeared in *Vilho Eskelinen and others v. Finland*,[38] in which a group of Finish policemen had brought a case before domestic courts, relating to their salaries. The procedure took place before Finish administrative courts. The Court had already established precedents that led to the conclusion that the character of domestic procedure was not decisive. A legal suit of an administrative nature, could, according to domestic rules, be reasonably considered as concerning *civil rights and obligations* in terms of Article 6 of the Convention.[39]

In *Eskelinen* the Court ruled in favour of a presumption of applicability of Article 6 of the Convention to ordinary labour disputes. Therefore it was not deemed sufficient for a State to establish that a civil servant participated in the exercise of public power just in order to avoid application of Article 6 of the Convention. A responding government with a tendency to avoid Article 6 of the Convention had to prove fulfilment of two conditions. Firstly, access to court must be expressly excluded in national law, and secondly such exclusion must be justified on objective grounds in the State's interest. The latter is by all means subject to the Court's scrutiny. The Court held in *Eskelinen* that Article 6 of the Convention was applicable to the case and found its violation.

The rule in *Eskelinen* therefore somehow rectified the one in the *Pelegrin Case,* and made it less rigid. Its final outcome is certain redressing of the concept of *civil rights and obligations* in respect of Article 6 of the Convention. It does not any more necessarily exclude the protection of persons linked to a State by special bonds of loyalty. The scope of the concept may now extend even to the law suits of civil servants performing part of the State sovereign power. That is, of course, under the conditions of the *Eskelinen rule.*

---

37 *Cf.* D. Popović, Pravo na pravnu sigurnost i pravedno Postupanje, *in* V. Dimitrijević *et al.* (Eds.), Međunarodno pravo ljudskih prava [International Law of Human Rights] 189 (2006).

38 Vilho Eskelinen and others *v*. Finland, app. No. 63235/00 (2007).

39 *Cf.* Menitto *v*. Italy, Reports of Judgments and Decisions, 2000-X. As a matter of fact, that was also the case in *Ringeisen.*

3. Autonomous Concepts and the Interpretation of the Convention

Autonomous concepts are, in their essence, an important means of interpreting the Convention, often used by the Court. In connection to their function two main questions arise. The first one concerns limits to the field of application of autonomous concepts created by the Court. The second one appears to be another facet of the same image. It pertains to the Court's scope of discretion and its way of reasoning during the process of achieving verdicts and decisions. Both questions are theoretic in character and demand broader research. Hence it is only a short sketch of possible answers that can be drawn below.

Starting with the second problem, one of the main issues in this respect is the relation between the original ideas of the drafters of the Convention and its additional protocols and the interpretation that can be attributed to their creations today. The Court's position on the subject is clear, for it has repeated on many occasions that it considered the Convention to be a living instrument. This formula stems from the late seventies of the last century, when the Court referred to it in a British case, which, though somewhat peculiar, well presented the fundamental dilemma.

The Court's earliest reference to the Convention as a living instrument was made in the case *Tyrer v. The United Kingdom*,[40] regarding the long lasting practice of corporal punishment of juveniles, which at the time still existed at the Isle of Man, one of the Channel Islands, belonging to the British Crown. The applicant was a minor who had assaulted and occasioned bodily harm to a senior pupil at his school, because the victim had reported the applicant for having brought beer into the school.

The applicant was sentenced to three strokes of a birch according to relevant legislation in force on the island. The applicant was birched in a police station, in the presence of his father and a medical practitioner. He had to take down his trousers and underpants and bend over a table, being held by two policemen, whilst the third administered the punishment.

The Court held that the judicial corporal punishment inflicted on the applicant amounted to degrading punishment within the meaning of Article 3 of the Convention and found a violation of that provision. It was in paragraph 31 of the judgment that the Court first expressed the idea of the Convention as a living instrument. The respondent government's thesis was that the judicial corporal punishment was not in breach of the Convention, "since it did not outrage the public opinion in the Island." The Court rejected that line of reasoning and stated: "the Convention is a living instrument which must be interpreted in the light of present-day conditions." Therefore, the fact that a certain practice had been long-lasting – and even enjoyed support of

[40] Tyrer *v*. The United Kingdom, Judgments and Decisions A26 (1978).

the population - could neither justify maintaining such practice, nor render it compliant with the Convention. In other words, following Mahoney, the main idea was that a practice or custom once perhaps permitted was subsequently prohibited.[41]

The living instrument approach of the Court to the problem of interpreting the Convention leads to consideration of the relation between its text and the Court's findings and conclusions. The effect of the Court's approach is very similar to the one produced by the use of autonomous concepts. It has been observed by scholars that "the Convention's provisions are abstract and sparse" and that therefore "the key to resolving individual complaints ultimately lies in how the text is interpreted."[42]

The Court has evidently gone beyond strict and unconditional fidelity to the Convention's text, i.e. an approach of interpretation sometimes labelled as originalism or textualism.[43] On many occasions the Court has been inclined to read into the text certain meanings, which apparently, or even linguistically, do not fit its ordinary meaning. From this point of view, the technique of autonomous concepts seems to have a somewhat reconciliatory role. Creating them means, in a certain sense, preserving the Court's fidelity to the Convention's text.

At this point a previous example can be invoked. The Court provides protection of property under Article 1 First Protocol. The concept of *property* or *possessions*, as demonstrated above, embraces among other notions, legitimate expectations. By including the latter into the concept of property the Court could remain faithful to the text. In so doing, the Court has gone beyond the 'original' or 'usual' meaning of the notion of *property* or *possessions* in order to apply a certain provision, contained in the text. In order to be able to apply the provision the Court had to keep to an autonomous concept, thus broadening the 'original' meaning of a notion used in the Convention's text.

Thus, the Court's fidelity to the text of the Convention is achieved by a slightly different perception of certain notions of the drafters' original intentions and meanings. This demonstrates, to a certain extent, the creativity of the Court, which should, however, be exercised within rational limits. These are posed by social needs and various challenges of the modern world. It has been stressed in the doctrine that the Court is inspired in this respect by Article 31(1) of the Vienna Convention on the Law of Treaties, which provides that a treaty shall be interpreted "in the light of its object and purpose."[44]

As to the second question mentioned earlier, one may conclude at this point that the Court is entitled to discretion in constructing autonomous concepts.

---

[41] *Cf.* Mahoney, *supra* note 4, at 147; *see also* Letsas, *supra* note 5, at 61.

[42] S. Greer, The European Convention on Human Rights – Achievements, Problems and Prospects 193 (2006) (with reference to C. Gearty, article of 1993).

[43] Letsas, *supra* note 5, at 59-60.

[44] Jacobs & White, *supra* note 1, at 34-35.

However, the first question, on how far the Court can go in its introduction of limits to the field of application of the autonomous concepts, does still remain. It should always be borne in mind that the two questions are closely linked to each other and can not be separated. Whenever the Court creates an autonomous concept the problem of its boundaries will inevitably emerge. This encompasses the border of judicial self-restraint.

The Court's creativity and judicial discretion are questions of a broader interest. They should not be posed exclusively with regard to the field of human rights, although very often those rights and their implementation served as a challenge for courts to break through with new and fresh ideas. Notwithstanding its occurrence at national level too, the question is raised to a level of specific significance in an international court of law.

As far as the Court's interpretation of the Convention is concerned, it should be pointed out that there were and probably still are, judges who are to some extent hostile to a broadening view on autonomous concepts. Analyzing such attitudes, Letsas has arrived at the crucial question he most eloquently formulated: "Do autonomous concepts constitute a case of illegitimate judicial legislation?"[45]

At this point I agree with Letsas. He argues that judicial discretion originates in disagreement on possible interpretations of the text of the Convention. Judges merely opt for one of the possibilities offered by logic. They are obliged to provide reasons for their judgments *i.e.* for the choices they made, but the judicial discretion as such cannot be put in question.[46] It is clear that before the Court of Strasbourg, as well as in all other courts of law, irrespective of the level – national or international – parties put forward different interpretations of legal provisions. Rendering justice in a particular case substantially means nothing but making a choice among possible interpretations.

The use of autonomous concepts in the European Human Rights Law, as it has developed in the case-law of the Court, therefore provokes the question of the starting points of interpretation, as to what would happen if the Court were to decide in a complete absence of a text. One could imagine a court of law, vested with the power to render justice, either at national or international level, without a text in the sense of some provisions to which to adhere. Such a body could, to my mind at least, administer justice. It would have to start providing judgments and decisions and subsequently be considered to be bound by these. This, in turn, brings out the difficulty of the role of precedents and the *stare decisis* in the case-law of the Court.[47] This is a complex matter that has not yet been given much attention from scholars and certainly demands more reflection than can be lowed in this paper.

[45] Letsas, *supra* note 5, at 49.

[46] *Id.*, at 53-54.

[47] *See* Popović, *supra* note 32, at 105-109.

4. Handling Autonomous Concepts at National Levels

It has been pointed out that autonomous concepts mainly find their origins in expressions of national legal systems of the member States to the Convention. Terms that serve as starting points for creating autonomous concepts remain in use at the level of domestic law and in litigations before domestic courts. At the same time the Convention represents a source of law in the member States, and is implemented by the domestic courts of law. The autonomous concepts therefore co-exist with the terms representing their origins, and should be equally implemented.

The situation of parallel existence of autonomous concepts and domestic legal terms at national level calls for an explanation. One of the major points concerns modes of incorporating the Convention into domestic legal order.[48] Countries with a monistic approach to the relations between international and national law will in this respect probably differ from those following a dualist approach.

A topic that justly calls for reflection is whether and to what extent the autonomous concepts of the European Law of Human Rights are capable of leading to transformation of domestic legal concepts. This process is a rather complex one and merits specific research before conclusions of a general nature can be drawn, but it must be said that efforts of this kind are already appearing in the doctrine.[49]

As the autonomous concepts are applicable at national level, they should figure in legal studies in order to prepare future lawyers to deal with these concepts. This is, of course, valid above all for judges, but no less for practicing lawyers and public prosecutors, which leads to the conclusion that teaching awareness of and knowledge on autonomous concepts should find its place in the curricula of law schools. The autonomous concepts of the European Human Rights Law most certainly fall within the category of concepts of those reputed as having a universal vocation as well as a certain status in positive law,[50] which is why they should be spearheaded in universities.

Early study of autonomous concepts is also highly recommendable, since they are applied and exist at national level, along with national legal concepts from which, in spite of their apparent similarity, they inevitably differ. National and European concepts are better taught in parallel, rather than having the former represent a dogma that law students subsequently have to question and seek deviation from. At this point the present author agrees with Legrand who proposes that students should be initiated in comparative law not only to escape the phenomenon he calls 'l'imperium des textes' but also to avoid the

48 On modes of incorporation *see* Grabenwarter, *supra* note 1, at 18-25.
49 *Cf.* n. 16.
50 *Cf.* S. Cassese, Oltre lo Stato 107 (2006).

customary apodictic character of their national law.[51] This represents a great challenge to modern legal studies, particularly in view of certain peculiarities that come to the fore when traditional and new democracies are considered and compared.[52]

5. Conclusions

Autonomous concepts are susceptible of evolution on their own within the European Human Rights Law. They escape definitions, established legal theory and comparative law. They are typical products of a judge-made law.

Autonomous concepts serve as a tool for the interpretation of the Convention as carried out by the Court. They are rooted in judicial creativity, an apparently appropriate answer to the various challenges of today's world.

Autonomous concepts influence legal developments at national level and should benefit from thorough consideration in the drafting process of university curricula. Autonomous concepts still require extensive research. The more academia spends on researching the limits and consequences of autonomous concepts, the more efficient protection of human rights in Europe will be.

[51] P. Legrand, Le droit comparé 69 (1999).

[52] *Cf.* D. Popović, *La raison comparatiste et la liberté. Problème de renforcement du pouvoir judiciaire dans les nouvelles démocraties*, *in* J. du Bois de Gaudusson *et al.*, Mélanges en l'honneur de Slobodan Milacic – Démocratie et liberté: tension, dialogue, confrontation 239, at 244-246 (2007).

Aleksandar Gajić

International Criminal Tribunal for the Former Yugoslavia – Human Rights Perspective

"This is a critical period for international criminal justice; a twilight era which will prove to be either the dawn of international law justice or its dusk."[1]

1. Introductory Remarks

The Universal Declaration on Human Rights, even though not binding, served and is still serving as a leading instrument in the estimation of the achievements of human rights standards in domestic and international arena. As stated in the preamble of the Universal Declaration: "Human rights should be protected by the rule of law." Today, no one can argue that international law does not sufficiently protect human rights in criminal proceedings. Whether those rights are fully enforced is another question, and equally arises in respect of both international and municipal criminal systems. International and municipal legal systems face various difficulties and are open to criticism. The 60th anniversary of the most important human rights instrument in the history of humanity is a good opportunity to present a few critical remarks on the law and practice of the International Criminal Tribunal for the Former Yugoslavia (ICTY) from a human rights perspective.

Naturally, an in-depth elaboration of all the issues that deserve discussion is impossible in one article; rather a whole library could be designated to that topic. In this presentation I will attempt to make a few remarks on several issues that certainly belong to the category of the most important.

1 A. Cassese, *Opinion: The International Criminal Tribunal for the Former Yugoslavia and Human Rights*, 2 European Human Rights Law Review 329, at 352 (1997).

Miodrag Jovanović & Ivana Krstić (Eds.), Human Rights Today – 60 Years of the Universal Declaration, 127-142.

* * *

There is no doubt that jurisprudence of the ICTY plays a crucial role in further development of international criminal law. However, the ICTY is an *ad hoc* tribunal; its decisions have no binding effect of precedent on other courts and tribunals, except for a possible persuasive authority of *ratio decidendi* of its decisions, which is highly dependant on the answer to the question whether the jurisprudence of the ICTY is fully in line with internationally recognized human rights norms and standards. As Judge David Hunt observed:

> The Tribunal will not be judged by the number of convictions which it enters, or by the speed with which it concludes the completion strategy which the Security Council endorsed, but by fairness of the trials.[2]

Fairness of the trials and protection of human rights in criminal proceedings can only be estimated in the light of the internationally recognized human rights norms and standards. Not to neglect the rights of the victims to know the truth, and protection of the witnesses[3], it has to be pointed out that

> if the rights of the accused, as defined in an international setting, are a step back from those same rights in the national setting, than the ICTY will be wavering from its course.[4]

The ICTY's jurisprudence is, and certainly will continue to be, under the magnifying glass of critical analysis, particularly in an attempt to build a solid basis for the imminent International Criminal Court (ICC) jurisprudence. The ICC faces certain problems, and some of which have been successfully resolved in the recent jurisprudence,[5] and it does not seem surprising that the ICC jurisprudence does not follow the solutions established in the ICTY

---

[2] *Dissenting Opinion of Judge David Hunt on Admissibility of Evidence in Chief in the Form of Written Statement, Prosecutor v. Slobodan Milosevic,* 21 October 2003, para. 22.

[3] *See e.g.* P. Chifflet, *The Rule and Status of the Victim, in* G. Boas & W. A. Schabas (Eds.), International Criminal Law Developments in the Case Law of the ICTY 75 (2003). Statute of the International Criminal Court provides opportunity for the full participation of victims in the trials, who will be represented by their own legal representatives.

[4] J. Sloan, *The International Criminal Tribunal for the Former Yugoslavia and Fair Trial Rights*, 9 Leiden Journal of International Law 479, at 501 (1996). Judge Schomburg explicitly stated that

> [a] person who is accused before ICTY or ICTR cannot have more limited protection of his human rights only because his trial is conducted by an international criminal tribunal instead of a national one.

W. Schomburg, *The Protection of Human Rights of the Accused Before the International Criminal Tribunals for the Former Yugoslavia (ICTY) and Rwanda (ICTR), in* K. Bard & R. Soyer (Eds.), Internationale Strafgerichtsbrakeit – Status quo und Perspektiven 76 (2005).

[5] Many substantial aspects of the crimes against humanity and war crimes have been successfully resolved. However, the ICTY, unlike the International Criminal Court, made a little distinction between the rules applied in international and non-international armed conflicts.

jurisprudence.[6] However, it is too early to draw conclusions since ICC has just begun its work.[7]

From the jurisprudence of the ICTY both positive and negative experience could be drawn. Since the furtherance of human rights is the preoccupation of utmost importance, those which may be considered as negative experiences have to be addressed first, in order to avoid further departures from the rule of law, to improve human rights protection, and not any less important, to serve as a basis for possible reconsideration of the judgments and decisions rendered by the ICTY Appeals Chamber.[8]

2. The ICTY's General Approach to Human Rights

For a proper understanding of the ICTY's jurisprudence it is necessary to have in mind ICTY's general approach to human right issues as expressed in the ICTY decisions. This is necessary in order to understand the problem concerning the methods by which the ICTY has sought to protect human rights of the accused, the victims and witnesses who appear before it, and whether this protection is in line with required internationally recognized norms and standards. This general approach was formulated in the ICTY's first case (*Prosecutor v. Tadić*),[9] and deviation from the expressed standpoints is hard to find.

The Trial Chamber I in this instance, held that it was not bound by universal human rights principles as interpreted by other human rights bodies, because of its unique structure and the nature of the subject matter it dealt with. Particularly the Chamber emphasized that Article 14 of the ICCPR and Article 6 of the ECHR

---

6 For example, on the matters of proving the witnesses, disclosure obligations of the Prosecution, duties of the Prosecution during investigations, system of the protection of victims and witnesses etc. In addition, Statute of the International Criminal Court was not based on the ICTY jurisprudence, thought ICTY jurisprudence was of great importance. Many substantive law issues, concerning for example, forms of liability and *mens rea* requirements, different approach to internal and international armed conflicts etc, have been regulated in a completely different manner than expressed in the ICTY's jurisprudence.

7 The first trial opened on 26 January 2009 in the Prosecutor *v*. Thomas Lubanga Dyilo (ICC-01/04-01/06).

8 In general, the Appeals Chamber has the power to reconsider past decisions, particularly "where it was realized that the previous decision was erroneous or where it has caused an injustice." Hovewer, ICTY Statute provide very narrow framework for the reconsideration of final judgments (admissible only in the case of newly discovered fact). (*See e.g.* Prosecutor *v*. Delalić et. al., Case No. IT/96/R/R119, Appeals Chamber, Decision on Motion for review, 25 April 2002, paras. 16-17, Prosecutor *v.* Jelisić, Case No. IT-95-10-R, Appeals Chamber, Decision on Motion for Review, 2 May 2002).

9 Prosecutor *v.* Tadić, Decision on Prosecutor's Motion Requesting Protective Measures For Victims and Witnesses, Trial Chamber, Case No. IT-94-1-T, 10 August 1995.

> are meant to apply to ordinary criminal [...] adjudications. By contrast, the International Tribunal is adjudicating crimes which are considered so horrific as to warrant universal jurisdiction. The International Tribunal is, in certain respect, comparable to a military tribunal, which often has a limited right of due process and more lenient rules of evidence[10]

and added that

> [a]s such, the interpretation given by the other judicial bodies to Article 14 of the ICCPR and Article 6 of the ECHR is only of limited relevance in applying the provisions of the Statute and Rules of International Tribunal as these bodies interpret their provisions in the context of their own legal framework.[11]

The Chamber concluded that those universal human rights principles were not applicable in the same way in which they were applicable to municipal jurisdictions and suggested that it was more akin to a military tribunal and as such, it would adopt a contextual approach to the interpretation of human rights.

Whether this approach is in line with the universally recognized human rights norms is more than doubtful, particularly having regard to the concerns expressed by various human rights bodies regarding military tribunals,[12] doubts whether the contextual approach is a correct method of interpretation (and its rejection by the International Law Commission), and particularly the expectations that the ICTY would fully respect the internationally recognized human rights standards. That expectation was unambiguously expressed in the UN Secretary General Report concerning the establishment of the ICTY:

> It is axiomatic that the International Tribunal must fully respect internationally recognized standards regarding the rights of the accused at all stages of its proceedings. In the view of the Secretary General, such internationally recognized standards are, in particular, contained in Article 14 of the International Covenant on Civil and Political Rights.[13]

Certain members of the Appeals Chamber seem to be in disagreement with this general approach, though not expressly, and even when they vote in favor of the decisions that are fully in line with the previous jurisprudence. For

---

[10] *Id.*, para 27. In Prosecutor *v.* Kupreškić the Appeals Chamber has stated

> [i]n sum, international criminal courts such as the International Tribunal must always carefully appraise the decisions of other courts before relying on their persuasive authority as to the existing law.

Judgment, 14 January 2000, para. 542.

[11] *Id.*

[12] *See* G. McIntyre, *Defending Human Right in the Arena of International Humanitarian Law: Human Rights in the Jurisprudence of the ICTY*, *in* G. Boas & W. A. Schabas (Eds.), International Criminal Law Developments in the Case Law of the ICTY 195 (2003).

[13] *Report of the Secretary General Pursuant to Paragraph 2 of Security Council Resolution 808 (1993)*, S/25704, para. 106.

example, in one of his scholarly works published during his mandate as a Judge of the Appeals Chamber, Judge Wolfgang Schomburg wrote:

> A person who is accused before ICTY [...] cannot have more limited protection of human rights only because his trial is conducted by an international criminal tribunal instead of a national one.[14]

This approach seems to be the correct one, and it is based on Judge Schomburg's explicit statement that the standards enriched the International Covenant on Civil and Political Rights "provide a clear guidance not only for the ad hoc Tribunals."[15] Unfortunately, the practice is not always in line with the approach suggested (but not applied) by Judge Schomburg.[16]

The rights of the accused as established by the International Covenant on Civil and Political Rights are of such a nature that the international court has no power of derogation, because they are recognized as minimum standards, and no deviation is allowed (except of those expressly regulated by these conventions) whatever subject matter of the criminal proceedings is. As Gabrielle McIntyre, one of the Legal Officers for the Appeals Chamber at the ICTY has stated that "by justifying departure from universal principles recognized by the international community, it is arguable that the Tribunal establishes hierarchy of law to which those universal norms can be subverted."[17]

The ICTY has no real predecessor on which it could rely for jurisprudence and estimate the rules previously applied.

> The Nuremberg and Tokyo tribunals belong to an era that preceded codified human rights. Under international law the rights guaranteed to the defendants were rudimentary and, in practice, were not always fully respected.[18]

However, the ICTY belongs to an era of codified human rights, clarified by various human rights bodies, and it seems that its task should be enforcement of the achieved human rights standards, not deviations from it. On the other

---

14 Schomburg, *supra* note 4, at 76.

15 *Id.*, at 74-75.

16 Judge Schomburg did not make any reference to the ICTY's decisions in which views that are opposite to those he expressed in his scholarly work were expressed.

17 McIntyre, *supra* note 12, at 194-195.

18 A. Cassese, *supra* note 1, at 331. *See also* Decision on the Prosecutor's Motion Requesting Protective Measures for Victims and Witnesses, The Prosecutor *v.* Tadić, 10 August 1995, paras. 20-21:

> As a body unique in international law, the International Tribunal has little precedent to guide it. The international criminal tribunals at Nuremberg and Tokyo both had only rudimentary rules of procedure.

Decision on the Prosecutor's Motion Requesting Protective Measures for Victims and Witnesses, The Prosecutor *v.* Tadić, 10 August 1995, para 20.

hand, whether the ICTY's jurisprudence is, or is not, in line with these standards cannot be judged on a mere general basis and opinions, but through a thorough analysis.

3. Certain Substantive Law Issues (*Nullum Crimen Sine Lege*)

The contextual approach has the potential to seriously endanger the rights of the accused. What remains problematic is the context not only in relation to procedural rights but also in relation to substantive law, particularly in determining the rules of the International Humanitarian Law and forms of criminal liability. A few examples are enough to substantiate that concern, and to raise many questions about applicability of nullum crimen sine lege principle by the ICTY.

* * *

Certain aspects of the law of reprisals are a good starting point, because it seems that it is not in line with well established international customary law, and that the ICTY in applying contextual approach in interpretation allowed itself freedom to overrate the influence of the newly formed international criminal justice system.

The Appeals Chamber has argued:

> [...] while reprisals could have had a modicum of justification in the past, when they constituted practically the only effective means of compelling the enemy to abandon unlawful acts of warfare and to comply in future with international law, at present they can no longer be justified in this manner. A means of inducing compliance with international law is at present more widely available and, more importantly, is beginning to prove fairly efficacious: the prosecution and punishment of war crimes and crimes against humanity by national or international courts. This means serves the purpose of bringing to justice those who are responsible for any such crime, as well as, albeit to a limited extent, the purpose of deterring at least the most blatant violations of international humanitarian law.[19]

The very existence of the international criminal jurisdiction cannot be an element of the context that the Tribunal has to take into account when examining the law that has to be applied. Everyone familiar with the law on reprisals know that reprisals, in order not to be unlawful have to be conducted as a measure of last resort, when serious violation of international humanitarian law is in progress, and only as a means to stop violations and to compel the other side in the conflict to obey the rules.[20] This is primarily the measure to

[19] The Prosecutor *v*. Zoran Kupreškić, Judgment 14 January 2000, para. 530.

[20] *See e.g.* C. Greenwood, *The Law of War (International Humanitarian Law)*, *in* M. Evans

stop violations of international humanitarian law, and these counter-measures are necessary having regard to the development of the situation in which the prosecution and punishment are far away from the reality of the moment when such measures have to be conducted in order to save lives and other human values.[21] Furthermore, international criminal jurisdiction is far from being as effective in a manner argued by the Appeals Chamber. As the practice shows, its effectiveness can be estimated only in the context of the post conflict situation and willingness of the states to cooperate with the prosecution. No one can argue that international criminal tribunals are fully effective during the armed conflict, or at least when those who are accused are in power.

* * *

One of the ICTY's key departures from the contemporary international law of armed conflict seems to be an effort to apply almost completely the same rules with regard to both international and non-international armed conflict. Making the same rules for both types of conflict certainly is a trend. However, this trend has not achieved the status of *lex lata*. The Statute of the ICC, contrary to the ICTY jurisprudence, separates the law applicable to an international armed conflict from that applicable to an internal armed conflict.

* * *

Forms of liabilities employed by the ICTY seem inconsistent with the rules of international law. Of particular concern is the third type of joint criminal enterprise (JCE) as a form of criminal responsibility, which is complete innovation of the Tribunals jurisprudence. Since space does not allow even elementary discussion about this form of liability, it seems proper to underline that the ICTY applies law mens rea requirement in order to convict a person for the most horrific crimes. Namely, without statutory provision, through contextual interpretation of the Statute, the ICTY introduced three types of joint criminal enterprise, allowing a possibility for finding the accused guilty for crimes that he did not commit, did not order or participate in their commission. In order to find the accused guilty

(Ed.), International Law 789, at 820 (2003). Additional Protocol I to the Geneva Conventions prohibits reprisals against civilian population, civilian objects and certain other items (Arts. 51(6), 52(1), 53(2) and 56 (4). Greenwood stated that "[t]hese provisions, however, are controversial and are not generally regarded as a part of customary international law." *Id.*

[21] Even the former president of the ICTY, Antonio Cassese admitted that the ICTY

> has not deterred persons from committing further crimes […]. Nor has it significantly contributed to restoring peace or to reconciling the opposite ethnic and religious groups.

A. Cassese, *The ICTY: A Living and Vital Reality*, 2 Journal of International Criminal Justice 585, at 596-597 (2004).

> for the third form of JCE, the accused is held responsible for a crime outside the common purpose if, under the circumstances of the case, (i) it was feasible that such a crime might be perpetrated by one or the other members of the group and (ii) the accused willingly took that risk (*dolus eventualis*).[22]

This conception is hardly *lex lata* of the contemporary international law and it is not surprising that the acronym of this mode of liability (JCE) has achieved a colloquial interpretation – just convict everybody. Contrary to the ICTY's judge made law, the Statute of the International Criminal Court (it is an international treaty that reflects positive international law and progressive development) does not allow recklessness as a culpable mens rea. Article 30 of the ICC Statute defines the mental element to be consisting of intent and knowledge, allowing exceptions only if otherwise provided by the Statute.[23] The ICTY Statute does not provide exceptions that culpable mens rea may be other than intent and knowledge.

It seems that the boundaries of command responsibility as a form of liability that has its clear basis in international customary and treaty law was too narrow for the conviction of the so called 'high level accused'. While the basic idea of JCE is not deprived of its validity (responsibility for participation in an enterprise that as its goal has commission of crimes, or pretend to achieve lawful goal by commission of crimes) and is incorporated in the Statute of the ICC,[24] the idea is ruined with the introduction of elements antithetical to the very nature of war crimes and crimes against humanity.

---

22 *See e.g.* Prosecutor *v.* Martić, Trial Chamber Judgment, 12 June 2007, para. 439; Judgment, Appeals Chamber, 8 October 2008, para. 68.

23

> Unless otherwise provided, a person shall be criminally responsible and liable for punishment for a crime within the jurisdiction of the Court only if the material elements are committed with intent and knowledge.
>
> For the Purpose of this article a person has intent where a) In relation to conduct, the person means to engage in the conduct; b) in relation to the consequence, the person means to cause that consequence or is aware that it will occur in the ordinary course of events.
>
> For purpose of this article, 'knowledge' means awareness that a circumstance exists or a consequence will occur in the ordinary course of events.

24

> The Rome Statute of the International Criminal Court (ICC) states that an individual is criminally responsible for a crime if he commits, orders, or aids and abets the crime, or '[i]n any other way contributes to the commission or attempted commission of such a crime by a group of persons acting with a common purpose.' Thus, JCE, under one of its alternative names (common purpose doctrine), falls within the ambit of the ICC Statute. This feature of the ICC Statute does not derive from the JCE jurisprudence of the ICTY, which postdates the negotiation of the ICC Statute, but instead from language borrowed from the International Convention for the Suppression of Terrorist Bombings.

A. Marston Danner & J. S. Martinez, *Joint Criminal Enterprise, Command Responsibility and the Development of International Criminal Law*, 93 California Law Review 75, at 154 (2005).

As Prof. A.M. Danner pointed out,

> [i]n practice, JCE represents an enormous transfer of power from international judges to prosecutors, who have enormous discretion to decide how much wrongdoing to tie to any particular defendant. Because the doctrine is so loose, JCE approaches dangerously close to guilt by association. This is particularly troubling in the light of the still-tenuous legitimacy of international criminal law.[25]

Paradoxically, JCE theory is "established as a form of liability within the meaning of 'commission' under Article 7(1) of the Statute." So, the accused may be found guilty for the commission of the crime, even if he was not aware that the crime actually happened, even if he did not support that crime, even if he could not be found guilty for aiding and abetting the crime. By introducing the concept of JCE the Prosecution is sure that no one of the high level accused (political and military leaders) can escape conviction.

4. Form of Investigation, Disclosure and Ability of the Accused to Prepare His Defence (Equality of Arms Principle)

The starting point of every discussion about the nature of certain criminal procedure is the system of investigation, particularly the role of the main investigative body, in the case of ICTY, the Prosecution. It is generally accepted that the form of investigation to a significant degree determines the obligation of the parties in later stages of the proceedings and the form of presentation of evidence. The form of investigation has a significant effect on the accused and could serve as the criteria whether the proceedings (in both pre-trial and trial phase) offer an opportunity to enable the accused to be in the position of equality of arms, which is one of the basic principles of the right to a fair trial.

At the ICTY, the investigation is completely one-sided. The system is adversarial; that characteristic of the ICTY proceedings is very problematic.[26]

---

[25] A. Marston Danner, *Joint Criminal Enterprise and Contemporary International Criminal Law*, The American Society of International Law Proceedings of the 98th Annual Meeting 31 March-April 2004, Washington, DC, at 188.

[26]

> In most common law jurisdictions the police and prosecution are under a duty to carry out all reasonable investigations into an alleged crime and if exculpatory material is found that must be noted to the defense. However, in civil law, the prosecution has an obligation to seek for such material.

V. Tochilovsky, *Proceedings in the International Criminal Court: Some Lessons to Learn From ICTY Experience*, 10 European Journal of Crime, Criminal Law and Criminal Justice 268, at 269, n. 6 (2002).

In other words, what the Prosecution did and does is investigation in order to make and substantiate charges, not an investigation which will encompass both incriminating and exonerating materials.[27]

The Prosecution has an obligation, under Rule 68, to disclose to the Defense all exculpating and mitigating materials they have in their possession. However, Rule 68 creates difficulties since the Prosecution determines what is against its position,[28] and there is no real possibility for the Accused to properly examine the materials collected by the Prosecution. As the Trial Chamber observed:

> Rule 68 [...] does not translate into a right for the Defense to receive all of the Prosecution's evidence that could be useful in the defense against charges in the indictment.[29]

The Appeals Chamber has stated that

---

[27] *See* Tochilovsky (Trial Attorney of the Prosecution of the ICTY and its representative at the conference establishing the ICC), *supra* note 27, at 269. It is worth to note Tochilovsky's remark (at the same page):

> Such a one sided investigation is rather foreign to a lower from a civil law jurisdiction. For example, in a case before the ICTY, a civil law defense counsel reacted to such an allegedly 'one sided' investigation by the prosecutor in the following words 'We asked the investigators to come to Vitez and not to interview just one side [...]. It was the first time I came across the problem of my witnesses and your witnesses, because in the area in which we worked, we usually had witnesses of the court [...].' (Transcript, 27 August 1998, Kupreškić, IT-95-16-T). In most common law jurisdictions the police and prosecution are under a duty to carry out all reasonable investigations into an alleged crime and if exculpatory material is found that must be notified to the defense.

Id., nn. 5 and 6.

[28] The Trial Chamber relies on the Prosecution's good faith, and at the same time recognizes that there is some subjectivity in determining what information or evidence is exculpatory. Prosecutor *v*. Tihomir Blaškić, Decision of April 1998.

On the other hand

> [t]he Prosecution is under no legal obligation to consult with an accused to reach a decision on what material suggests the innocence or mitigates the guilt of an accused or affects the credibility of the Prosecutor's evidence. The issue of what evidence might be exculpatory is primarily a fact-based judgment made by and under the responsibility of the Prosecution.

Prosecutor *v*. Blaškić, Judgment, Case No. IT-95-14-A, 29 July 2004, para. 264. *See also* Prosecutor *v*. Brđanin and Talić, Case No. IT-99-36-T, Decision on Motion for Relief from Rule 68 Violations by the Prosecutor and for Sanctions to be Imposed Pursuant to Rule 68bis and Motion for Adjournment While Matters Affecting Justice and a Fair Trial Can be Resolved, 30 Oct. 2002, para. 30.

[29] Prosecutor *v*. Blagojević *et al.*, case No. IT-02-60-PT, Trial Chamber II, Joint Decision on Motions Related to Production of Evidence, 12 December 2002, para. 26.

> [i]t is on the Prosecution to determine whether or not the evidence is exculpatory. The Chamber does not intervene in the exercise of this discretion by the Prosecution, unless it is shown that the Prosecution abused its discretion.[30]

The Defence and the Trial Chambers do not have full access to the Prosecution's dossier. The Prosecution's obligation of disclosure is determined by the Prosecution (Prosecution as a judge in its own case), because the criteria of what is and what is not in favour of the Defence is completely on the Prosecution[31] and the Defence is not allowed to be engaged in the so called 'fishing expedition' searching material in possession of the Prosecution. Namely, the Chamber will not allow access to the materials in possession of the Prosecution "unless the Defense shows that the requested items are material for the preparation of the defense case and that the Prosecution has custody or control over the evidence."[32]

Categorization of the materials as incriminating or exculpatory is determined by the Prosecution, not by the Defence or the Trial Chamber. Sometimes, what is incriminating or exonerating depends on the interpretation, and both parties may rely on the same documents for the support of their cases. It appears that significant improvement of the equality of arms principle would be if the material, in the pre trial stage, can be classified as relevant or irrelevant, and available to the Defence from the very beginning of the pre-trial procedure. The ICC system accepts, or is very near to, the solution that all of the materials relevant to the case are available to all the parties involved in the case, including the trial and pre-trail chambers.

Contrary to the ICTY system, the ICC Statute expressly regulates the duties of the Prosecution, which are fully in line with the principle of fair trial and equality of arms. Article 54 of the ICC Statute expressly regulates that

> [i]n order to establish the truth, extend the investigation to cover all facts and evidence relevant to an assessment of whether there is criminal responsibility under this Statute, and, in doing so, investigate incriminating and exonerating circumstances equally.

---

30 *See e.g.* Prosecutor *v.* Brdjanin, Decision on Appellant's Motion for Disclosure Pursuant to Rule 68 and Motion for an Order to the Registry to Disclose Certain Materials, Case No. IT-99-36/A, Appeals Chamber, 7 December 2004, at 3, Prosecutor *v.* Blaškić, Judgment, Appeals Chamber, Case No. IT/95/14/A, 29 July 2004, para. 264.

31 Exculpatory material is

> material which is known to the Prosecutor and which is favorable to the accused in the sense that it tends to suggest the innocence or mitigate the guilt of the accused or may affect the credibility of prosecution evidence.

Prosecutor *v.* Tihomir Blaškić, Decision on the Production of Discovery Materials, 1997, para. 12.

32 *See e.g.* Prosecution *v.* Delalić and others, Decision on the Motion by the Accused Zjenil Delalić for the Disclosure of Evidence, Case No. IT-96-21-PT, September 1996, para. 9.

This provision is not without appropriate control, since the Pre-Trial Chamber may request that the Prosecution search for exonerating evidence, for example to interview a witness,[33] or to decide to stay the proceedings unless the Prosecution discloses to the Defence, or made available to the Judges important potentially exculpatory material.[34]

In this context, equality of arms cannot be found at the ICTY, since the Prosecution is in much better position in terms of personnel, funds, external support, and particularly the obligation of the States to cooperate with the Prosecution. No such opportunities and no equivalent obligation of the States are present on the side of the Defence. Such structural defects were eliminated from the ICC.

While at the ICC the very idea of the Prosecution is to be an independent body searching for the truth, at the ICTY the Prosecution is an organ of the Tribunal whose primary goal is conviction of the accused. While the nature of the Prosecution's position is that it runs for conviction of the accused, the obligations imposed on the ICC Prosecution's investigation eliminates to the highest degree the differences in factual abilities of the Prosecution and Defence to conduct investigations, and in any case make procedure just and the principle of equality of arms achievable to the maximum possible extent.

At the ICTY, the Chambers treated the principle of equality of arms only as a procedural equality[35] and introduced serious limitations to that principle. The ICTY has not considered the obvious inequality between the Prosecution and Defence with respect to their ability to prepare their cases.[36] Institutional advantages of the Prosecutor's Office, in terms of funds, personnel, continuous duties of the States to cooperate with the OTP, continuous investigations, support from various NGO etc., and preparations for the case even before the indictment, and at the same time without the duty to investigate incriminating and exonerating materials equally. Particularly, the self represented accused has very limited abilities, more limited than when they are represented by a Counsel.[37]

---

[33] Tochilovsky, *supra* note 27, at 269.

[34] The Prosecutor *v.* Thomas Lubanga Dyilo, Trial Chamber 1, Decision of 13 June 2008.

[35] For analysis of this principle in the jurisprudence of the ICTY, *see e.g.* Prosecutor *v.* Tadić, Appeal Judgment, 15 July 1999, paras. 48-50.

[36] G. McIntyre, *Equality of Arms – Defending Human Rights in the Jurisprudence of the International Criminal Tribunal for the Former Yugoslavia*, 16 Leiden Journal of International Law 269, at 272 (2003). She argued that

> this inequality results from the Tribunal's procedures and is a consequence of the institutional advantages of the Office of the Prosecutor as an organ of the Tribunal. It will be argued that in the context of the Tribunal, if the full ambit of the principle of equality of arms is to be respected and criminal proceedings at the Tribunal are to be fair proceedings, than the principle should be interpreted in a much boarder way than as actual procedural equality.

[37] Self represented accused has the right to two legal associates, one investigator, one case

5. Standard of Proof 'Beyond Reasonable Doubt' and Standard of Appellant Review of the Trial Chamber's Factual Findings

As Judge Richard May wrote, the standard of proof beyond reasonable doubt is the factor "which has gone toward preserving fairness and equality between the parties in international criminal tribunals."[38] That standard of proof has its clear basis in the Statute and the Rules of the Procedure and Evidence, but still, at least some trial chambers do not apply them correctly.

For example, in Martić Trial Judgment, the Trial Chamber reveals its position regarding relevant standard of proof not in the main text but in the footnote. As stated in the Judgment: "The Trial Chamber interprets the standard 'beyond reasonable doubt' to mean a high degree of probability; it does not mean certainty or proof beyond a shadow of a doubt."[39]

The Trial Chamber explicitly stated that proof beyond reasonable doubt, which is the highest standard possible, does not mean 'certainty.' Recent jurisprudence of the International Court of Justice provides cogent reasons that the definition of the standard of proof beyond reasonable doubt given by the Trial Chamber I is erroneous. In the *Bosnian genocide* case standard of proof was clarified in sufficient manner:

> In respect of the Applicant's claim that the Respondent has breached its undertakings to prevent genocide and to punish and extradite persons charged with genocide, the Court requires *proof at a high level of certainty appropriate to the seriousness of the allegation.*[40]

In other words, proof beyond reasonable doubt is nothing else *than the high level of certainty*, or high degree of cogency. That is well known and well established in the practice of various courts as well as in the relevant literature.[41]

---

manager and one translator to be appointed by the Registry, while at the same time a huge team is on the side of the Prosecution with many investigators, trial attorneys, legal associates, technical staff etc.

[38] R. May & M. Wierda, *Trends in International Criminal Evidence: Nuremberg, Tokyo, the Hague and Arusha*, 37 Columbian Journal of Transnational Law 725, at 725 (1999).

[39] Prosecutor *v.* Milan Martić, IT-95-11, Trial Chamber I, Judgment,12 June 2007, n. 19.

[40] Case Concerning the Application of the Convention on the Prevention and Punishment of the Crime of Genocide (*Bosnia and Herzegovina v. Serbia and Montenegro*), Judgment 26 February 2007, para. 210.

[41] Traditionally, in international adjudication, apart from prima facie evidence which is reserved for preliminary proceedings, two standards of proof are applied, proof beyond reasonable doubt, which requires *a high degree of cogency*, and preponderance of evidence. The latter means that the appreciation of evidence points into a particular direction although there remains reasonable or even more than reasonable doubt. International courts or tribunals have not confined themselves strictly to these standards but have combined or modified them where

Even if the Trial Chamber's position regarding standard of proof was declared by the Appeals Chamber "as confusing and not in accordance with the standard of proof of a criminal trial,"[42] grounds for appeal (erroneous application of the applicable law) have been rejected.[43] The Appeals Chamber argued that "despite making reference to a probability standard one in the footnote, the Trial Chamber's other statements regarding the standard of proof established that it properly understood the requisite standard"[44] referring in the footnote no. 141 to the Trial Judgment footnote references on the relevant paragraphs of the Judgment rendered in *the Prosecutor v. Limaj et al.*

Inappropriate articulation of the standard proof beyond reasonable doubt causes difficulties even on the proceeding on appeal. The standard of appellate review is a judge made law, narrowly constructed. When the Defence or the Prosecution lodge the appeal on the grounds of an error of fact which has occasioned a miscarriage of justice, it has to demonstrate that "no reasonable trier of fact *could have made* the impugned finding." In other words, when the Defence lodges an appeal, "[t]he Appeals Chamber will determine whether no reasonable trier of fact could have reached the conclusion of guilt beyond reasonable doubt" in the sense that factual conclusion "could not have been accepted by any reasonable Tribunal."

As summarized by the Appeals Chamber:

> When considering alleged errors of fact, the Appeals Chamber will determine whether *no reasonable trier of fact could have reached the verdict of guilt beyond reasonable doubt.* The Appeals Chamber bears in mind that, in determining whether or not the Trial Chamber's finding *was reasonable*, it 'will not lightly disturb findings of fact by the Trial Chamber.'

The Appeals Chamber applies the same standard of reasonableness to alleged errors of fact regardless of whether the finding of fact was based on direct or circumstantial evidence. Furthermore, the Appeals Chamber recalls, as a general principle, the approach adopted in *Kupreškić et al.*, wherein it was stated that:

---

justifiable under the circumstances of the respective case. "[W]ell founded in fact and law" as referred to in Art. 28 of the Statute is not a standard of proof in the sense of 'preponderance of evidence', it is rather comparable to the standard of proof in the sense of 'proof beyond reasonable doubt' as applied in many national legal systems (*see* M. Kazazi, Burden of Proof and Related Issues 324 (1997)); Separate Opinion of Vice-President Wolfrum, The M/V 'Saiga' (no. 2) Case (Saint Vincent and the Grenadines *v*. Guinea), International Tribunal for the Law of the Sea, Merits, para. 12. *See also* C. F. Amerasinghe, Evidence in International Litigation 235-238 (2005).

42 Prosecutor *v*. Milan Martić, Judgment, Appeals Chamber, 8 October 2008, para. 58.

43 The Appeals Chamber, unfortunately has found that the "Martić has failed to show the Trial Chamber actually erred in its application of the standard of proof", even if challenged finding does not concern error in facts (that was reserved in other grounds of appeal) but an error in law.

44 *Id.*, para. 59.

> Pursuant to the jurisprudence of the Tribunal, the task of hearing, assessing and weighing the evidence presented at the trial is left primarily to the Trial Chamber. Thus, the Appeals Chamber must give a margin of deference to a finding of fact reached by the Trial Chamber. Only where the evidence relied on by the Trial Chamber *could not have been accepted by any reasonable tribunal of fact* or where the evaluation of the evidence is '*wholly erroneous*' may the Appeals Chamber substitute its own finding for that of the Trial Chamber.[45]

At least two problems arise. The first is hidden in the Appeals Chamber consideration that even two trial chambers acting in good faith and applying the same standard may reach different conclusions. The standard of appellant review is not whether the Appeals Chamber is satisfied that the Trial Chamber reached conclusion beyond reasonable doubt, but whether the Trial Chamber *could have reached* the conclusion beyond reasonable doubt. What the Appeals Chamber actually examines is whether the challenged factual findings are reasonable, not whether is it in line with the standard of proof 'beyond reasonable doubt'.

The second consideration concerns the nature of appellant procedure. The standard of appellant review completely corresponds to the standard of the appellant review of the common law systems where adjudicating functions are divided between the judge and lay jury. Since the judge is not the one who makes factual determinations, but the lay jury, the standard of appellant review could not be whether they applied proper standard of proof, but whether a judge gave appropriate direction to the jury regarding standard of proof beyond reasonable doubt and in order to grant an appeal, "the Court of Appeal has to be satisfied that no reasonable jury could have come to a different conclusion."[46]

While this standard is appropriate in a system where factual determinations are reserved for the lay jury, in the system where professional judges make both factual and legal findings, the appropriate standard has to be – whether the Trial Chamber reached conclusion 'beyond reasonable doubt'.

The standard of appellate review uniformly applied by the Appeals Chamber significantly restricts the right of appeal.[47] From the standard of appellate review it follows that an error of fact which has occasioned a miscarriage of justice does not exist where the Trial Chamber reached the conclusion which is not in accordance with the standard of proof beyond reasonable doubt, but

---

45 *Kupreškić et al.*, Appeal Judgment, para. 30.

46 *See. e.g.*, R. Clyton & H. Thomlinston, Fair Trial Rights vii (2001).

47

> The Secretary-General is of the view that the right of appeal should be provided for under the Statute. Such a right is a fundamental element of individual civil and political rights and has been incorporated, inter alia, in the International Covenant on Civil and Political Rights. For this reason, the Secretary-General has proposed that there should be an Appeals Chamber.

Secretary General Report, para. 116.

where an error of fact is a manifest or of such a nature that "*could not have been accepted by any reasonable tribunal*." It seems that this approach is not consistent with the nature of the ICTY adjudicating bodies (Chambers) that are composed of professional judges, nor in accordance with Article 25 of the Statute of the ICTY.

6. Concluding Remark

Unfortunately, many people understand the mandate of the ICTY in terms of convictions, excluding acquittals. The mandate of every court is and has to be to conduct fair trials, to apply law in force and to preserve its judicial integrity. The ICTY is an *ad hoc* tribunal and its decisions have no binding effect of precedent on other courts and tribunals, except for a possible persuasive authority of *ratio decidendi* of its decisions, which is highly dependant on the answer to the question whether the jurisprudence of the ICTY is fully in line with the internationally recognized human rights norms and standards. To quote once again Judge David Hunt who observed that "[t]he Tribunal will not be judged by the number of convictions which it enters [...] but by fairness of the trials."[48]

[48] Dissenting Opinion of Judge David Hunt on Admissibility of Evidence in Chief in the Form of Written Statement, Prosecutor *v*. Slobodan Milosevic, 21 October 2003, para. 22.

Part III

Developments and Challenges in Human Rights Law

Patrick Thornberry

'Bringing the Victims to Light' Under the International Convention on the Elimination of All Forms of Racial Discrimination[1]

1. Introduction[2]

The present paper focuses on the work done by the Committee on the Elimination of Discrimination (CERD) in elaborating its understanding of the range of persons and communities entitled to protection under the Convention on the Elimination of All Forms of Racial Discrimination. The approach is analytical and conceptual. The descriptive elements in the paper do not purport to amount to a history of the Committee, though sundry historical moments in its lengthy existence are called into play to illustrate some of the abiding themes of the Convention. The paper briefly accounts for the context

1 'The Convention' or 'ICERD' in this paper.

2 Overviews of the Convention and interrogation of specific aspects have been presented by, *inter alia*, M. Banton, International Action Against Racial Discrimination (1996), and M. Banton, *Decision-taking in the Committee on the Elimination of Racial Discrimination, in* P. Alston & J. Crawford (Eds.), The Future of UN Human Rights Treaty Monitoring 55 (2000); N. Lerner, The UN Convention on the Elimination of All Forms of Racial Discrimination (1980); T. Meron, *The Meaning and Reach of the International Convention on the Elimination of All Forms of Racial Discrimination*, 79 American Journal of International Law 283 (1985); K. J. Partsch, *The Committee on the Elimination of Racial Discrimination, in* P. Alston (Ed.), The United Nations and Human Rights: A Critical Appraisal 339 (1992); E. Schwelb, *The International Convention on the Elimination of All Forms of Racial Discrimination*, 15 International and Comparative Law Quarterly 996 (1966); P. Thornberry, *Confronting Racial Discrimination: A CERD Perspective*, 5 Human Rights Law Review 239 (2005). Many aspects of the Convention are addressed in S. Fredman (Ed.), Discrimination and Human Rights (2001) – *see in particular* K. Boyle & A. Baldaccini, *A Critical Evaluation of International Human Rights Approaches to Racism* 135, *id.*; *see also* W. Vandenhole, Non-Discrimination and Equality in the view of the UN Human Rights Treaty Bodies (2005).

Miodrag Jovanović & Ivana Krstić (Eds.), Human Rights Today – 60 Years of the Universal Declaration, 145-170.

in which the Convention emerged, the relevant norms of the Convention, the range of procedures utilised by the Committee, the range of 'victims' of racial discrimination identified in its practice, and the *problematique* of Convention policy on cultural diversity and multiculturalism. The paper concludes with reflection on current challenges facing the Committee (and human rights systems more widely), commenting on likely immediate developments in the Committee's work, and areas of concern warranting its closer attention.[3]

2. Context

The prohibition of racial discrimination in international law finds expression in Articles of the Charter of the United Nations which prohibit distinctions in the enjoyment of human rights based on 'race, sex, language or religion'. The inventory of prohibited grounds of discrimination is amplified in later human rights instruments, but the essential prohibition of racial discrimination features in key contemporary listings. The inclusion in the Charter of a proscription of racial discrimination contrasts with the silence of the Covenant of the League of Nations, despite the efforts of Japan to insert a provision therein on the equality of nations and peoples,[4] a silence which suggests that 'hierarchical' thinking about peoples and nations was not uncongenial in the early twentieth century, dominated as it was by the subjugation of large segments of humanity in vast colonial systems.[5] The UN proscription of racial discrimination represented a quantum leap in international legal endeavours: the League of Nations system for the protection of minorities (developed parallel to the Covenant) had previously sought to address 'racial, religious and linguistic' issues in a structured fashion, but its geographical range of application was more limited than the 'universal' instruments of the UN canon.

The United Nations Sub-Commission on the Prevention of Discrimination and Protection of Minorities conceptualised the 'prevention of discrimination' limb of its mandate as "the prevention of any action which denies to individuals or groups equality of treatment which they may wish."[6] A memorandum of the Secretary-General added that

[3] References to 'victims' in the present chapter relate to the 'unpacking' by CERD of categories of groups and persons protected by the Convention; this should not be confused with the narrower issue of 'who is a victim?' under the Convention's Article 14 communications procedure. For reflection on the latter, *see* in particular POEM and FASM *v.* Denmark, Communication No. 22/2002, A/58/18, Annex III A; Documentation and Advisory Centre on Racial Discrimination *v.* Denmark, Communication No. 28/2003, A/58/18, Annex III B; The Jewish Community of Oslo *et al.* *v.* Norway, A/60/18, Annex III B.

[4] W. A. McKean, Equality and Discrimination under International Law 16-19 (1983).

[5] B. Boxill (Ed.), Race and Racism (2001).

[6] E/CN.4/52, Section V.

> [t]o prevent discrimination, therefore, some means had to be found to suppress or eliminate inequality of treatment which many have harmful results, aiming to prevent any act or conduct which implies that an unfavourable distinction is made between individuals solely because they belong to certain categories or groups in society.[7]

On this interpretation, equality is to be achieved by suppressing or eliminating certain forms of conduct rather than through a positive 'politics of difference'[8] and recognition of specific groups. The relationship between non-discrimination and minority and indigenous rights, between the 'elimination' pole of non-discrimination and the 'recognition pole' of minority and indigenous rights, has been only partially elaborated within the praxis of the Convention.

The Declaration on the Elimination of All Forms of Racial Discrimination[9] was adopted by the UN General Assembly in 1963; it did not contain a definition of 'racial discrimination'. Concepts developed in the limited field of employment and occupation were utilised in ICERD.[10] Following a brief but complex preamble, Part I of the Convention sets out a straightforward normative structure: a definition of racial discrimination (Article 1), followed by a broad undertaking to eliminate racial discrimination "in all its forms" (Article 2), a condemnation of racial segregation and Apartheid (Article 3), a draconian Article 4 on hate speech, a non-exhaustive list of rights to which the principle of non-discrimination attaches (Article 5), a short article on remedies (Article 6), and an article on pro-tolerance and anti-racist education (Article 7). Part II of the Convention sets up the Committee on the Elimination of Racial Discrimination and introduces its procedures. At the time of writing, there are 173 States parties to the Convention.

3. CERD and Its Procedures: A Summary

The 18-member Committee works principally by analysing and commenting on reports by States which are obliged, according to Article 9(1) of the Convention, to report

> (a) within one year after the entry into force of the Convention for the State concerned; and (b) every two years and whenever the Committee so requests. The Committee may request further information from the States Parties.

Each dialogue with a State Party is followed by a set of concluding observations by the Committee which contain elements of praise, statements of concern and recommendations for further action.[11] Where appropriate, the Committee will

---

7 *The Main Types and Causes of Discrimination*, UN Sales No. 49.XIV.3, paras. 6 and 7.

8 I. M. Young, Justice and the Politics of Difference (1990).

9 Contained in General Assembly resolution 1904 (XVIII), 20 November 1963.

10 Discrimination (Employment and Occupation) Convention 1958, ILO Convention No. 111.

11 In the 'overview' of the methods of work of the Committee in 2001, the case was made

also recognise the difficulties States have had in implementing the Convention on account of sundry disasters, including man-made ones. The system utilises members of the Committee as country rapporteurs who take the responsibility of leading the dialogue with the reporting government. CERD sessions are normally held in Geneva: country visits are not part of its regular *modus operandi*. Reports five years or more overdue may be subjected to the review procedure, under which CERD may decide to examine a country situation in the absence of a report. The 'threat' of a review usually brings forth either a report or a reason for not submitting one. The Committee decided in 1996 that, in the absence of an initial report,

> the Committee shall consider as an initial report all information submitted by the State Party to other organs of the United Nations or, in the absence of such material, reports and information prepared by organs of the United Nations.[12]

The Committee has recently added a follow-up procedure to check through on implementation of its recommendations: a coordinator and an alternate were appointed by the Committee at its 65th session in 2004.[13] Additional to the main dialogues, CERD 'summarises' its views and practice on particular issues relating to racial discrimination in general recommendations, of which 31 have been issued in the life of the Committee.[14]

Two complaints systems are envisaged in the Convention. The first of these, the inter-State complaints procedure in Articles 11-13 of the Convention, has not been activated, whereas the procedure provided for in Article 22, whereby disputes relating to 'the interpretation or application of this Convention' can be referred to the International Court of Justice, has recently been engaged by Georgia against the Russian Federation.[15] The communications procedure for "individuals or groups of individuals [...] claiming to be victims of a violation" is set out in Article 14 of the Convention. The understanding of who can make a communication under Article 14 has exercised the Committee in recent sessions.[16] Communications under Article 14 have not occupied the Committee to the same extent as analogous procedures under for example the International Covenant on Civil and Political Rights 1966 (ICCPR). The

---

that "in the interest of transparency the adoption of concluding observations in public meetings should continue," A/56/18, para. 479. However, the 'overview' of 2003 recites that the "meetings of the Committee to adopt the concluding observations will be held in private." A/58/18, Annex IV.

12 A/51/18, para. 608.

13 *See* Rule 65.2. of the rules of procedure, and Guidelines on follow-up to concluding observations and recommendations, A/61/18, Annex VI.

14 Compilation of General Comments and General Recommendations adopted by Human Rights treaty Bodies, HRI/GEN/1/Rev. 9, 27 May 2008.

15 International Court of Justice press release 2008/23, 12 August 2008.

16 *See*, *inter alia*, Jewish Community of Oslo et al. *v.* Norway, A/60/18, Annex III B, para. 7.4.

case law is, in consequence, sparse, focusing on a basic understanding of the concepts, structures and norms to address them.[17]

CERD adopted early warning and urgent action guidelines in 1993[18] and refined them in 2007.[19] The Guidelines are presented as a revision of the 1993 paper "in the light of the practice of the Committee since 1993 and of the current needs and recent developments."[20] In view of their overall preventive ethos,[21] the guidelines make explicit linkage to the prevention of genocide in their recall of the 2004 'Stockholm' speech of the Secretary-General on prevention of genocide,[22] reference to persistent patterns of racial discrimination "in some cases with genocidal dimensions,"[23] and to the Special Adviser of the Secretary-General on the prevention of genocide.[24] Most situations addressed by the guidelines will fall short of genocide, and the 'indicators' for triggering the procedure include the important qualification that, since such indicators

> may be present in situations not requiring immediate attention to prevent and limit serious violations of the Convention, the Committee shall assess their significance *in light of the gravity and scale of the situation*,[25] including the escalation of violence or irreparable harm that may be caused to victims of discrimination on the grounds of race, colour, descent or national or ethnic origin.[26]

4. The Concept of Discrimination

On the core notion of discrimination, CERD General Recommendation XIV (42)[27] observed that "differentiation of treatment will not constitute discrimination if the criteria for such differentiation, judged against the objectives and purposes of the Convention, are legitimate." *A contrario*, differential treatment will constitute discrimination

---

17 The Committee has also developed a follow-up procedure to individual communications: A/61/18, Chapter VII.

18 A/48/18, Annex III (early warning guidelines).

19 A/62/18, Annex III (revised early warning guidelines).

20 Revised early warning guidelines, para. 3.

21 References are made, *inter alia*, to the report of the Secretary-General, 'In Larger Freedom' emphasising prevention of human rights violations (A/59/2005, para. 106), the call from the Secretary-General to the UN High Commissioner for Human Rights for a plan of action in which she emphasised the importance of prevention (A/59/2005/Add.3).

22 Revised early warning guidelines, para. 4.

23 *Id.*, para. 7.

24 *Id.*, para. 14.

25 Emphasis added.

26 *Id.*, para. 12.

27 A/48/18, Chapter VIII B.

> if the criteria for such differentiation, judged in the light of the objectives and purposes of the Convention, are not applied pursuant to a legitimate aim, and are not proportional to the achievement of this aim.[28]

The Committee has made recommendations both on discrimination among ethnic groups, and discrimination against persons belonging to the groups. 'Discrimination' should not signify uniformity if there are relevant differences in situation between one person or group and another. The Committee has insisted that, in appraising discrimination, "the specific characteristics of ethnic, religious and cultural groups be taken into consideration,"[29] and that, inter alia, "policies of forced assimilation amount to racial discrimination."[30] The demand in General Recommendation 24[31] for uniform application of criteria to determine the existence of ethnic groups on the territory of the State, avoiding 'differing treatment' for various population groups, does not go against its nuanced approach to discrimination. The recommendation does not suggest that all groups be treated the same regardless of circumstances, but is a plea for uniformity of approach to existence criteria for groups,[32] who otherwise might be arbitrarily excluded by government *fiat* from the operation of the principle of non-discrimination. Forms of discrimination caught by the Convention are many and various. Explicitly, the Convention addresses discrimination in "purpose or effect"[33] so that CERD may critique State practices which unintentionally discriminate. CERD has also employed the vocabulary of direct and indirect discrimination,[34] discrimination *de jure* and *de facto*,[35] systematic[36] or structural discrimination,[37] as well as the cases of double for multiple discrimination on the basis of intersectionality.[38]

The Convention addresses discrimination in 'public life', a term left undefined in the Convention but which must take its colour from the full

---

[28] CERD General Recommendation 30 on Discrimination Against Non-Citizens, para. 4.

[29] A/60/18, para. 169 (Laos).

[30] A/60/18, para. 318 (Turkmenistan).

[31] A/54/18, Annex V; Vandenhole, *supra* note 2, at 100-101.

[32] The summary records make clear that the context of the draft (introduced by Committee member Diaconu) is one of 'demographic information' rather than substantive treatment – CERD/C/SR.1281, para. 27.

[33] For a critique of basic concepts, *see* L. Hannikainen & E. Nykanen (Eds.), New Trends in Discrimination Law – International Perspectives (1999).

[34] 'Indirect' discrimination is not explicitly used in ICERD. The 'purpose or effect' distinction is not necessarily the same as that between 'direct and indirect' discrimination: for example, both direct and indirect discrimination could be 'purposive'. CERD explicated some relevant distinctions in Ms L.R. *v.* Slovakia, Communication No. 31/2003, A/60/18, Annex III A, para. 10.4.

[35] Vandenhole, *supra* note 2, at 38-39.

[36] For example Concluding Observations on Laos, A/60/18, para. 168, making relevant distinctions.

[37] For example A/59/18, para. 57 (Brazil).

[38] Discussed, *infra*.

range of activities implicated in Convention prohibitions, and is not for example confined to discrimination in the sphere of public administration.[39] The Convention obliges States to intervene in cases of discrimination by non-State actors – by, for example, prohibiting and bringing to an end "racial discrimination by any persons, group or organization";[40] public spaces are explicitly referred to in Article 5(f) prohibiting discrimination in "[t]he right of access to any place or service intended for use by the general public, such as transport, hotels, restaurants, cafes, theatres and parks." The text of the Convention does not however delineate the private from the public with any degree of precision, and it should be recalled that 'freedom of association' is a right protected from discrimination by the Convention: the implications of this may cut across more 'interventionist' notions, especially for 'organizations' on a smaller scale. According to one authority, the reference to 'public life' 'was inserted to remove from the scope of the Convention discrimination within private relations.'[41] While it did not trouble the drafters of the Convention when compared with for example the discussions on 'national or ethnic origin' or 'descent' in Article 1, it was an issue particularly with Western governments, including in cases relating to Article 4 of the Convention.[42] An extensive discussion took place in the Committee in 1993 in response to a draft 'recommendation on public life',[43] during which points were made on the widening scope of the Convention in the light of phenomena such as 'the privatization of public life',[44] and 'privatized discrimination'.[45] There was support for the extension of the Convention into inter-individual relationships and relations between individuals and non-State entities.[46]

---

[39] Meron, *supra* note 2, at 293.

[40] Art. 2(d). *See also* Art. 4(a). In General Recommendation 20 – A/51/18, Annex VIII – the Committee States (para. 4):

> To the extent that private institutions influence the exercise of rights or the availability of opportunities, the State Party must ensure that the result has neither the purpose nor the effect of creating or perpetuating racial discrimination.

[41] M. Banton, International Action Against Racial Discrimination 195 (1996).

[42] The point was trenchantly made by the representative of Australia in the Third Committee of the General Assembly who recalled an earlier statement that Australia could not be expected to

> pass a special law to prosecute and punish under criminal law every person who utters a remark capable of being interpreted as advocacy of racial discrimination [...] to do so might well make martyrs out of people whose objectionable ideas would otherwise be rejected by reasoned argument, or more probably by ridicule

A/C.3/SR.1306, para. 5. *See also e.g.* A/C.3/SR. 1315, para. 1-3 (UK); SR.1316, paras. 3-4 (the Netherlands); and SR.1318, para. 56 (Ireland).

[43] CERD/C/SR.969, paras. 19-44.

[44] SR.969, para. 26 (van Boven).

[45] *Id.*, para. 39 (Agha Shahi).

[46] *Id.*, para. 29 (Diaconu).

In this sphere, the case of business corporations currently exercises the Committee to a perceptible extent. Their case may be easier to capture in the Convention in view of the quasi-public functions exercised by the corporate sector, especially where powerful transnational corporations are concerned. The Committee has found the State ultimately responsible for discrimination caused by private business, especially in cases concerning indigenous peoples[47] and the Roma,[48] but potentially also to 'descent' or other groups.[49] The proposition that business corporations should respect State laws on racial discrimination is implicit in CERD recommendations, though the question of how such responsibility intersects with the principle of State responsibility is relatively undeveloped. Elaborations of principle have recently been made in connection with indigenous peoples in cases including those of Canada and the United States. In concluding observations on Canada, CERD combined an observation on transnational corporations with an observation on 'extraterritoriality', recommending that "the State party explore ways to hold transnational corporations registered in Canada accountable," requesting information in its next periodic report "on the effects of activities of transnational corporations registered in Canada on indigenous peoples abroad and on any measures taken."[50] The activities of corporations in relation to indigenous lands and territories are a significant focus in CERD's early warning and urgent action procedure.

5. Special Measures

The Convention goes beyond this exemption of special measures from the prohibition of discrimination. In the context of the undertaking of States in to "pursue by all appropriate means and without delay a policy of eliminating

[47] *See e.g.* concluding observations on Guatemala, A/61/18, para. 119; Guyana, *id.*, para. 147; Nigeria, A60/18, para. 294; and Suriname, A/59/18, paras. 194 and 198 – the last paragraph is particularly striking, with the Committee recommending

> the inclusion in agreements with large business ventures – in consultation with the peoples concerned – of language specifying how those ventures will contribute to the promotion of human rights in areas such as education.

[48] The 'case law' of the Committee has addressed discrimination by banks, clubs, etc., on a number of occasions. *See* Dragan Durmic *v.* Serbia and Montenegro, Communication No. 29/2003, A/61/18, Annex IV; *see also* CERD's concluding observations on Bosnia and Herzegovina, A/61/18, para. 38, and General Recommendation 27 on Discrimination Against Roma, A/55/18, Annex V.C.

[49] CERD General Recommendation 29 on article 1, para. 1 (Descent), A/57/18, Chapter XI F.

[50] A/62/18, para. 78. *See also* the 2007 concluding observations on the USA, CERD/C/USA/CO/6, para. 30.

racial discrimination,"[51] Article 2.2. makes *obligatory*[52] the taking of "special and concrete measures to ensure the adequate development and protection of certain racial groups or individuals belonging to them [...] when the circumstances so warrant." The formula in Article 1.4. is adapted to ensure that such measures "shall in no case entail [...] the maintenance of unequal or separate rights for different racial groups after the objectives for which they were taken have been achieved." In the drafting of the convention, a number of States expressed reservations concerning the inclusion of special measures – claiming, *inter alia*, that they would perpetuate separation from the wider community,[53] would open the door to all sorts of "legal manoeuvring to justify various kinds of racial discrimination,"[54] etc. The notion of special measures now sits more comfortably in the general discourse of human rights.

In terms of substance, Fredman cites Keller for the suggestion that ICERD provision on special measures "does not require more than redress of past discrimination."[55] Similarly, Boyle and Baldaccini assert that the affirmative action provisions recognise "the need to accommodate diversity and to redress disadvantage emanating from past discriminatory policies and practices, which have developed into structural patterns of injustice."[56] Leaving aside the obvious point that all present discrimination arises from some practice, 'historic' or more recent, it is not unreasonable to suggest that the provisions should be applied in a pro-active future-oriented manner in order to prevent fresh institutionalizations of racism and protect new victims of disadvantage. The point is made clear by CERD in its General recommendation 32 on the meaning and scope of special measures, paragraph 22 of which states that it "is not necessary to prove 'historic' discrimination in order to validate a programme of special measures; the emphasis should be placed on correcting present disparities and on preventing further imbalances from arising."[57] The open-ended 'justifications' for special measures in the Convention are merely the 'adequate advancement' or 'adequate development and protection' of certain groups or individuals, and the obligation to act is triggered by the lambent phrase 'when the circumstances so warrant'.

---

[51] Art. 2.1. There is also a Convention requirement to promote interracial understanding. CERD has observed that, towards the ends of eliminating discrimination and promoting understanding "States must be prepared to use both coercion and persuasion – utilizing the power of the law to prohibit and punish, as well as the power of education and information to enlighten and persuade." General Recommendation 14, A/48/18, chapter VIII B.

[52] Emphasis added.

[53] Chile, E/CN.4/Sub.2/SR.416, para. 13.

[54] Ivory Coast, A/C.3/SR.1306, para. 23.

[55] S. Fredman, *Combating Racism With Human Rights: the Right to Equality*, *in* S. Fredman (Ed.), Discrimination and Human Rights 9, at 42 (2001). The author cited is P. Keller, *Rethinking Ethnic and Cultural Rights in Europe*, 18 Oxford Journal of Legal Studies 55 (1998).

[56] Boyle & Baldaccini, *supra* note 2, at 157.

[57] CERD/C/75/Misc.7/Rev.2 (2009, unedited version, on file with OHCHR Secretariat).

6. Grounds and Victims of Racial Discrimination

While 'race' as such is not defined, the term 'racial discrimination' is defined as

> any distinction, exclusion, restriction or preference based on race, colour, descent, or national or ethnic origin which has the purpose or effect of nullifying or impairing the recognition, enjoyment or exercise, on an equal footing, of human rights and fundamental freedoms in the political, economic, social, cultural or any other field of public life.[58]

The umbrella term in the Convention is not 'race' but 'racial discrimination'. 'Race' was a specifically European way of addressing and subordinating those perceived to be different; the Convention adds the four other 'grounds' in *pari materia*. While the additions lessen the difficulty of deploying 'race' in the Convention,[59] the concept has prompted some States parties to explain the limitations of it use.[60] The Committee nonetheless encourages States to include race as a ground of discrimination in domestic law as an aspect of 'the full substance' of the Convention.[61] CERD devotes attention to a wide range of groups – the contemporary victims of racial discrimination; the 'others' of the contemporary imaginary. Victims of racial discrimination emerge from processes of globalization as well as from traditional enmities and practices, historical inequities, and traditional systems which continue to produce dehumanising effects. The emergence of victims into the light has not occurred simply on account of the brute force of 'events' but is also a product of developments in recognition of differentiated categories of human rights holders since the Universal Declaration of Human Rights in terms of their status, gender, history, culture and identity. The differentiation of categories has enabled the Committee to deepen its enquiries into the realities of discrimination as they affect situated human beings rather than abstractions.

---

[58] Art. 1.1.

[59] T. Todorov, *Race, Writing and Culture*, *in* H. L. Gates, Jr., Race, Writing and Difference 370 (1986).

[60] *See e.g.* the recent (2008) statement by Germany in its eighteenth periodic report:

> The German government applies the term 'racial discrimination' as defined in the Convention. In no way does that mean that it supports theories or doctrines which claim that there are different human races. The German government thus makes reference to the declaration made on behalf of the European Union at the World Conference against Racism on 7 September 2001.

CERD/C/DEU/18, at 7, n 1.

[61] For example, A/58/18, para. 530 (United Kingdom). The same set of concluding observations uses the terms 'racial prejudice' (para. 532) and 'racial minorities' (para. 538); the imperative to include all grounds specified in Art. 1 is related to the avoidance of 'differential levels of protection' (para. 534).

7. Minorities

CERD has not issued a general recommendation on the relationship between the convention and minority rights and perhaps ought to do so.[62] However, the Committee has devoted considerable time to minorities, even though the Convention does not make specific reference to minorities – nor to indigenous peoples. Underpinning the Committee's approach to the non-discrimination norms is the demand for a truthful account of diversity, and scepticism towards claims of homogeneity. It is now rare (though not unknown)[63] for governments to claim complete homogeneity of population – or that racial discrimination is unknown on the State territory. In response, the Committee constantly presses for demographic information. In terms of the span of groups recognized by States parties, the critical statements in General recommendation 24[64] concerning recognition by States parties of some ethnic groups while disregarding others have already been noted, including the plea for uniform existence criteria. The Committee has not set out general existence criteria for all Article 1 groups, though it has done this for descent/caste groups in General Recommendation 29. CERD understands individual self-identification as the *prima facie* working principle as regards membership of racial or ethnic groups.[65] *Inter alia*, the Committee has also challenged government use of terminology and may fore example decide to question States parties as to whether the designation of the group appearing in State reports matches the preferences of the community in question.[66] In such cases, the Committee concern is that inappropriate terminology may represent an attempt to submerge identities, clouding the application of the principle of non-discrimination.

CERD has questioned states on the terminology of 'national minorities' contrasted with 'ethnic groups' to determine what standards of rights are implicated in the choice of usage.[67] Cases where the State would exclude the operation of the Convention through recognising groups only as 'social' and not 'cultural' groups are scrutinised with particular care by the Committee,[68]

62 Thornberry, *supra* note 2, at 257-266.

63 For recent examples of CERD observations on such a claim, *see* A/61/18, para. 84 – concluding observations on El Salvador; *id.*, para. 359 (Oman); Yemen, *id.*, para. 442.

64 A/54/18, Annex V.

65 General Recommendation 8, A/45/18, Chapter VIII 1.

66 A/61/18, para. 138, suggesting clarification by Guyana whether description of communities as 'Amerindians' was preferred by them. The general preference for addressing groups by their preferred names appears in General Recommendation 27 on the Roma: A/55/18, Annex V.C., para. 3.

67 A/61/18, para. 166 – concluding observations on Lithuania; *id.*, para. 271 on Estonia. *See also* concluding observations on Slovenia, A58/18, para. 234.

68 A/60/18, para. 144; CERD/C/SR.1687, para. 35 – concerning the Traveller community in the Republic of Ireland.

especially where concepts of 'cultural difference' are effectively downgraded to those of 'the socially problematic'.[69] In relation to minorities, virtually all aspects of specific minority rights, as well as their relationship to general human rights norms, have been the subject of recommendations at one time or another. Civil and political rights, economic and social rights, segregation practices, and language and cultural rights, persistently figure in Committee practice.[70] Among minorities, the Roma figure prominently in the work of CERD, with many aspects of their rights accounted for, from specific issues such as education in 'special schools'[71] to broader, holistic profiles of discrimination.[72] The climate of opinion within societies, including the ethos generated by politicians and the media, has also been subject of comment. In the case of Italy, the Committee recommended

> that the State party increase its efforts to prevent racially motivated offences and hate speech, and ensure that relevant criminal law provisions are effectively implemented. The Committee recalls that the exercise of the right to freedom of expression carries special duties and responsibilities, in particular the obligation not to disseminate racist ideas. It also recommends that the State party take resolute action to counter any tendency, especially from politicians, to target, stigmatize, stereotype or profile people on the basis of race, colour, descent and national or ethnic origin or to use racist propaganda for political purposes.[73]

It may be observed that discussion of Roma questions is not confined to Europe; for example observations on Brazil made reference to 'gypsies',[74] and those on Ecuador to Roma.[75]

8. Indigenous Peoples

Discrimination against indigenous peoples also frequently engages the Committee, which issued General Recommendation 23 on indigenous peoples in 1997.[76] *Inter alia*, the recommendation recalls the affirmation

[69] *See* concerning the fifteenth and sixteenth periodic reports of the Yemen, CERD/C/SR.1765, para. 39; A/61/18, para. 449 (concerning the Al-Akhdam).
[70] Vandenhole, *supra* note 2, at 96-100.
[71] Concluding observations on Hungary, A/57/18, para. 382; Czech Republic, A/58/18, para. 386.
[72] The Committee's approach is reflected in General Recommendation 27, A/55/18, Annex V C. Rights of Roma persons were found to have been violated in Koptova *v.* Slovakia, 13/1998, Annex II B; Ms L. R. et al. *v.* Slovakia, 31/2003, A/60/18, Annex III A; and Dragan Durmic *v.* Serbia and Montenegro, A/61/18, annex IV. For follow-up action in relation to all three of these cases, *see* A/62/18, Annex VI.
[73] CERD/C/ITA/CO/15, para. 15; *see also*, *id.*, para. 16.
[74] A/59/18, para. 62.
[75] CERD/C/ECU/CO/19, para. 11 (2008).
[76] General Recommendation 23, A/52/18, Annex V. Para. 4(b) of the Recommendation refers to discrimination based on 'indigenous origin or identity'.

by the General Assembly that the provisions of ICERD apply to indigenous peoples. The Committee frequently invites States that have not done so to ratify ILO Convention 169, a text which avoids the troublesome language of self-determination,[77] and latterly has also begun to recommend the use of the more ambitious 2007 UN Declaration on the Rights of Indigenous Peoples[78] which does address self-determination, as a guide to interpreting obligations under the Convention towards indigenous peoples.[79] Additional to concluding observations on State reports, a string of situations concerning indigenous groups have been and are being addressed under CERD's early warning and urgent action procedure, including Committee decisions concerning the New Zealand Foreshore and Seabed Act 2004,[80] and on the United States of America in the case of the Western Shoshone.[81]

On occasions, the Committee has set out an expansive interpretation of indigenous rights, particularly in its utilization of the concept of 'informed consent'. The Committee forcefully articulated its position on informed consent in General Recommendation 23: States parties are recommended to

> ensure that members of indigenous peoples have equal rights in respect of effective participation in public life and that no decisions directly relating to their rights and interests are taken without their informed consent.[82]

The provisions on informed consent were a particular focus of discussion in the Committee. Whereas some members recalled the limitations in ILO Convention 169[83] on informed consent – i.e. that the Convention did not imply a right of veto on the part of indigenous peoples,[84] others took a stronger

[77] M. Tomei & L. Swepston, Indigenous and Tribal Peoples: A Guide to ILO Convention No. 169, at 8-9 (1996).

[78] A/61/L/67, Annex.

[79] CERD/C/USA/CO/6, para. 29; *see also* concluding observations on Fiji, CERD/C/FJI/CO/17, para. 13. The Committee's views on the right to self-determination were articulated in General Recommendation 21, A/51/18, Annex VIII B.

[80] A/60/18, Chapter II.

[81] A/61/18, Chapter II.

[82] General Recommendation 23, para. 4.d. *See also* para. 5.

[83] Arts. 6 and 7 of Convention 169 are particularly relevant here, establishing modalities for 'consultation' and 'participation of indigenous peoples in applying the principles of the Convention.

[84] CERD member Diaconu raised the point that "the idea of consent implied the right to veto, which was not in conformity with the spirit of ILO Convention No. 169, which was based, rather, on the idea of consultation through the appropriate channels. In some cases [...] there was cause to insist on prior consensus but there were many other cases where a small community could hinder the taking of decisions that would be of benefit to all citizens. The Committee should be careful not to innovate in that regard." CERD/C/SR.1235, para. 69; and, *id.*, para. 78. Caution was also expressed by members Ahmadu (*id.*, para. 70), Shahi (*id.*, para. 73), Van Boven (*id.*, para. 71). The notion of a right to veto was supported specifically by CERD members Aboul-Nasr (*id.*, para. 72), Valencia Rodriguez (*id.*, para. 77), Wolfrum, (*id.*, paras. 67, 74, 80), and Garvalov (*id.*, para. 82).

line.[85] On the substance of the recommendation, members appear to have been influenced by the draft UN Declaration on the rights of indigenous peoples, as well as developments in Latin America.[86] Paragraph 4 distinguishes between a 'general' right of effective participation in public life and a narrower principle insisting on informed consent when 'decisions' directly relating to the rights and interests of indigenous peoples are concerned.[87] 'Informed consent' was expressly preferred to 'informed participation'.[88] In concrete cases, the Committee has not always rigorously insisted on principles of informed consent, even in cases where there was a clear opportunity to follow this principle and where General Recommendation 23 is recalled by the Committee;[89] in other cases the principle is expressly accorded prominence.[90] References to 'free, prior and informed consent' permeate the text of the UN Declaration on the Rights of Indigenous Peoples.[91]

---

[85] According to Garvalov (CERD/C/SR.1235, para. 82),

> the two terms 'consent' and 'participation' meant entirely different things. If indigenous peoples were to give their 'consent' they musty agree to the proposal; they could 'participate' and express their approval or disapproval, without actually having any power over the final decision. He preferred the word 'consent'.

[86] Wolfrum, SR.1235, para. 93.

[87] *See* comments by Wolfrum, SR.1235, paras. 67, 74 and 75; and Aboul-Nasr, *id.*, para. 72.

[88] CERD/C/SR.1235, para. 60 (Wolfrum, referring to a proposal by Diaconu).

[89] For example in its 2004 concluding observations on Suriname, concerning forestry and mining concessions, the Committee, while noting the State party's assertion that "there are mechanisms guaranteeing that indigenous and tribal peoples are notified and consulted before any forestry and or mining concessions within their lands are awarded", expressed concern that "consultation of that kind is rare." Accordingly, the Committee invited the authorities

> to check that the established mechanisms for notifying and consulting the indigenous and tribal peoples are working, and recommends that the State party strive to reach agreements with the peoples concerned, as far as possible, before awarding any concessions.

A/59/18, para. 192. While General recommendation 23 is recalled in para. 202 of the observations, we may note the absence of a principle of informed consent in the above and in other elements of these observations, especially paras. 188-202.

[90] For example in concluding observations on the USA, in a paragraph which expressed concern, *inter alia*, at information on plans for expansion of mining and nuclear waste storage on Western Shoshone ancestral land, the Committee drew that attention of the State party

> to general recommendation 23 on indigenous peoples which stresses the importance of securing the 'informed consent' of indigenous communities and calls […] for recognition and compensation for loss.

A/56/18, para. 400.

[91] Declaration on Indigenous Peoples, Arts. 10, 11, 19, 28 and 29; Art. 32 refers to 'free and informed consent'.

9. Minorities, Cultural Diversity and Convention Policy

CERD's frequent grappling with issues of cultural diversity leads to questioning of the extent to which the Convention's discourse of equality can be 'married' with the discourse of diversity. It can be framed as a debate on integration and assimilation, on equality and special measures, on non-discrimination and minority rights, or – fashionably – as an exploration of the 'ism' of 'multiculturalism'. CERD lacks a 'benchmark' General Recommendation on minorities and multiculturalism, despite suggestions from CERD members that the Committee should work towards the adoption of such a general recommendation.[92] The Committee discussed (inconclusively) the question of multiculturalism in 2005.[93] One member of the Committee[94] recalled the duty of CERD in the matter of non-discrimination and argued that some CERD recommendations have not served the cause of non-discrimination but may have served, on the contrary, to exacerbate societal differences. The member also suggested that ambitious models of minority rights 'made in Europe' may not be suitable for Africa and the Americas including for example practice in the field of multilingual education.[95] Other members stressed that the Committee's notion of integration was different from assimilation, and that processes of nation building must be based on broad respect for human rights and cultural diversity.[96] One member challenged the notion that nation building was hindered by policies respecting cultural diversity, and distinguished, as did other members, the policy of the Convention from programmes of assimilation.[97] There was broad support for the treatment of minority issues, including the area of language, on a case-by-case basis, with necessary flexibility.[98] On multiculturalism itself, the demographic reality of multicultural populations was generally recognised with different degrees of emphasis, though the policy implications flowing from this were understood in different ways. Criticism of 'the European model' of minority rights may have been based on a perception that 'European' standards envisaged the teaching of all minority languages in the State equally, irrespective of limiting circumstances.[99] It is not clear in practice that CERD (or any other treaty body)

---

92 Thornberry, CERD/C/SR.1724, para. 11; Agha Shahi, *id.*, para. 26.

93 CERD/C/SR.1694, 8 March 2005; CERD/C/SR.1724, 17 August 2005.

94 Lindgren Alves: CERD/C/SR.1724, paras. 2-4.

95

> [...] by applying the European model to Africa or Latin America, the Committee only served to foster fragmentation in countries which had been struggling to create unity.

SR.1724 para. 3.

96 Thornberry, SR.1724, para. 7.

97 Pillai, SR.1724, paras. 17-19; Valencia Rodriguez, SR.1694, paras. 25-26.

98 For example Sicilianos, SR.1724, para. 12.

99

> Was it reasonable or realistic to request the Nigerian Government to recognise

has adopted a 'broad brush' approach, making unreasonable demands on States with limited resources; on the contrary, it may well be claimed that its approach has paid close attention to circumstances and avoided unreasonable prescriptions to resource-limited States.[100] Emerging from the debates in a mixed understanding of multiculturalism, ranging from a necessary expression of the reality of cultural diversity to a recipe for segregation and social fragmentation.

10. Special Measures: Application to Minorities, Indigenous Peoples et al.

Indigenous groups and minorities enjoy their own rights in international law which stand independently of Convention provisions (discussed above) on special measures. The Committee does not always distinguish cases of 'recognition of specific minority/indigenous rights' from 'special measures', but recommendations to States parties concerning indigenous groups may be made within and without the special measures paradigm.[101] A renewed surge of interest in the concept of special measures and how it relates to minority and indigenous rights is evident from Committee discussion of the seventeenth periodic report of New Zealand.[102] The report incorporated an extensive section on special measures in accordance with Article 2.2. of the Convention which included a range of information on, *inter alia*, Maori fisheries, the Foreshore and Seabed Act, the Maori Land Act, Maori and Pasifika education, Maori language, etc.[103] The extent of the materials included under special measures provoked a question by the country rapporteur on why the State party considered that historical treaty settlements on why the State party considered that historical treaty settlements constituted special measures. The issue was pressed by other Committee members who argued that distinctions should be drawn between such special measures and indigenous as well as minority rights, notably that special measures under Article 2.2. were exceptional and temporary in nature whereas indigenous and minority rights were to be enjoyed

> all the 250 minority groups which lived on its territory and to provide education in all minority languages?

Lindgren Alves, SR.1724, para. 3.

[100] *The Practice of the Committee on the Elimination of Racial Discrimination With Respect to Multiculturalism*, CERD/C/67/Misc. 5, 3 August 2005.

[101] *See e.g.* the Concluding Observations on Bangladesh on special measures – A/56/18, para. 66. For a more wide-ranging set of recommendations, including many not confined to a 'special measures' or 'affirmative action' framework, *see* A/57/18, paras. 315-43 – Concluding Observations on Canada.

[102] Fifteenth, sixteenth and seventeenth reports of New Zealand, submitted as one document, CERD/C/NZL/17, 18 July 2006.

[103] CERD/C/NZL/17, paras. 51-172.

when the communities in question enjoyed a presence in the State party.[104] A Statement by the New Zealand Race Relations Commissioner supported the members' critique in this respect – the Commissioner had "made it clear that special measures should not be confused with the Government's treaty obligations, indigenous rights, or general social and economic measures tailored to particular ethnic groups."[105] The response of the New Zealand delegation suggested that, in light of comments by Committee members, the scope of special measures, the matter would be reconsidered.

The concerns of the Committee related in part to the potential fragility of historical settlements (including the Treaty of Waitangi) if included, even implicitly, as a temporary measure, a perception advanced by Maori groups in their submissions to the Committee.[106] In the concluding observations on New Zealand the Committee stated its concern that "in the report of the State party, historical treaty settlements have been categorized as special measures for the adequate development and protection of Maori," while noting "the statement made by the delegation that such categorization should indeed be reconsidered." Accordingly, the Committee drew the attention of the State party

> to the distinction to be drawn between special and temporary measures for the advancement of ethnic groups on the one hand and permanent rights of indigenous peoples on the other hand.[107]

The importance of distinguishing between permanent rights of indigenous and other groups and special measures has been further clarified by CERD General Recommendation 32 which advises that special measures

> should not be confused with specific rights pertaining to certain categories of person or community, such as, for example, the rights of persons belonging to minorities … the rights of indigenous peoples … and rights of women to non identical treatment with men … Such rights are permanent rights … States parties should carefully observe distinctions between special measures and permanent human rights in their law and practice. The distinction between special measures and permanent rights implies that those entitled to permanent rights may also enjoy the benefits of special measures.[108]

---

104 Discussions at the 1821st and 1822nd meetings, 31 July and 2 August 2007.

105 Statement by Joris de Bres, Race relations Commissioner, New Zealand Human Rights Commission (on file with author). *See also Guidelines on Measures to Ensure Equality*, prepared by the New Zealand Human Rights Commission (undated, on file with author).

106 Treaty Tribes Coalition, Aotearoa Indigenous Rights Trust, Maori Party, Te Whanau a Apanui and Peace Movement Aotearoa.

107 CERD/C/NZL/CO/17, 15 August 2007, para. 15.

108 CERD/C/75/Misc.7/Rev.2, para. 15, *supra* note 57.

11. Descent and Caste

On its face, 'descent' is a broad ground of discrimination, only partly unpacked by the Committee in relation to caste and analogous systems of stratification.[109] The essence of the Committee's approach to caste groups is to call up 'descent' rather than 'race', although there have been 'race' inflections in Dalit interventions at the UN, and a slippage of categories in much historical and contemporary writing on caste.[110] Besides race and history narratives, and the processes of self-identification and self-description they imply, the exogamous ascription or fixing of caste attributes onto populations recalls ascriptive processes attaching to 'race', 'colour' or 'ethnicity' based allegedly on immutable characteristics or incorrigible 'otherness'.[111] In other words, caste or analogous forms of social stratification is on a par with the other descriptors in Article 1 and appropriately brought within its frame.[112]

Adopted following a vivid thematic discussion in 2002,[113] General Recommendation 29 on descent based discrimination,[114] encourages States to recognise the problems and address them in law and practice. The General Recommendation followed the Durban World Conference on Racism where the caste issue was talked out after vigorous diplomacy by India. The Committee had independent reasons to explore the issue in order to understand better a key term in the Convention and continues to grapple with caste and descent-based discrimination.[115] India contests the application of the Convention to matters of caste on grounds that 'race' is distinct from 'caste'.[116] Following CERD's recent reaffirmation that 'discrimination based on caste is fully covered by the Convention',[117] India once more responded that the Convention does not cover caste.[118] Japan has made analogous observations concerning the Buraku

[109] P. Thornberry, *The Convention on the Elimination of Racial Discrimination, Indigenous Peoples and Caste/Descent-Based Discrimination*, *in* J. Castellino & N. Walsh (Eds), International Law and Indigenous Peoples 17 (2005); Banton, *supra* note 41, at 151 recalls the CERD use of 'descent' in the case of conflicts in Somalia.

[110] *See* the multiple references to the intersection of 'race' and 'caste' *in* S. Bayly, Caste, Society and Politics in India (1999).

[111] K. Booth, *Three Tyrannies*, *in* T. Dunne & N. J. Wheeler (Eds.), Human Rights in Global Politics 31 (1999).

[112] *See* A. Sicilianos, *L'Actualité et les potentialités de la Convention pour l'élimination de la discrimination raciale*, 64 Revue Trimestrelle des Droits de L'Homme 869 (2005).

[113] CERD/C/SR.1531.

[114] A/57/18, Chapter XI F.

[115] Concluding observations on Mali, A/57/18, para. 406; Senegal, *id.* para. 445; the UK, A58/18, para. 544; Nepal, A/59/18, paras. 119, 120, 127, 129 and 130; Madagascar, paras. 315, 320; Mauritania, *id.*, para. 342; and Nigeria, A/60/18, para. 290.

[116] Nineteenth periodic report of India, CERD/C/IND/19, 29 March 2006, paras. 15-17.

[117] A/62/18, para. 166.

[118] *Id.*, Annex X: comments of States parties on the concluding observations adopted by the Committee.

question in more limited terms.[119] The issue is an aspect of a larger question of determinations of group status, including claims by States to uniqueness in social arrangements, endeavouring to elude capture by the purportedly trans-cultural categories of international law. It is instructive in this last respect that India does not accept that the Convention covers the situation of its 'scheduled tribes',[120] which, whatever the state of the argument as to the coverage of caste, are, it is submitted, clearly within the scope of the Convention.

12. Non-Citizens

Article 1.2. of the Convention provides that it "shall not apply to distinctions, exclusions, restrictions or preferences between citizens and non-citizens," but in practice, CERD has given this provision a narrow interpretation. The Committee has addressed discrimination against immigrants/asylum-seekers, and sundry non-citizens and people in movement, including that arising from counter-terrorism measures, which may hit asylum-seekers and other immigrants particularly hard,[121] urging States to respect fundamental rights when combating terrorism.[122] In General Recommendation 11 (1993),[123] CERD reminded States parties that Article 1.2. must not be interpreted to detract from rights and freedoms enunciated in other instruments. General Recommendation 30[124] on discrimination against non-citizens addresses issues such as hate speech and racial violence, access to citizenship, administration of justice, expulsion and deportation and economic, social and cultural rights. The recommendation reinforces General Recommendation 11 in emphasising that any limiting features of the Convention in Article 1 must not undermine human rights in general including the principle of equality.[125]

[119] For the concluding observations, *see* A/56/18, para. 166: "the Committee, contrary to the State party, considers that the term 'descent' has its own meaning, and is not to be confused with race or ethnic or national origin."
[120] A/62/18, Annex X.
[121] For Committee comments, *see* concluding observations on Canada, A/57/18, para. 338; New Zealand, *id.* para. 427; Russian Federation, A/58/18, para. 192; Norway, *id.*, para. 473; the UK, *id.*, para. 536; Sweden, A/59/18, para. 225; Kazakhstan, *id.*, para. 294; and Australia, A/60/18, para. 33.
[122] Statement on racial discrimination and measures to combat terrorism, A/57/18, Chapter XI C.
[123] A/48/18, Chapter VIII B.
[124] A/59/18, Annex VIII.
[125] *See also* General Recommendation 22 on Article 5 and refuges and displaced persons, A/51/18, Annex VIII C.

13. Intersectionality 1: Religion

According to one commentator, CERD tends to take it as read that national, ethnic, linguistic and religious minorities or cultural groups of various kinds come within the frame of Article 1.[126] There is however an important *caveat* in the case of religion, namely that the Committee searches for an 'ethnic' or other connection or element of intersectionality between racial and religious discrimination before it regards its mandate as engaged.[127] This situation arises from the peculiarity that, although the Convention is structured to address racial discrimination, freedom of thought, conscience and religion figures, as noted above, among the protected rights in Article 5. Thus, the Convention requires conceptualization of *racial* discrimination in the enjoyment of *religious* freedom. As an attempted resolution of this jumbling of categories, CERD has made it clear that: "Religious questions are of relevance to the Committee when they are linked with issues of ethnicity and racial discrimination."[128] The Committee has made references in its concluding observations to phenomena such as Islamophobia (including reports thereof following the attacks of 11 September 2001),[129] discrimination against Jews and Sikhs, discrimination against indigenous religions and desecration of sacred sites, etc., etc. – cases where it has sensed an overlap between religion and ethnicity.[130]

The 'intersection' was further examined in two cases in 2007, both involving allegations of hate speech. *P.S.N. v Denmark*,[131] concerned alleged violations of Article 1(d), 4 and 6 of the Convention through statements published on a website by an MP against immigration and Muslims, under the headline 'articles no one dares to publish'.[132] The opinions expressed were reiterated in an interview given to a newspaper, and some had been previously published in a book. The petitioner filed three complaints under the Danish Criminal Code, section 266b of which prohibits racial statements, on the grounds that the website statements targeted a specific group – Muslims, were degrading and propagandistic, and were published to a large audience; analogous complaints related to the book and the interview. The State party argued against admissibility in that the case fell outside the scope of Article 1 of the Convention in referring to Muslims, while acknowledging that

[126] "CERD tends to treat discrimination against minorities as a distinct theme, regardless of which prohibited grounds are specified." Vandenhole, *supra* note 2, at 95.

[127] Concluding observations stressing intersectionality include A/58/18, para. 539 (United Kingdom); A/60/18, para. 142 (Ireland); *id.*, para. 246 (Georgia); *id.*, para. 295 (Nigeria); *id.*, para. 323 (Turkmenistan).

[128] A/60/18, para. 246 (Georgia).

[129] A58/18, para. 540 (United Kingdom).

[130] In some cases the language used does not make the 'intersection' very clear: A61/18, para. 418, referring to reported 'anti-Muslim' statements.

[131] Communication No. 36/2006, A/62/18, Annex V.

[132] *P.S.N. v Denmark*, para. 1.1.

> it is possible to argue to a certain extent that the statements refer to second-generation immigrants and set up a conflict between 'the Danes' and them, thereby falling to some degree within the scope of the Convention.[133]

The petitioner on the other hand contended that "Islamophobia, just like attacks against Jews, has manifested itself as a form of racism in many European countries."[134] Hatred, it was claimed, had been stirred up against peoples of Arab and Muslim background, and "culture and religion are connected in Islam."[135] In its admissibility decision, CERD observed that "the impugned statements specifically refer to the Koran, to Islam and to Muslims in General," without any reference to the five grounds set out in Article 1 of the Convention.[136] Further, while the elements in the case file did not allow the Committee to ascertain the intention of the statements, "it remains that no specific national or ethnic groups were directly targeted," and that "Muslims currently living in the State party are of heterogeneous origin."[137] The Committee recognised "the importance of the interface between race and religion" and stated that "it would be competent to consider a claim of 'double' discrimination on the basis of religion and another ground specifically provided for in Article 1," which was not the case with the current petition.[138] The petition according to the Committee was based on religion alone, and "Islam is not a religion practised solely by a particular group."[139] The communication was therefore declared inadmissible. In *A.W.R.A.P. v Denmark*,[140] the Committee declared inadmissible a communication on similar grounds to its decision in *P.S.N.*

It may be suggested that in future cases likely to arise more could be made of the concepts of 'discrimination in effect' or 'indirect discrimination' and heavier reliance placed the self-perception of communities. Cases can arise where the hate speech discourse is careful to avoid direct racial or ethnic insult, and may have 'switched' its language from the racial/ethnic to the religious in relation to the same targeted community. The Committee is, it is submitted, eminently capable of addressing such re-phrasing of hate speech from within its present interpretative resources. It is not always possible in any case to draw sharp distinctions between racial discrimination and discrimination on grounds of religion: as a former Special Rapporteur on Religious Intolerance put it, "religion shares something of the definition of ethnicity, just as ethnicity

133 *Id.*, para. 4.1. The State party also contended (*id.*, para. 4.12) that "the right to freedom of expression is particularly imperative for an elected representative of the people."
134 *Id.*, para. 5.3.
135 *Id.*, para. 5.3. The petitioner cited (*id.*, para. 5.3.) the Committee's concluding observations of 2002 and 2006 linking people of 'Arab and Muslim' background.
136 *Id.*, para. 6.2.
137 *Id.*, para. 6.2.
138 *Id.*, para. 6.3.
139 *Id.*, para. 6.3.
140 Communication No. 37/2006, A/62/18, Annex V.

is basic to religious identity."[141] For many communities addressed by CERD, there are no clear lines between culture or tradition and religion, and efforts to separate out culture from religion could result in grafting a 'structure' on to a community which is artificial and inadequately responsive to community self-perception.[142]Further, since the bases of racism may be ethnic and cultural hostility as much as 'race' or colour, the norms and spiritual practices integral to group identity are likely to be subjected to the same discrimination as other facets of culture.

14. Intersectionality 2: Gender

In General Recommendation 25 on gender-related dimensions of racial discrimination,[143] the Committee invited States to analyse the relation or intersectionality between race and gender by considering the form and manifestation of racial discrimination; the circumstances in which discrimination occurs; the consequences of such discrimination; and the availability of remedies and complaint mechanisms.[144] Questions of 'gender, race and discrimination' are part of the regular discourse of the Committee. Sessions have addressed, besides issues of trafficking of women and girls – in many cases a thoroughly racialized phenomenon in relation to the country of origin as well as the countries of passage and destination[145] – HIV/AIDS,[146] discrimination against Roma and Traveller women,[147] transmission of nationality through the male line,[148] customs and practices of certain groups,[149] imprisonment rates for indigenous women,[150] and problems of

[141] Report by Abdelfattah Amor for the Durban World Conference on Racism, A/CONF.189/PC.1/7, 13 April 2000, para. 122.

[142] In such cases, it is submitted, the notion of an 'intersection' also resembles an external imposition of a pastern discerned by outsiders.

[143] A/55/18, Annex V A.

[144] The Committee welcomed Sweden's Action Plan to Combat Racism, Xenophobia, Homophobia and Discrimination – a rare mention of a sexual orientation issue, A/59/18, para. 213.

[145] Recent concluding observations on trafficking include, in 2004, A/59/18, para. 244 (Argentina); *id.*, para. 265 (Belarus); *id.*, para. 293 (Kazakhstan); in 2005, A/60/18, para. 59 (Azerbaijan).

[146] Concluding observations on Uganda, A/58/18, paras. 263-86; Suriname, A/59/18, paras. 180-210.

[147] Concluding observations on Czech Republic, A/58/18, paras. 373-93; Slovakia, A/59/18, paras. 378-95; Ireland, A/60/18, para. 147.

[148] Concluding observations on Bahamas, A/59/18, paras. 18-45; Lebanon, *id.*, paras. 46-72; Mauritania, *id.*, paras. 328-57; and Madagascar, *id.*, paras. 304-27.

[149] *See* concluding observations on Nepal, A/59/18, paras. 116-40; Mauritania, *id.,* paras. 328-57; Suriname, *id.*, paras. 180-210; and Tanzania, A/60/18, para. 348.

[150] Concluding observations on Australia, A/60/18, para. 41.

female domestic workers.[151] The gender-race intersection bears out the often complex motivations for oppressive action in real-life situations.[152] In order to engage the prohibitions in the Convention, racial discrimination need only be a significant element in the construction of such situations; it need not be the 'sole' ground of action.[153]

15. Conclusions and Questions

The abstract 'grounds' of discrimination in Article 1 did not immediately translate themselves into the targeted communities recognised in CERD practice. There are overlaps among the Article 1 descriptors, as the *travaux* suggest that not every descriptor was understood to mark out a sharply defined conceptual space.[154] The *travaux* evidence intensive discussion on terms such as 'national origin' but comparatively little on others, such including 'descent'. The grounds of discrimination in the article were nonetheless judged as being *in pari materia* by the drafters, as relating to distinctions which "do not take account of the particular characteristics of the individual [...] but [...] only [to] collective qualifications deriving from [...] membership in a certain social or other group'.[155]

In terms of it approach to the interpretation of the Convention, CERD has said on more than one occasion that "the Convention, as a living instrument, must be interpreted and applied taking into account the circumstance of contemporary society."[156] Interpretation by CERD of important areas of concern has travelled a distance since the inception of the Committee, which began work in an international environment differing considerably from the present, not least in the fact that colonial systems were still a fact of international life, and that the new wave of post-colonial nation-building tended towards the assimilation of sub-state ethnic groups. Committee analyses of the spectrum of situations capable of generating discriminatory practices evidence a more complex reality than that accounted for by the drafters of the Convention.

In light of a complex practice, it is perhaps supererogatory to attempt to determine, in the terminology of the Vienna Convention on the Law of Treaties, whether CERD practice is best described in terms of 'ordinary meaning', or

151 For example concluding observations on Bahrain, A/60/18, para. 85.

152 The Committee refers to double discrimination against 'children and women' in concluding observations on Mali, A/57/18, para. 404.

153 Concluding observations on Austria, A/57/18, para. 28, where the Austrian legal prohibition on distinctions on the 'sole' grounds of race, colour, etc., were regarded by the Committee as "representing a narrower prohibition of discrimination than is provided in the Convention."

154 I. Diaconu, *supra* note 32, *The Definitions of Racial Discrimination*, para. 17.

155 UN Secretary-General, *supra* note 7, para. 6.

156 *Stephen Hagan v Australia*, Communication no. 26/2002, A/58/18, Annex III A, para. 7.3.

'object and purpose', to say nothing of the concept of subsequent practice.[157] 'Ordinary meaning' is not contradicted, as the terms of the Convention, or aspects of it, are short and open to explanation; and 'object and purpose' equally describes the approach to some extent. Over the life of the Convention we may fairly describe the Committee's approach to interpretation as in general purposive and adaptive,[158] as paying attention to the principle of effective interpretation – making the treaty work for its intended beneficiaries – and as receptive to movements in the wider world of human rights. States are of course entitled to disagree with the interpretations, but the Committee has held its lines with tolerable consistency, and expects States to respond to the Convention in light of its practice. The contexts of discrimination outlined above illustrate how the Committee has 'unpacked' some 'forms' of discrimination implied in the title of the Convention, if not 'all forms' of racial discrimination.

Continuing interpretative challenges emerge in many contemporary contexts. Issues arise or continue regarding the consequences of population migrations including economic migration, from war and conflict involving massive displacement of persons and communities, from succession and creation of States, from despoliation of indigenous territories in search of 'natural resources', from the continuation of traditional enmities as well as finding new enemies, from actions of States and others in counter-terrorism, from perceptions of threats to cultural and religious identity, and from hate speech, including that disseminated through the internet and other technologies, etc., etc. Within its engagement with the traditional canons of State responsibility, the Committee has encountered an expanding range of situations that have compelled it to reflection the reach of the Convention in relation to business corporations and other private actors: the approach is innovative but we await concrete results.

Other kinds of difficulty also arise. For a diversity of cultural or ethnic groups, the question of the Convention's reach into the 'private' sphere intersects with issues concerning the reach of human rights into cultural space, into cultural relations and traditions. The inconclusive nature of the Committee's ruminations on 'multiculturalism' have already been described

---

[157] Vienna Convention on the Law of Treaties, 1155 U.N.T.S. 331, Arts. 31 and 32. On the subsequent practice point, and without wishing to press the point further in the present paper, it may be suggested that Committee determinations can be taken as constituting "subsequent practice in the application of the treaty which establishes the agreement of the parties regarding its interpretation" in the sense of Art. 31(3)(b) of the Vienna Convention on the Law of Treaties; alternatively, the acquiescence of States parties in those determinations may constitute or contribute to the constitution of such practice.

[158] The Committee's approach to Art. 4 has been more literal than its approach regarding the grounds of prohibited discrimination.

above. Concerning the CERD approach to some traditional practices in light of the realities of ethnic and cultural diversity, one dilemma was aired by CERD member de Gouttes in the Committee's 2005 debate on multiculturalism:

> Although the Committee was called upon to recognize the inherent value of each culture, it was nevertheless necessary to impose a limit on that recognition. That limit could be understood as the universality of human rights, which was the need to ensure universal respect for fundamental human rights, regardless of region, culture, tradition, etc. What that meant was that the Committee should not go so far as to support cultures that engaged in practices or customs that ran counter to the core human rights, as defined by United Nations human rights treaties. He believed that all Committee members could agree on such a limit.[159]

Questions on culture and customs often connect with rights of women, although their scope is wider and have included for example questions relating to the caste system. Committee decision-making depends on verifying the existence of a practice or questioning the practice in the light of human rights standards, and deciding what to do about practices which the Committee regards as challenging human rights principles. In many cases, a particular determination that the principle has been violated will not always immediately suggest itself. It should not be assumed that culture is 'inherently' opposed to human rights: a degree of reciprocity is also implied since local understandings and application of norms will be mediated through cultural lenses. While the Committee generally treads lightly and mediates criticism of cultural practices through the lens of State responsibility, when it is faced with situations where the claims of culture are weakened (in cases of mass defection or where the notion of cultural 'belonging' is otherwise challenged), it may be emboldened to take a stronger line. Unanswered questions regarding the public and private reach of the Convention attain particular poignancy in the 'cultural' sphere.

In terms of what still needs to be done, there are *lacunae* in the Committee's corpus of work. Leaving aside the need for constant improvement of the mechanics of monitoring, CERD has not definitively pronounced on the relationship between minority and indigenous rights and the principle of non-discrimination, including a review of what should be understood by the notion of 'integration'. The conceptual relationships here are likely to be complicated in future by the emergence of the Declaration on the Rights of Indigenous Peoples with its notably strong stance on collective rights. There is no general recommendation thus far on the role of education in combating discrimination, and one could be useful if only to underscore the contribution of education to the promotion of tolerance; comparatively speaking, the Committee has made much more of Article 4 of the Convention on hate speech. Thinking on the role of transnational corporations operating discriminatory practices extraterritorially – particularly against indigenous peoples – is embryonic; drafting a general recommendation jointly with another treaty body might usefully highlight

[159] CERD/C/SR.1724, para. 23.

commonalities in the threats posed to indigenous existence and identity. The Committee has thus far avoided a clarifying thematic discussion on racial and religious discrimination, a point of increasing importance in light of episodes such as the 'Danish cartoons' case, and the moves in the General Assembly and the Human Rights Council to address 'defamation of religions'.

A reading of the work of CERD reveals a continuing complex identification of victims of discriminatory practices, in light of the raw human data and continually refined normative lenses, coupled with a less than dogmatic approach to analysis of the problems and possible remedies. The intellectual framework of the 1960s exercises a pull on the Committee through the bare bones of the text but the normative certainties of that era are not for revisiting. The expansion of perceived loci of discrimination from colonial contexts and the apparatuses of racist states to the world at large renders more difficult the application of simple prescriptions. A defensible archive of human rights work, including CERD, would synthesise the question of whether the understanding of the situations of discrimination is adequate with that of the adequacy of the response to the situations perceived. Whether CERD has identified the victims of discrimination appropriately, whether the victims have seen their dignity recognised and been brought into the light, and whether the Committee has 'made a difference' in the real world, are critical questions which should certainly be asked. They could also be asked of all who operate in the field of human rights, laymen, journeymen and pontiffs alike.[160]

[160] Based on A. J. Ayer's 'classification' of philosophers into laymen, journeymen and pontiffs.

Matthias Hartwig

Human Rights in Times of War

1. Introduction

For a long time the doctrine of international law drew a clear line between the law régime applicable in the time of peace and the law régime applicable in the time of war. War was treateded as a situation in which all rules of humanity were suspended. Grotius concluded: "Vis ac terror maxime propria bellorum."[1] Augustinus compared big empires – especially if at war – with criminal gangs: "Remota itaque iustitia quid sunt regna nisi magna latrocinia?"[2] States behaved as outlaws. Times of war were conceived as an exceptional situation in which the law, especially international law only played a minor role. Law was somehow suspended by war. International law resumed its force only with the end of the war. In line with this reasoning the prevailing practice and doctrine declared that the application of treaties ended with the outbreak of a war.[3]

The introduction of legal restrictions on the conduct of States in times of war is a relatively recent development dating back to the 19th century. The main point to be observed is that these rules developed within the laws of war, they should contribute to the 'civilization' of war by reducing the evil and not by aiming at the good; they became part of this 'state of emergency' that war constitutes. Most importantly, they were not derived from civil rights beyond the laws of war, especially not from human rights or other rules protecting individuals. Instead they formed an autonomous legal order applicable exclusively in the times of war.

1 H. Grotius, De iure belli ac pacis, Lib. III cap. I §VI 1.

2 Augustinus, De civitate dei, Book IV.

3 J. Delbrück, *War, Effect on Treaties*, *in* R. Bernhardt (Ed.), IV Encyclopedia of Public International Law 1367 (2000); B. Schäfer, Zum Verhältnis Menschenrechte und humanitäres Völkerrecht 10 (2006).

Miodrag Jovanović & Ivana Krstić (Eds.), Human Rights Today – 60 Years of the Universal Declaration, 171-186.

The history of international human rights is quite different and, above all much shorter. In a way one can say that it started only after World War II with the UN-Charter and the Universal declaration of the Human Rights in 1948, and the regional instruments for the protection of human rights and international covenants. The introduction of human rights into international law was an answer to grave breaches of human principles before and during the World War II. They constituted a rejection of totalitarian States oppressing the liberties and freedoms of their citizens. They established a basic standard for the relationship between the individual and the State. The objective of the fundamental rights, however, led to difficult questions. The line between human rights as norms under international law and the principle of non-intervention as laid down in internal affairs in Article 2 paragraph 7 of the UN-Charter was difficult to determine. Whereas the non-intervention principle guarantees the sovereignty of States, which includes the determination of its form of governance, human rights establish some standards for the relationship between government and citizens. The principle of non-intervention was introduced in order to rule out any form of infringement in the internal affairs of a State. The maintenance of peace being the main objective of the UN, in a first period after the foundation of the UN the enforcement of human rights was given lesser priority.

The Universal Declaration was adopted as a non-binding resolution of the UN-General Assembly. In the regional human rights systems the member States accepted the jurisdiction of courts in case of individual applications only with hesitance.[4] For these reasons, the implementation of human rights documents was doubtful. Taking into account the potentially far reaching impact of human rights, States were very reluctant in assuming obligations that could be enforced by international organs.[5] Especially because human rights implied far reaching intentions, i.e. the establishment of a civil order within the States, and because human rights were not limited to the restriction of certain behavior in a specific situation the States recorded many reservations on the application of human rights documents. The prudent application of the human rights in peace time blocked the discussion of the role human rights could play in times of war.

This situation changed for various reasons. First, wars took on another character. Classically, wars were conflicts between States. After 1945, however, wars became increasingly a mixture of civil strife, insurrection, civil

[4] The individual complaint before the Human Rights Committee is based on the Optional Protocol which entered into force only in 1976; the European Convention on Human Rights introduced a mandatory proceeding for individual complaints in 1998, the American Convention on Human Rights does not give individuals a standing before the Inter-American Court of Human Rights.

[5] For this reason, all international organs dealing with human rights may only declare the incompatibility between national acts and the respective human rights instrument, they are not authorized to quash such an act.

war and the participation of foreign powers. Classical wars between two States are an exception.[6] If humanitarian law regulates the conduct of States in times of war, then the object of such regulation is disappearing due to the described change in the character of war. The question arose whether humanitarian law can be applied to the new forms of war.

The Geneva Conventions of 1949 took this problem into consideration, but they gave a very reluctant answer, that is still in line with international law's preoccupation with interstate relationships. Article 3 of the Geneva Conventions provided for the application of a minimum standard of humanitarian law in non-international conflicts. It was quite clear that humanitarian law would not grant the same protection in such a war as in an international conflict. Article 3 of the Geneva Convention defines itself as an exemption from the general rule of humanitarian law which is applicable only to international conflicts.

The second development concerned the position of human rights in international law. Originally, human rights dealt with the relationship between individuals and States. This relationship is classically defined as a part of the internal affairs in which international law should not intervene. However, with the adoption in 1966 of the UN-Covenants human rights definitively became a matter of binding universal international law. At the same time the UN Security Council started its practice of declaring grave violations of human rights to be a threat to peace.[7] Respect for human rights no longer fell exclusively into the realm of internal affairs but emerged as a matter of international law. If human rights form part of the international legal order then the question may be raised: are they applicable in conflicts, especially where the humanitarian law does not grant sufficient protection, as it might be the case in internal armed conflicts. The application of human rights in times of war seems well founded especially because human rights and humanitarian law share the common goal of protecting the individual against the violence of the State. Therefore, international organs such as the Human Rights Commission declared that human rights and the international humanitarian law were converging.[8]

In the following discussion three aspects will be analyzed:

a) The general application of human rights in time of war

b) The territorial application of human rights instruments

c) The relationship between human rights and humanitarian right

---

[6] As example may serve the war between Great Britain and Argentina in 1982 (Falkland war) or the war of the coalition against Iraq in 1991.

[7] *See e.g.* UN Security Council Resolution 794 (Somalia); 940 (Haiti); 1199 (Serbia).

[8] Resolution 1989/26 H. J. Heintze, *ECtHR and Human Rights Standards During Armed Conflicts*, 45 German Yearbook of International Law 60, at 61 (2002).

2. The General Application of Human Rights in Time of War

2.1. The Application of Human Rights Norms in Times of War According to the Human Rights Treaties

International human rights have been catalogued in international universal and regional treaties and non-binding instruments such as the Universal Declaration of Human Rights. To the degree that human rights norms have become customary international law they did so essentially on the basis of treaties. The applicability of human rights norms in times of war can be studied best in the respective treaties.

Almost all human rights instruments contain a provision dealing with the question of the application of the human rights in times of war. The respective clause provides for the possibility of a derogation of certain guarantees.

Article 15 of the European Convention on Human Rights is an example:

> In time of war or other public emergency threatening the life of the nation any High Contracting Party may take measures derogating from its obligations under this Convention to the extent strictly required by the exigencies of the situation, provided that such measures are not inconsistent with its other obligations under international law.

This provision implies two consequences. First, as an exceptional clause, it supposes that the convention on the protection of human rights is applicable even in time of war. Second, the suspension of the application of certain convention rights is possible only under certain material and procedural conditions. There must be a war; this is subject to control by the organs of the convention, even if they regularly declare that the State has a great margin of appreciation in this context. There also is a procedural prerequisite, *i.e.* the State has to inform the Secretary General of the European Council on the measures taken. All these measures are subject to the principle of proportionality.[9]

The interrelation between human rights and humanitarian law becomes even more evident with respect to the protection of life. Article 15 ECHR provides: "No derogation from Article 2, except in respect of deaths resulting from lawful acts of war shall be made." Life is protected also in time of war, which might be astonishing, but Parties can derogate from this guarantee as far as the rules of war justify the killing of a person. The laws of war establish a restriction to the application of the human right.

The American Convention on Human Rights encompasses an equivalent provision in its Article. 27. Article 4 of the International Covenant on Civil and Political Rights also provides for the possibility of a derogation of the guarantees of the covenant in time of a public emergency; emergency is construed as embracing also the case of war. The provision exempts some

---

[9] A similar provision may be found in Art. 27 ACHR.

rights from the possibility of derogation such as the prohibition of torture, the right to life, the prohibition of slavery and others. It means that these rights are applicable in times of war under all circumstances.

The Convention against Torture declares in Article 2:

> No exceptional circumstances whatsoever, whether a state of war or a threat of war, internal political in stability or any other public emergency, may be invoked as a justification of torture.

Again this implies the applicability of this Convention in times of war.

But not only human rights instruments provide for their applicability in the times of war. Humanitarian law also refers to the international guarantees of human rights: Article 72 of the Additional Protocol I to the Geneva Conventions provides:

> The provisions of this Section are additional to the rules concerning humanitarian protection of civilians and civilian objects in the power of a Party to the conflict contained in the Fourth Convention, particularly Parts I and m thereof, as well as to other applicable rules of international law relating to the protection of fundamental human rights during international armed conflict.

This provision does not declare human rights norms of international law generally applicable in time of war but it presupposes that such norms exist.

The Additional Protocol II to the Geneva Conventions recalls in the preamble that international instruments relating to human rights offer basic protection to the human person. This protocol is dedicated exclusively to the law of warfare. By referring to human rights it includes them into the group of norms that are applicable in wartimes. The Commentary on the Additional Protocols of 8 June 1977 to the Geneva Convention of 12 August 1949 declares that the Universal Declaration of Human Rights, the international covenants, in particular the Covenant on Civil and Political Rights, the instruments concerning specific aspects of the protection of human rights, such as the Convention on Genocide and the regional instruments relating to human rights fall under this term.[10] Thereby the Protocol underlines the operationability of human rights instruments in times of war, which directly follows from the respective documents, and is now recognized by humanitarian law.

The application of human rights treaties in times of war has been critizised in scholarship and by some States.[11] It is pointed out that human rights regulate the relation between citizens and the State, whereas humanitarian law deals with the regulation of the conduct of war between States. However,

[10] Y. Sandoz, C. Swiniarski & B. Zimmerman (Eds.), Commentary on the Additional Protocols of 8 June 1977 to the Geneva Convention of 12 August 1949, at 1339-1340 (1987).

[11] J. Pictet, Development and Principles of International Humanitarian Law 3 (1985); position of Israel before the Human Rights Committee UN Doc. CCPR/C/ISR/2001/2; the position of the United States in Response of the United States to Request for Precautionary Measures – Detainees in Guantanamo Bay, Cuba, 15 April 2002, 41 International Legal Materials 1015, at 1019 *et seq*. (2002).

this critique overlooks the above described development: First, human rights are not limited to the relationship between the State and its citizens. Even if historically they might have formed part of the 'contrat social' – as laid down in the American Declaration of Independence or the French Déclaration des droits de l'homme et du citoyen – it has become common ground that human rights are basic principles that extend beyond the relationship between the State and its citizens. They are applicable to foreigners; many States declare that the fundamental rights codified in national constitutions also apply when the State through its organs and officials acts abroad *vis-à-vis* non-citizens.[12] It is especially necessary to consider that human rights exist not only for times of peace, as the derogation clauses show. This is in the logic of the system, as human rights guarantees are most endangered in emergency situations, and it would be counterproductive to limit or even to eliminate their applicability when they are most necessary. It is also necessary to remark that the law of war penetrates, ever more extensively, into internatl conflicts. Starting with Article 3 common to all four Geneva Conventions of 1949, the regulation of internal conflicts by humanitarian law was later enshrined in the Additional Protocol II to the Geneva Conventions of 1977. Extending humanitarian law to internal conflicts where indisputably human rights are applicable implies the recognition that human rights do not end their regulatory force in times of conflict. In the end, the classical dichotomy between human rights in times of peace and humanitarian law in times of war is no longer supportable. The texts of the international human rights instruments and the interpretation and application of these instruments by international courts do not support the old dichotomy.

2.2. International Jurisprudence With Respect to the Applicability of Human Rights in Times of War

The International Court of Justice decided for the first time in its Advisory Opinion on the Legality of the Use of Nuclear Weapons on the applicability

[12] *E.g.* the Bundesverfassungsgericht (the German Constitutional Court) decided that German organs when exercising State power abroad, have to respect the fundamental rights laid down in the German constitution, BVerfGE (decisions of the Federal Constitutional Court) Vol. 94, 315 (324 s.); the British High Court came to the conclusion in the case The Queen on the application of Al Skeini et al. *v.* Secretary of State for Defences (Case No. CO/2242/2004), Judgment of 14 December 2004, England and Wales High Court, that the conduct of British Armed Forces in a military camp may be scrutinized under the Human Rights Act. The US Supreme Court held in recent decisions on the detainees in Guantànamo: "Even when the United States acts outside its borders, its powers are not 'absolute and unlimited' but are subject 'to such restrictions as are expressed in the Constitution'.", 553 U.S. Supreme Court (2008), at 35, Lakhdar Boumediene et al. *v.* George W. Bush, Judgement of 12 June 2008.

of human rights in times of war. Basing its arguments on a positivistic interpretation of the ICCPR it stated:

> The Court observes that the protection of the International Covenant of Civil and Political Rights does not cease in times of war, except by operation of Article 4 of the Covenant whereby certain provisions may be derogated from in a time of national emergency.[13]

This jurisprudence was continued in the Advisory Opinion on the construction of the wall in Palestine:

> More generally, the Court considers that the protection offered by human rights conventions does not cease in case of armed conflict, save the effect of provisions for derogation of the kind to be found in Article 4 of the International Covenant on Civil and Political Rights.[14]

In the frame of the American Convention on Human Rights the Inter-American Court stated:

> The American Convention, as well as other universal and regional human rights instruments, and the 1949 Geneva Conventions share a common nucleus of non-derogable rights and a common purpose of protecting human life and dignity. These human rights treaties apply both in peacetime, and during situations of armed conflict.[15]

The Inter-American court reaches its conclusions by identifying the objectives of the two fields of international law, *i.e.* the protection of human life and dignity. If the scopes of human rights law and of humanitarian law are the same it would not make sense to claim a mutual exclusiveness.

Similarly, the European Court of Human Rights did not hesitate in declaring the applicability of human rights law under a war régime. In the famous *Loizidou* Case it held that Turkey as an occupying power has to respect the obligations of the European Convention on Human Rights. The Court did not even deal with the question of the applicability of international human rights law in time of war, focusing exclusively on the question if Turkey is exercising jurisdiction in Northern Cyprus taking the applicability for granted.

In the *Ilaşcu* Case of 2004 the European Court attributed responsibility to the Russian Federation for the violation of the European Convention of Human Rights due to the fact that Russian troops were – illegally – in Transnistria and supported the separatist movement there. The same year the European Court applied the provisions of the European Convention on Human Rights to Turkish military activities in Northern Iraq. Again, the Court did not

[13] ICJ, *Advisory Opinion on the Legality of the Use of Nuclear Weapons*, para. 25.
[14] ICJ, *Advisory Opinion on the Legal Consequences of the Construction of a Wall in the Occupied Palestinian Territory*, para. 106; quoted *in* ICJ, *Judgelment on Armed Activities on the Territory of the Congo*, para. 216.
[15] *Juan Carlos Abella v. Argentina*, Case 11.137, Report Nº 55/97, Inter-Am. C.H.R., OEA/Ser.L/V/II.95 Doc. 7 rev. at 271 (1997) para. 158.

discuss whether the ECHR could be applied to such a situation, but it took the ECHR's applicability for granted. The Court stated: "The essential question to be examined in the instant case is whether at the relevant time Turkish troops conducted operations in the area where the killings took place."[16]

This case-law demonstrates that international courts now consider human rights applicable in times of war. They have arrived at this conclusion without extensive reasoning.

3. The Territorial Extension of the Application of Human Rights Documents

Having accepted the general applicability of human rights in times of war jurisprudence has, however, had some difficulty with the questions of the applicability of human rights instruments in wartime beyond the territory of the Member States to the respective instruments. No specific problem arises with respect to State conduct in its own territory, because there is an assumption that a State exercises jurisdiction over its territory. The situation becomes more complicated if military activities abroad are at stake. As military activities in war times often take place beyond the borders of a State the problem of the application of human rights instruments in wartime regularly and not only exceptionally arises. It is due to the provisions of some of these treaties on their territorial applicability. Article 2 CCPR reads:

> Each State Party to the present Covenant undertakes to respect and to ensure to all individuals within its territory and subject to its jurisdiction the rights recognized in the present Covenant;

Article 1 of the ECHR provides:

> The High Contracting Parties shall secure to everyone within their jurisdiction the rights and freedoms defined in Section I of this Convention.

Article 1 of the American Convention on Human Rights also limits the applicability of the convention to the persons under the jurisdiction of a member State. This raised the question whether extraterritorial actions of a State are covered by the respective Human righs instrument. Having a look especially at the wording of Article 2 CCPR one may have some doubts. Extraterritorial actions seem to be expressly excluded. Many member States insisted on this limitation of the applicability of human rights instruments and did not want their extraterritorial actions to be checked under the parameters of the CCPR.[17] The ICJ in its advisory opinion on the legal consequences of the

---

[16] ECtHR, *Issa et al. v. Turkey*, para. 75, Judgment of 16 November 2004.

[17] USA, UN Doc. CCPR/C/SR.1405 (1995), Israel, Belgium, UN Doc. CCPR/CO/81/BEL (2004), § 6 Netherlands UN Doc. CCPR/CO /72/NET/Add. 1 (2003).

construction of a wall in the occupied Palestinian territories analysed the object and purpose of the covenant and came to the conclusion "that the International Covenant on Civil and Political Rights is applicable in respect of acts done by a State in the exercise of its jurisdiction outside its own territory."[18] It found this result in line with the practice of the Human Rights Committee, which had arrived ath the same interpretation.[19] Taking note of the Israeli position according to which the Covenant does not apply in the occupied territories, the ICJ quoted a comment of the Human Rights Committee that stated that the Covenant is applicable in the territories.[20] The scholarship defends this position, interpreting the "and" as disjunctive, including persons on the State's territory and persons under a State jurisdiction. It would run counter to the objectives of the Covenant if persons in occupied territories who are most exposed to human rights violations, were excluded from any protection.[21]

A rich line of decisions from international tribunals may be found in the regional human rights instruments. The organs of the Inter-American system answered the question of the extraterritorial application of the American Convention positively,[22] focusing on the exercise of jurisdiction. The European Court of Human Rights likewise held in the above mentioned *Loizidou Case* that jurisdiction is not equivalent with territoriality.[23] In exceptional case – such as an occupation – States exercise their jurisdiction beyond their State borders. The European Court of Human Rights underlines that the responsibility for the respect of the guarantees of the European Convention derives from the control that the occupying power exercises in the occupied territories. The responsibility in such a case is independent from the fact that control is exercised by the State's armed forces or through a subordinate local authority. This line of reasoning was interrupted in the famous *Banković Case* dealing with the responsibility of ECHR Members States over Serbian territory leading to loss of lives and material damages. The European court rejected the claim of the Serbian citizens that the NATO-member States were exercising jurisdiction by bombing a foreign territory. The starting point of the Court's reasoning was

[18] ICJ *Advisory Opinion on the Legal Consequences of the Construction of a Wall in the Occupied Palestinian Territories*, para. 111.

[19] Human Rights Committee, *Saldías de López v. Uruguay*, Communication No. 52/1979.

[20] "[I]n the current circumstances, the provisions of the Covenant apply to the benefit of the population of the Occupied Territories, for all conduct by the State party's authorities or agents in those territories that affect the enjoyment of rights enshrined in the Covenant and fall within the ambit of State responsibility of Israel under the principles of public international law," CCPR/C0/78/1SR, para. 11.

[21] T. Buergenthal, *To Respect and to Ensure: State Obligations and Permissible Derogations*, *in* L. Henkin (Ed.), The International Bill of Rights: the Covenant on Civil and Political Rights 72, at 72, 81 (1981).

[22] Inter-American Commission of Human Rights, *Coard v. U.S.A*, Case No. 10.951, Report No. 109/99; Alejandre Jr. et al. *v*. Cuba, Case No. 11.589, Report No. 86/99.

[23] ECtHR, *Loizidou v. Turkey*, (preliminary objections, judgment of 23 March 1995 Series A 310, §71.

that as a rule jurisdiction and territoriality are identical. Whereas the European Court in the *Loizidou Case* pointed out the difference between territoriality and jurisdiction in the *Banković Case* the Court underlined that, as a rule, jurisdiction is exercised on the territory of a State. It considered the extra-territorial exercise of the jurisdiction as an exception. The European Court found confirmation for this view in the *travaux préparatoires*. It underlined that the member States never referred to art. 15 when using their armed forces abroad. The Court linked the notion of jurisdiction with the notion of control that might be exercised in case of an occupation or if a person is arrested abroad,[24] but not when bombing a foreign State.

However, this interpretation of the notion of jurisdiction is not convincing and does not fit into the former line of decisions. The reference to the *Loizidou Case* is doubtful. In this case the question was whether acts undertaken on a foreign territory by a local administration are attributable to Turkey. The European Court answered in the positive pointing out the control that the occupying power exercises in the occupied territory. It held that the control entailed the obligation to secure the guarantees of the Convention, and this responsibility exists irrespective of who is acting – the organs of the occupying forces or local organs. In the *Banković Case* the situation was quite different. The question was not whether specific acts undertaken in a foreign territory are attributable to a State. It was beyond doubt that the bombing was an act of the respective Member States of the European Convention. One could even say that the decision for the act in question was not taken abroad but on the territory of the Member States. Since the *Soering* decision of the European Court of Human Rights it is generally recognized that the guarantees of the European Convention can be violated by Member States even if the violation materializes abroad.[25] The real question in the *Banković Case* was whether the Serbian victims were under the jurisdiction of the Member States participating in the bombing. Contrary to the European Court's holding in the *Banković Case*, jurisdiction abroad does not require an absolute control over the foreign territory. In the *Issa Case* the European Court decided that although Turkish troops had not established general control over Northern Iraq, responsibility under the ECHR was nontheless established because Turkish troops were acting.[26] The same line of reasoning can be seen in the *Öcalan* decision, in which the European Court decided that the detention of a person abroad means that this person is under the jurisdiction of the arresting State.[27] The European Court tried to distinguish the *Banković Case* by pointing out that Öcalan after his detention was forced to return to Turkey. But this aspect cannot be

24 ECtHR, *Öcalan v. Turkey*, Judgment of 12 March 2003.

25 In the *Soering Case* the question was if the extradition of a person to the USA where he risked to be condemned to death was a violation of Art. 3 ECHR.

26 ECtHR, *Issa et al. v. Turkey*, para. 75, Judgment of 16 November 2004.

27 ECtHR, *Öcalan v. Turkey*, Judgement of 12 March 2003, para. 93.

relevant because the detention under review took place in Kenya and the following events could not establish jurisdiction that did not exist when the person was arrested. If Öcalan had not been arrested but killed in Kenya, then the applicability of the ECHR would be the same. It follows that a person is "under the jurisdiction" of a State if he or she is affected by an act of State power that interferes with one of the freedoms guaranteed by the European Convention. Bombing is the exercise of State power in the same sense as the arrest of a person is; it is an even more extreme form of the exercise of State power.

The link between jurisdiction and State territory might be the rule; but no normative conclusions can be drawn there from. It is recognized in international law that the two notions are not identical. There are situations where a State has no – or only a restricted – jurisdiction in its own territory, *i.e.* in cases of occupation. There are also cases where jurisdiction is exercised beyond the State territory, *e.g.* on ships and aircraft under the flag of the State, or through the acts of embassies and consulates abroad.[28] The textual interpretation of Article 1 of the ECHR does not permit another result. The provision does not use the notion of territory, as does Article 2 of the CCPR. It just speaks of jurisdiction; restricting this notion by the introduction of the criteria of territory cannot be justified. The European Court could have drawn some support by looking at the decisions interpreting other human rights instruments such as the CCPR and the ACHR. In spite of the reference to the 'territory' in Article 2 CCPR the Human Rights Committee decided that this treaty applies to events that took place abroad.[29] The Inter-American Commission decided that the ACHR is not limited to acts undertaken on the territory of a respondent State.[30] The interpretation of jurisdiction in this broad sense is in line with the purpose of human rights guarantees, which should grant protection whenever and wherever a State is acting. The restriction of the effects of these guarantees to the State's territory would create a gap because it would exempt State acts undertaken abroad from the legal limitations that impose human rights protecting as limits on State power.

A further argument has to be taken into account. Once the applicability of the human rights instruments in time of war accepted answering the question of the human rights instruments to extraterritorial acts in the negative would entail an unequal treatment of the armed forces defending the territory of a State and invading forces which have not established a control. Under such conditions the defending forces would have to respect the human rights

[28] J. Frowein & W. Peukert, Europäische Menschenrechtskonvention (1996), Art. 1, para. 5.

[29] Human Rights Committee, *Saldías de López v. Uruguay*, Communication No. 52/1979.

[30] Inter-American Commission of Human Rights, Alejandre jr. et al. *v.* Cuba, Case 11.589, Report 86/99, para. 23; the case dealt with the destruction of two civilian aircrafts above the high see by a Cuban military aircraft; therefore, it is comparable to the situation in the *Banković Case*, however, the Inter-American Commission of Human Rights arrived at other conclusions than the European Court of Human Rights.

provisions but the invading forces operating abroad would not. Such an unequal treatment of two parties involved in the same war and fighting on the same territory would not be in line with the general idea of the law in times of war, which imposes the same obligations on all parties.

Finally, it would seem strange that States declared that acts of State organs taken abroad fall under the State jurisdiction and therefore are not exempt from a control under the respective fundamental rights laid down in the constitution[31] whereas international courts would declare that persons concerned by these acts are not under the jurisdiction of the respective State in the sense of the international instrument.

Coming back to the *Banković Case* one has to reach the conclusion that there was no reason to exclude the applicability of the ECHR. In deciding in this way, the ECtHR tried to avoid a political storm. At the time in question, Serbia was not a member of the ECHR and no Serbian judge was member of the European Court of Human Rights. There is always a risk of a *Siegerjustiz* (victor's justice) when not all parties involved in a war are sitting on the bench of judges that have to decide on the conduct of the parties in the war.

4. The Relationship Between Human Rights and Humanitarian Law

In spite of the different historical and philosophical backgrounds the interconnection between human rights and the humanitarian law was quite evident from the very beginning. The impact of human rights trying to protect basic human values in times of war, which aims precisely at jeopardizing these values must be clarified.

The question of the exact relationship between the humanitarian law and the human rights law is difficult to answer. The question cannot be settled in a single response. A differentiation between various situations has to be made. No problem arises if the requirements of human rights law and humanitarian law are identical.[32] Here, the two rights are boosting each other. However, if the guarantees of both branches of law conflict or have a different range, the question arises which law will prevail. It is generally said that humanitarian law forms a sort of *lex specialis* with respect to human rights.[33] The ICJ joined

[31] *See supra* note 12.

[32] *E.g.* Art. 105 of the Geneva Convention III protects similar values as Art. 14 CPPR; the prohibition of serfdom, Art. 8 CPPR, Art. 4 ECHR, Art. 6 ACHR matches provisions of humanitarian law, prohibiting forced labour, D. Schindler, *Le Comité international de la Croix-Rouge et les droits de l'homme*, 1979 Revue internationale de la Croix-Rouge 3, at 10 (1979).

[33] J. Frowein, *The Relationship Between Human Rights Regimes and Regimes of Belligerent Occupation*, 28 Israel Yearbook on Human Rights 1, at 9 (1998).

this opinion. It held in the *Advisory Opinion on the Legal Consequences of the Construction of a Wall in the Occupied Palestinian Territories*:

> As regards the relationship between international humanitarian law and human rights law, there are thus three possible situations: some rights may be exclusively matters of international humanitarian law; others may be exclusively matters of human rights law; yet others may be matters of both these branches of international law. In order to answer the question put to it, the Court will have to take into consideration both these branches of international law, namely human rights law and, as *lex specialis* and international humanitarian law.[34]

As *lex specialis* humanitarian law would have to be applied insofar as it is contradicting human rights. However, one may raise the question whether the notion of *lex specialis* fits the relationship between humanitarian law and human rights law in all cases. The *lex specialis* is a norm that encompasses all prerequisites of the *lex generalis* for the application, and at least one additional element. If one adopts this definition one may wonder whether humanitarian law really qualifies as a *lex specialis* of human rights law. Is the permission to kill a combatant in time of war really a *lex specialis* to the guarantee of life under human rights régimes? It would be the same to hold that the law of censorship is a *lex specialis* to the freedom of expression. If the *lex specialis* rule were stringent, then one could not explain the above mentioned derogation clauses in the human rights instruments. For in a conflict humanitarian law would simply prevail.Furthermore, one has to consider the non derogable human rights guarantees, such as the prohibition of torture and slavery. Here, it is beyond doubt that humanitarian law does not prevail over the respective prohibitions, even if in some western countries this principle has come under discussion and sometimes has been violated. The ICJ itself, by the way, did not apply its jurisprudence on the qualification of humanitarian law as a *lex specialis* in a very stringent way. As the *Advisory Opinion on the Legal Consequences on the Construction of the Wall in the Occupied Palestinian Territories* shows, the Court balances human rights and military necessity, and in the given case human rights prevailed.[35] Balancing conflicting interests will be the method most often used in order to overcome a conflict between opposing norms of the two branches of law, as far as it is not excluded from the very beginning.

As far as human rights norms and humanitarian norms do not exclude each other, they may serve as a means of interpretation of the norms of the other branch. Two examples are discussed in the following sections beginning with the protection of life and followed by the derogation clauses.

Article 6 of the ICCPR does not permit a derogation of the right to life. This could insinuate that life is protected also in time of war. As a matter

---

[34] ICJ, *Advisory Opinion on the Legal Consequences of the Construction of a Wall*, para. 106.,

[35] ICJ, *Advisory Opinion on the Legal Consequences of the Construction of the Wall in the Occupied Palestinian Territories*, para. 134.

of fact, the Human Rights Committee in its General Comment on Article 6 ICCPR condemned wars as a scourge of humanity, because they destroy innocent lives. The Committee concludes that States have an obligation under Article 6 ICCPR to prevent war.[36] In 1984 the Committee went so far as to declare that designing, testing, manufacturing, possession and deployment of nuclear weapons is one of the greatest threats to the right of life,[37] implying that Article 6 of the ICCPR is applicable to these acts extending its application to the prewar armament.

However, Article 6 does not lead to the exclusion of all forms of war although war unavoidably entails human losses, it even aims at them.. Article 6 paragraph 1 last paragraph reads: "No one shall be arbitrarily deprived of his life." In a common reading of this provision the killing of persons is not considered to be an arbitrary deprivation of life as far as the State is respecting the rules of warfare. This is reflected in Article 15 paragraph 2 of the ECHR:

> No derogation from Article 2, except in respect of deaths resulting from lawful acts of war, or from Articles 3, 4 (paragraph 1) and 7 shall be made under this provision.

The ICJ decided in the *Advisory Opinion on the Legality of the Use of Nuclear Weapons*:

> The test of what is an arbitrary deprivation of life, however, then falls to be determined by the applicable *lex specialis,* namely, the law applicable in armed conflict which is designed to regulate the conduct of hostilities. Thus whether a particular loss of life, through the use of a certain weapon in warfare, is to be considered an arbitrary deprivation of life contrary to Article 6 of the Covenant, can only be decided by reference to the law applicable in armed conflict and not deduced from the terms of the Covenant itself.[38]

It lies in the line of this reasoning that killings in an unlawful war might be regarded as a violation of Article 6 of the ICCPR.[39] However, this conclusion, drawn from the perspective of human rights law and the interpretation of arbitrary deprivation, runs counter to a very basic principle of humanitarian law, *i.e.* the strict separation between *ius ad bellum* and *ius in bello*. If the qualification of State acts under *ius ad bellum* had an impact on the qualification under *ius in bello*, the attempt to limit the atrocities in wartime by an equal treatment of all lawful combatants would come to an end.[40] In times of war,

---

[36] Human Rights Committee, General Comment No. 6 of 30 April 1982.

[37] Human Rights Committee, General Comment No. 14 of 9 November 1984.

[38] ICJ, *Advisory Opinion on the Legality of the Use of Nuclear Weapons,* para. 25.

[39] M. Nowak, U.N. Covenant on Civil and Political Rights – CCPR Commentary 125 (2005); K. Bennoune, *Toward a Human Rights Approach to Armed Conflict: Iraq 2003*, 11 U.C. Davis Journal of International Law and Policy 171, at 215 (2004).

[40] H. J. Heintze, *Las Palmeras v. Bamaca-Velasquez und Bankovic v. Loiszidou? Widersprüchliche Entscheidungen zum Menschenrechtsschutz in bewaffneten Konflikten*, 18 Humanitäres Völkerrecht – Informationsschriften 177, at 182 (2005).

States always blame each other for breaching the prohibition of the use of force. Therefore, the combatants would lose any protection if they were judged in relation to the war in which they are participating. The civilization of war, more specifically of *ius in bello* depends upon the separation between *ius ad bellum* and *ius in bello*. Here, the extension of human rights law would lead to the diminishment of the protection. Therefore, when using the humanitarian law as the criteria for the interpretation of the human rights instruments, one has to respect the inner logic of this law.

Even more important is the interpretation of the derogation clauses in the respective human rights instruments. It is a common conviction that the application of the derogation clauses is subject to the principle of proportionality. A derogation from human rights guarantees is admissible in times of war only insofar as it is indispensable in order to defend the State and the common interest in wartime. If the rules of humanitarian law prohibit a certain conduct then the derogation of the respective guarantees of an instrument of human rights would be illegal and a breach of the treaty in question. States cannot refer to times of war in order to justify a restriction of human rights if the laws of war do not admit such restrictions. Here, one notices a certain parallelism between humanitarian law and the law of human rights. Human rights instruments must not lead to a more restrictive treatment of human rights than humanitarian law allows. In this sense the Inter-American Commission on Human Rights considering the admissibility of a derogation of guarantees under Article 27 ACHR, decided that such a derogation cannot be inconsistent with that State's other obligations under international law.[41] As far as humanitarian law influences the interpretation of human rights law, that regime has an impact on the application of humanitarian law. Especially, the general clauses of the humanitarian law are open to human rights input. The Common Article 3 of the Geneva Conventions requires the humane treatment of all persons who are not actively taking part in the hostilities. The interpretation of what is humane may be found with reference to the content of human rights guarantees. The Convention on the Rights of the Child may serve as a further example for the interconnection of human rights and humanitarian law. Article 38 of this convention obliges all parties to respect the humanitarian law as far as it protects children's rights. In this way, the respective humanitarian law is somehow incorporated into a Convention that primarily is understood as a guarantee of human rights of a particularly delicate group. Here, human rights law is applied under the perspective of humanitarian law.

A special opening clause for human rights at least as supplementary law that may be applied as far as the humanitarian law does not rule on a certain

[41] Juan Carlos Abella *v*. Argentina, Case 11.137, Report Nº 55/97, Inter-Am. C.H.R., OEA/Ser.L/V/II.95 Doc. 7 rev., at 271 (1997), http://www1.umn.edu/humanrts/cases/1997/argentina55-97a.html; in the same sense Buergenthal, *supra* note 21.

question, can be derived from the Martens' clause, which dates back to the origins of the humanitarian law.[42] It reads:

> Until a more complete code of the laws of war has been issued, the High Contracting Parties deem it expedient to declare that, in cases not included in the Regulations adopted by them, the inhabitants and the belligerents remain under the protection and the rule of the principles of the law of nations, as they result from the usages established among civilized peoples, from the laws of humanity, and the dictates of the public conscience.

5. Conclusions

Human rights matter in international law, they have gained such an importance that no branch of international law is immune to their force. Even the branch that is furthest away from material legality, the law of war, has come under the control of human rights law, at least to a certain degree. The applicability of human rights in time of war has become common place. However, a closer look reveals the real relationship between human rights and humanitarian law which turns out to be more intricate. The generally accepted doctrine of humanitarian law as *lex specialis* of human rights law cannot be sustained. The solution in cases of conflict has to be found in a balancing between military necessity and human rights values. This approach, however, introduces the value judgment of humanitarian law into the realm of human rights. It remains to be seen whether human rights law will have enough weight to set enforceable limits on the conduct of war. Human rights law and humanitarian law are not a one way relationship. By embracing humanitarian law human rights might become infected with the virus of military necessity. This is not just a theoretical problem. In 2006, the German constitutional court decided that a law authorizing the minister of defense to shoot down an airplane in a situation similar to the terrorist attacks in the United States on September 11, 2001, would violate the principle of human dignity.[43] This decision was criticized, because it is beyond doubt that, in time of war, humanitarian law allows the killing of A State's own citizens.[44] Are there two standards of dignity – a peacetime and a wartime standard? Or must the peacetime dignity be brought in line with the wartime dignity and will all end up in a reduction of the protected values?

There is hope that human rights as conceived in peacetime will prevail and might become a "gentle, however forceful civilizer" of the States in times of war.

---

[42] The Martens' Clause was inserted into the preambles to the Hague Convention II of 1899 and to the Convention IV of 1907 with respect to the Laws and Customs of War on Land.

[43] BVerfGE (decision of the Federal Constitutional Court), judgment of 15 February 2006, http://www.bundesverfassungsgericht.de/entscheidungen.

[44] A. Zimmermann & R. Geiss, *Die Tötung unbeteiligter Zivilisten: Menschenunwürdig im Frieden – menschenwürdig im Krieg?*, 46 Der Staat 377 (2007).

Daphne Barak-Erez

Terrorism and Human Rights: Challenges to the Foundations of the Legal Order

1. Introduction

The task of balancing human rights and government anti-terrorism action is often presented as a new challenge, although in many regards this is not the case. Terrorist actions taken in order to promote national and political goals have been an integral part of modern history. If this is so, why are we encountered by the perception of 'newness' with respect to terrorism and anti-terrorism? In part, this is due to the fact that terrorist actions transcend the boundaries of national and regional conflicts and posses the potential for far reaching consequences. However, It seems that the reasons are predominantly the challenges posed by both terrorism and anti-terrorism to the foundations of the regime of international law, as crystallized after the World War II, on the one hand, and to the axioms of criminal law and constitutional law in liberal democracies, on the other hand. The discussion that follows will highlight these legal uncertainties and anxieties.

2. Terrorism and the International Legal Sphere

First and foremost, the perception of the 'newness' of the current challenge of terrorism is connected to the manner in which World War II came to an end. The ending of the war, perceived at the time as the last major war, brought about a 'new world order', which came part and parcel with an underlying consensus on rights (as demonstrated by the Universal Declaration of Human Rights) and on the way to conduct wars (written into the Geneva Conventions of 1949). The terrorist attacks of 2001 and their aftermath were new in the sense that they threatened the basis of this world order. In contrast to the days

Miodrag Jovanović & Ivana Krstić (Eds.), Human Rights Today – 60 Years of the Universal Declaration, 187-194.

of the Cold War, which had cast its shadow on world stability in the past, the current sense of danger is related to the fact that not only has the identity of our enemies changed, but also their forms of actions and motivations. The enemy is not necessarily a country anymore, whereas the assumptions of the world order, as crystallized after World War II, were that the significant actors to be held accountable for their actions are states. The sense of danger is heightened due to the gloomy prospect that a new international consensus will be formed. The old documents do not represent modern reality, but the chances of their replacement are faint. The reason for this is connected to the disparate answers provided by different countries to the question: "who are the terrorists"? These differing views render it impossible to draft conventions in this area behind the so-called veil of ignorance. Indeed, there are many new conventions on terrorism, however they deal with specific terrorist-related activities and do not profess to change the basic norms of the laws of war.[1] Other new documents in the international arena apply only to a limited group of states (e.g. European initiatives which apply only to European states).[2] Security Council resolutions in this area[3] are authoritative but they do not necessarily reflect a broad international consensus.

The argument regarding the inadaptability of the consensus formed after World War II to the challenge of terrorism can be exemplified by focusing on the Geneva Conventions of 1949. The assumptions underlying these conventions are:

1) The main armed conflicts are wars between states;

2) The main combat forces are organized like national armies (with distinctive signs and a clear commanding chain);

3) As a general rule there is a clear division between combatants and non-combatants;

4) Wars have clear beginnings and endings (based on agreements to end hostilities);

5) Military-related operations are conducted in areas that are removed from the centers of civilian life.

---

1 *See e.g.* Convention on the Prevention and Punishment of Crimes Against Internationally Protected Persons, Including Diplomatic Agents, 1973; International Convention Against the Taking of Hostages, 1979; International Convention for the Suppression of Terrorist Bombings, 1997; International Convention for the Suppression of the Financing of Terrorism, 1999; International Convention for the Suppression of Acts of Nuclear Terrorism, 2005.

2 *See e.g.* Council of Europe Convention on the Prevention of Terrorism, 2005.

3 The main Security Council Resolutions to be mentioned in this context are Security Council Resolution 1267 (1999); Security Council Resolution 1373 (2001); and Security Council Resolution 1566 (2004).

Indeed, the Geneva Conventions view the possibility of deviations from this baseline, but these are structured as exceptions to the rule.

Examining present day reality from the perspective of the assumptions of the Geneva Conventions easily demonstrates their inapplicability:

1) In the primary conflict with which the main world power – the US – is involved in it does not confront another state, but rather Al-Qaeda, an international terrorist organization. Indeed, the US has invaded Afghanistan and Iraq but it did so, arguably, in relation to its main and underlying war (or conflict) with Al-Qaeda.

2) Members of terrorist organizations do not fulfill the conditions prescribed by the Geneva Conventions for combatants. This is due not merely to their failure to wear uniform, but often also to their operation through cells which are not organized in a way that presents a clear chain of command.

3) Terrorist organizations frequently operate within civilian population and terrorists benefit from support from their neighbors and friends who are not part and parcel of their organizations.[4]

4) Terrorist attacks appear sporadically and there are no clear beginnings or endings of hostilities.

5) Terrorists try to hit civilian targets and hence the line between battle zones and civilian areas is completely blurred.

To a certain extent, these problems emerged even before 2001 – in the wake of national-related terrorism, but they have intensified and become central to the main conflicts in the world (and not only to regional conflicts). In addition, it is worthwhile to note that the main effort to reform the Geneva Conventions – the Protocol Additional to the Geneva Conventions from 1977 – has failed to achieve universal acceptance, which would include those relevant countries which are embroiled in terrorist related conflicts.[5]

Many of the tensions between the regime of the Geneva Conventions and present day reality are connected to the uncertainty regarding the legal status of members of terrorist organizations. On the one hand, they are not soldiers, and presumably cannot be treated as such, but on the other hand, it seems absurd to award them with all the protections which apply to civilians. This impossibility to categorize them leads to various paradoxes, which are central to the practice of war, for example:

1) Killing – the main assumption of the law of war is that it is legal to kill members of the military forces. If terrorists are not combatants it is illegal

[4] For a case focusing on limits of using sanctions against such support awarded by relatives and friends, *see* Ajuri *v.* IDF Commander in West Bank 56(6) P.D. 352.

[5] Among the countries which did not join the protocol are the US and Israel.

to kill them, without a trial. Indeed, even in the context of the law of war it is legal to kill civilians when they are involved in hostilities, but this notion is restricted to the times in which a military confrontation is taking place.

2) Detentions – when caught, terrorists do not qualify as prisoners of war. This would mean that they should be brought to justice, although it may be impossible to prove their guilt based on the ordinary rules of criminal law, mainly due to evidential problems.

Both the US and Israel have tried, in different ways, to maintain that terrorists who are not combatants according to the definitions of the Geneva Conventions should not enjoy, for this reason, additional privileges and immunities that would result from their classification as civilians (if that is the only other category recognized). In the US, the application of this view allowed for combatants who were not soldiers of a national enemy military to be held in custody without being brought to criminal justice – based on the Authorization for Use of Military Force (AUMF) and the military order promulgated by President Bush. This US policy was justifiably criticized because it significantly involved human rights violations – the prisoners detained did not receive appropriate treatment and could not challenge the cause of their detention in court. However, this criticism on the US practice barred the discussion from addressing a deeper truth: the practice was wrong, but in fact also international law has failed by not offering a clear and workable system for dealing with these prisoners.

Instances from the Israeli context highlight the same problem. In order to deal with this challenge, Israel has enacted the Incarceration of Unlawful Combatants Law, 2002, which regulates the detention of combatants who do not qualify as prisoners of war. According to the law, they should be detained in humane conditions, and be entitled to judicial review of their detention by ordinary civilian courts within fourteen days, and thereafter, at the minimum of six month intervals. This system is, in many senses, a reasonable way to deal with the normative black hole of international law in this matter. Yet, it was challenged in the Israeli Supreme Court, for infringing the norms of international law, on the grounds that it introduces a so-called third category which does not exist in the relevant international conventions – that of unlawful combatants.[6] A similar argument was made in the Israeli Supreme Court in an earlier case, which involved Israel's policy of targeted killings of terrorists operating against Israel outside its territory. Also in this case, a major argument pursued was that Israel had ventured to create a third category of unlawful combatants and apply to it new norms, not recognized by international law.[7] Against this background it is interesting to note that the

[6] Cr. App. 6659/06 A *v.* State of Israel (11 June 2008).

[7] HCJ 769/02 The Public Committee against Torture in Israel *v.* The Government of Israel (13 December 2006).

Israeli Supreme Court legitimized (subject to conditions) the two practices, by arguing that both were grounded in the laws of war applicable to citizens involved in hostilities. Accordingly, the Israeli Supreme Court opined that terrorists are civilians engaged in hostilities against the state, an astute solution, but at the same time, to some extent, a contradiction in terms. It is no less interesting to point out that the decision of the Israeli Supreme Court concerning targeted killings, based itself on the First Protocol Additional to the Geneva Conventions, drafted in 1977,[8] which has not been joined by Israel itself,[9] in a manner that implies an admission that the original Conventions are outdated.

A counter argument to the one made thus far may be that the focus on the laws of war is inadequate – that terrorism is a crime which should be dealt with by law enforcement mechanisms, and therefore the call for reforming the laws of war is misguided. According to this view, the difficulty in applying the Geneva Conventions does not reflect shortcomings in the law but rather inadequate endeavors to apply it outside traditional wars. This is an important perspective that should be taken into consideration, but it does not dismiss entirely the preceding argument. Indeed, in many contexts, when terrorism presents itself in the commission of crimes in domestic surroundings, the correct way to approach it is to apply law enforcement mechanisms in general, and criminal law in particular, in order to trace the perpetrators and bring them to justice. Nevertheless, the questions regarding the manner in which to apply the laws of war are still relevant with regard to circumstances in which countries have to face terrorists in circumstances of battle-type confrontations, in their territories or even beyond their borders.

3. Terrorism and the National Legal Sphere

The basic concepts of national legal systems have also been shaken by the challenge of terrorism. Here, the main tensions touch on the possibility to use preventive measures against suspected terrorists without infringing on the foundations of criminal law, according to which limitations of individual liberty should be the result of past guilty behavior which had already crystallized, based on evidence proved in a court of law.

The tensions around the recourse to the paradigm of prevention can be demonstrated by the example of detentions for preventive purposes. In general, the use of administrative detentions of those suspected of posing a

[8] According to section 51(3) of the protocol, civilians shall not enjoy the protections usually afforded to them as civilians when they "take a direct part in hostilities", as long as they do so – that is "for such time". Accordingly, the court has focused its judgment on the definitions of the concepts of 'direct part', 'hostilities' and 'for such time'.

[9] *See supra* note 5.

threat to society has been traditionally considered an insult to the idea of a democratic regime committed to the rule of law, in which people are supposed to be brought to justice and either acquitted or found guilty. Administrative detentions have been used predominantly by colonial rulers and regimes of military occupation (that is, outside the domain of peace time). Accordingly, legal systems which were willing to adhere to the use of administrative detentions were highly criticized. Examples worth mentioning in this respect were the use of administrative detentions against people suspected as affiliated with the IRA in Britain,[10] and administrative detentions in Israel.[11]

With the rise of the new wave of terrorism, old criticisms against preventive measures have been partially forsaken. Indeed, administrative detentions were re-introduced in a way that principally targeted non-nationals, yet the possibility to employ them, also against nationals, was not completely overruled.[12] In Britain, the House of Lords declared that the administrative detentions regime, which had been enacted in the wake of international terrorism in 2001, infringed the Human Rights Act, 1998, due to its discriminatory application (that is, its limitation only to aliens).[13] However, this decision did not overrule the possibility of re-enacting the same regime without its discriminatory aspects. Eventually, the policy choice adopted in Britain was to introduce an alternative preventive measure, in the form of control orders, to be applied in a non-discriminatory manner.[14] This regime has been accepted by the House of Lords, subject to some narrowing of the scope of the limitations attached to the control order, and to an insistence that the person involved will know the essence of the allegations against him (but not on full disclosure of the relevant evidence).[15] In Canada, the Supreme Court was not willing to accept that an application of a detentions regime pertaining only to aliens constituted discrimination. It criticized the policy, only for its procedural shortcomings, in the sense that the detainees were completely excluded from reviewing the relevant evidence against them and therefore could not effectively defend themselves.[16] Thus, the concern was not with

10 Initially, the practice of administrative detentions was introduced with regard to Northern Ireland by the Civil Authorities (Special Powers) Act (Northern Ireland), 1922. Later on, more laws on this matter followed. Currently, Britain does not use a regime of administrative detentions.

11 Emergency Powers (Detentions) Law, 1979.

12 In England – this measure was introduced by Part 4 of the Anti-Terrorism, Crime and Security Act 2001, which was later on replaced with a control orders regime, as explained later; In Canada – this measure is part of the Immigration and Refugee Protection Act 2001 (sections 80-82).

13 A *v.* Secretary of State for the Home Department [2005] 2 W.L.R. 87.

14 According to the Prevention of Terrorism Act 2005.

15 The main precedents on the law of control orders are: Secretary of State for the Home Department *v.* JJ [2007] 3 WLR 642; Secretary of State for the Home Department *v.* MB [2007] 3 WLR 681; Secretary of State for the Home Department *v.* E [2007] 3 WLR 720.

16 Charkaoui *v.* Canada (Minister of Citizenship and Immigration) (2007) SCC 9.

the idea of preventive detention but rather with the specifics of the detention regime. In addition, the Canadian Supreme Court was willing to accept the legitimacy of introducing procedural safeguards that would fall short of the norm of criminal trials (such as adopting the procedure of appointing a special advocate to whom the evidence is disclosed and is entrusted to argue the case without revealing the evidence to the person involved). Taking these examples as a whole, the emerging lesson might be that it is better to acknowledge that preventive measures can be used to fight terrorism and then invest thought in how to regulate them in a manner that will secure effective judicial review. A complete denial of this new reality may not necessarily lead to a better protection of human rights, but rather to lawless uses of preventive measures.

Another example of the prevention paradigm is the controversy around the use of physical measures in interrogations. In principle, the use of such measures is considered illegal in all civilized systems in the context of law enforcement. Yet, there are some signs to some willingness to tolerate them in a limited manner when used for preventive purposes. In Israel, in 1999 the Supreme Court clearly rejected the use of physical measures in interrogations, but provided for an exception in the so-called ticking bomb scenario (in which the use of physical measures may be *ex post* excused based on the defense of necessity).[17] This decision, given prior to 2001, has been the sole example to this approach for several years. However, a later decision of the British House of Lords may demonstrate that the Israeli Supreme Court is not alone. In the celebrated decision in which the House of Lords dismissed the possibility of using evidence collected by third countries through torture, for the purpose of a judicial process in Britain, it still held that data of this sort may be used by enforcement agencies in order to prevent a bomb explosion in a public place.[18]

The rise of the preventive approach is expressed also in the tendency to enact new offences aimed at prohibiting actions considered to contribute to the escalation of terrorism. Offences of this sort deal with provocation or incitement to commit terrorist actions, recruitment for terrorism and training for terrorism.[19] Thus, they go beyond the tradition of criminal law, which mainly focused on harmful actions and was usually reluctant to criminalize preliminary phases and preparatory actions. In other words, such legislative initiatives take a phenomenon that used to be on the borderline of criminal law – offenses of preparation and conspiracy – and make it central to law enforcement in the area of anti-terrorism.

[17] H.C.J. 5100/94 The Public Committee Against Torture in Israel *v*. the Government of Israel 53(4) PD 817.

[18] A *v*. Secretary of State for the Home Department [2006] 2 AC 221.

[19] A central example to this approach is found in the Council of Europe Convention on the Prevention of Terrorism, 2005, *supra* note 2. *See also* Security Council Resolution 1624 (on incitement to terrorism).

4. Terrorism Law: Avoiding the Issues or Addressing Them

The new threat of terrorism has caught both international law and national laws unprepared. The question is whether jurists will choose to live in denial, or decide to confront the new challenges posed by the new reality, even at the risk of challenging assumptions and principles considered so far as fundamental. In the course of this process, human rights should not be compromised, but it is important to acknowledge the need to reconsider the forms of their application to new circumstances.

Henk Botha

Human Dignity: Constitutional Right, Absolute Ideal, or Contested Value?

"Recognition of the inherent dignity and of the equal and inalienable rights of all members of the human family is the foundation of freedom, justice and peace in the world."
Preamble to the Universal Declaration of Human Rights

"All human beings are born free and equal in dignity and rights."
Article 1 of the Universal Declaration of Human Rights

"Respect for the dignity of all human beings is particularly important in South Africa. For apartheid was a denial of a common humanity. Black people were refused respect and dignity and thereby the dignity of all South Africans was diminished. The new Constitution rejects this past and affirms the equal worth of all South Africans. Thus recognition and protection of human dignity is the touchstone of the new political order and is fundamental to the new Constitution."
S v. Makwanyane para. 329

1. Introduction

Human dignity occupies a special place in South Africa's Constitution.[1] Section 10 provides that "[e]veryone has inherent dignity and the right to have their dignity respected and protected." Dignity is also affirmed as one of the founding constitutional values[2] which must guide the interpretation of

1 Constitution of the Republic of South Africa, 1996.

2 Section 1(a) proclaims that the Republic of South Africa is founded, inter alia, on the values of "human dignity, the achievement of equality and the advancement of human rights and freedoms," while section 7(1) states that the Bill of Rights "affirms the democratic values of human dignity, equality and freedom."

Miodrag Jovanović & Ivana Krstić (Eds.), Human Rights Today – 60 Years of the Universal Declaration, 195-210.

constitutional rights[3] and is central to inquiries into the justifiability of rights limitations.[4]

The Constitutional Court has been instrumental in establishing the primacy of human dignity.[5] It has invoked dignity as a justiciable right, a supreme value, an interpretive *Leitmotiv*, an objective legal norm, a basis for the limitation of rights and freedoms, and a guide to the principled resolution of constitutional value conflicts. Consider, for instance, the following dictum:

> The Constitution asserts dignity to contradict our past in which human dignity for black South Africans was routinely and cruelly denied. It asserts it too to inform the future, to invest in our democracy respect for the intrinsic worth of all human beings. Human dignity therefore informs constitutional adjudication and interpretation at a range of levels. It is a value that informs the interpretation of many, possibly all, other rights. [...] Human dignity is also a constitutional value that is of central significance in the limitations analysis. Section 10, however, makes it clear that dignity is not only a *value* fundamental to our Constitution, it is a justiciable and enforceable *right* that must be respected and protected.[6]

Guided, on the one hand, by international and comparative law, and on the other by its understanding of South Africa's troubled past, the Court has placed dignity at the centre of its constitutional jurisprudence. Dignity, in the view of the Court, straddles the divide between the universality of human rights and their rootedness in particular local struggles. Dignity emphasises our common humanity in a world characterised by division, fear and distrust; it holds open the promise of transcendence amidst depressing socio-economic realities. Dignity, moreover, provides a principled basis for the negotiation of a series of tensions that have plagued constitutional democracy since its inception: between equality and freedom, between the individual and community, between the generality of law and the recognition of difference.[7]

The turn to dignity has, however, not been uncontroversial. The Court has not only been criticised for privileging dignity over other values, such

---

3 Section 39(1)(a) ("When interpreting the Bill of Rights, a court, tribunal or forum must promote the values that underlie an open and democratic society based on human dignity, equality and freedom").

4 Section 36(1) (fundamental rights may only be limited to the extent that the limitation is "reasonable and justifiable in an open and democratic society based on human dignity, equality and freedom").

5 In one of the first cases decided by it under the interim Constitution, the Court described dignity, together with the right to life, as "the most important of all human rights, and the source of all other personal rights" in the Bill of Rights. S *v.* Makwanyane 1995 (3) SA 391; 1995 (6) BCLR 665 (CC) para. 144.

6 Dawood; Shalabi; Thomas *v.* Minister of Home Affairs 2000 (3) SA 936 (CC); 2000 (8) BCLR 837 (CC) para. 35 (emphasis in the original).

7 *See e.g.* L. W. H. Ackermann, *Equality and the South African Constitution: The Role of Dignity*, 63 Heidelberg Journal of International Law 537 (2000).

as equality and democracy,[8] but it has also been claimed that dignity is so open-ended that it could be invoked to justify almost any outcome. Far from providing a neutral and uncontested vantage point for the resolution of normative conflicts, dignity, in this view, replicates within itself the very tensions it is supposed to mediate.[9]

These criticisms need to be taken seriously. Dignity provides no magical formula for the adjudication of value conflicts – and it certainly does not absolve us from the responsibility to make hard, even excruciating choices. I will, however, argue that it is precisely the paradoxical nature of human dignity that enables it to structure constitutional discourse. In the ensuing sections, I will focus on five paradoxes – or perhaps five aspects of the same paradox – lying at the heart of human dignity.

Throughout the paper, South Africa's experience will be juxtaposed to that of Germany. Germany's dignity jurisprudence offers a particularly interesting comparative counterpoint. This is so for a number of reasons. First of all, the scope and sophistication of the dignity jurisprudence of German courts and the depth of academic comment by German constitutional law scholars on the concept and uses of dignity are unparalleled in any other country. Secondly, both countries have embraced dignity as a supreme value as a direct response to a totalitarian and deeply traumatic past characterised by pervasive discrimination and human rights abuses.[10] And thirdly, despite some textual, historical and broadly philosophical similarities, the two Constitutions and the legal traditions in which they are embedded are sufficiently dissimilar to enable a rich dialogue on the meaning and uses of dignity, and the possibilities and limits of a dignity-based jurisprudence.

2. Absolute Ideal or Negotiable Right and Value?

Human dignity implies something inviolable, something which commands our highest respect regardless of the consequences, something which can neither be forfeited nor waived nor weighed up against clashing considerations. And yet, precisely because it is such a pervasive value which underlies a variety of

[8] *See e.g.* C. Albertyn & B. Goldblatt, *Facing the Challenge of Transformation: Difficulties in the Development of an Indigenous Jurisprudence of Equality*, 14 South African Journal on Human Rights 248 (1998) for criticisms of the Court's dignity-based interpretation of the right to equality. *See also* H. Botha, *Equality, Dignity, and the Politics of Interpretation, in* W. le Roux & K. van Marle (Eds.) Post-Apartheid Fragments: Law, Politics and Critique 148 (2007); *Equality, Plurality, and Structural Power*, 25 South African Journal on Human Rights (2009, forthcoming) for explorations of the relationship between human dignity, equality and democracy.

[9] *See e.g.* D. M. Davis, *Equality: The Majesty of Legoland Jurisprudence*, 116 South African Law Journal 398 (1999).

[10] Du Plessis *v.* De Klerk 1996 (3) SA 850 (CC); 1996 (5) BCLR 658 (CC) para. 92.

rights, dignity cannot escape being subjected to balancing, thus subverting its claim to an absolute status. We can call this the first paradox.

The German Basic Law and the South African Constitution represent different ways of coming to terms with this paradox. Article 1(1) of the German Basic Law declares human dignity to be 'inviolable'. No provision is made for its limitation by or in terms of legislation. This has been interpreted to mean that dignity is absolute and may not be weighed up against other rights or the public interest. But dignity is not only shielded from ordinary legislative incursions. The principles laid down in Article 1 are also shielded from constitutional amendment by Article 79(3). Dignity thus belongs, alongside democracy, federalism and the social state, to an unalterable core of constitutional values and principles.

The absolute protection granted to dignity has had a profound influence on its interpretation. Whether or not dignity constitutes a subjective right in addition to being an objective constitutional norm has, for instance, been the subject of much debate. In the view of some commentators, the role of dignity should be restricted to that of an objective legal norm which directly binds all state authority and guides the interpretation of all fundamental rights. Treating it as a subjective right could easily lead to its relativisation, as it would increase the pressure to balance dignity against countervailing rights and interests.[11] The notion of dignity as absolute and inviolable has also impacted on the scope and meaning given to it. It is often stated that the meaning of dignity should not be trivialised or inflated,[12] and that according dignity a too extensive meaning would either paralyse government or detract from the absolute nature of Article 1(1).[13]

The notion that dignity is not subject to balancing has, however, come under pressure. Because dignity is seen as the basis of human rights and because it is so often used in conjunction with more specific rights, dignity sometimes features on both sides of a dispute. In cases where dignity conflicts with dignity, a court has no choice but to engage in balancing. In the abortion cases, the Federal Constitutional Court weighed up the life and dignity of

[11] Proponents of this view include G. Dürig, *Der Grundrechtssatz von der Menschenwürde*, 81 AöR 117, at 118-120 (1956); H. Dreier, I Grundgesetz Kommentar 207-209 (2004); and J. Isensee, *Menschenwürde: die säkulare Gesellschaft auf der Suche nach dem Absoluten*, 131 AöR 173, at 209-210 (2006). *But see also* M. Herdegen, *Art. 1 Abs. 1*, *in* T. Maunz & G. Dürig (Eds.), Grundgesetz Kommentar 1, at 18-20 (2003/2005); K. Stern, IV Das Staatsrecht der Bundesrepublik Deutschland 61-64 (2006).

[12] In the words of Dürig, *supra* note 11, at 124, Art 1(1) "ist keine 'kleine Münze'." In his view, dignity is trivialised by attempts to use it to expand the protection of personal honour or to preserve common decency. *Id.*, at 124, 127. *See also* Dreier, *supra* note 11, at 164-165.

[13] An example of an alleged incursion which was found to be too trivial was the spelling of a name in a telephone invoice – which was processed electronically – by 'oe' instead of 'ö' (BVerwGE 31, 236 (1969)).

the foetus against the self-determination and dignity of the mother.[14] Similar conflicts occur where a person consents to treatment (*e.g.* in the case of 'peep shows' and 'dwarf tossing') which is considered to be objectifying and degrading. Here the state's duty to protect dignity – if needs be, even against self-degradation – conflicts with the autonomy and right of the individual to self-determination.[15]

The difficulties surrounding an absolute constitutional conception of dignity are illustrated by debates triggered by new advances within the fields of biotechnology and human genetics. Concerns about the instrumentalisation and objectification of human embryos or persons in the areas of assisted reproduction, pre-implantation diagnostics, research on superfluous embryos, stem cell research, genetic therapy and cloning have given rise to arguments that these procedures are inconsistent with human dignity and therefore unconstitutional. Some of these concerns are, admittedly, real, and it is understandable that dignity is invoked in these contexts. There is nevertheless a danger that the – absolute and eternal – guarantee of human dignity could be used to forestall democratic debate on highly complex ethical issues that are the subject of widespread and reasonable disagreement. The same goes for abortion – an area in which the Federal Constitutional Court has found on two occasions that existing legislation did not go far enough in protecting the life and dignity of the unborn.[16]

In contrast to the German Basic Law, the South African Constitution neither proscribes the limitation of dignity nor insulates it from constitutional amendment. All rights in the Bill of Rights are subject to limitation, provided that the limitation meets the requirements of section 36, the general limitation clause. Moreover, like all other provisions in the Constitution, section 10 is subject to constitutional amendment, provided that the amendment is passed with the prescribed majority and procedure.[17] This approach leads to fewer

[14] BVerfGE 39, 1 (1975); BVerfGE 88, 203 (1993).

[15] *See* BVerwGE 64, 274. While some commentators regard these conflicts as exceptional (*see* Dreier, *supra* note 11, at 210), others believe that they are far more common than previously imagined. It has even been argued that the right not to be tortured – always considered to be at the heart of the dignity guarantee – is not absolute, that there are circumstances in which it is outweighed by the dignity of others, and that in such cases the state is under an obligation to torture a person in order to save the lives of innocent persons. W. Brugger, *Vom unbedingten Verbot der Folter zum bedingten Recht auf Folter?*, 55 Juristen Zeitung 165 (2000).

[16] 39 BVerfGE 1 (1975); 88 BVerfGE 203 (1993). On the question whether these medical and research procedures impair human dignity, *see* Dreier, *supra* note 11, at 173-176, 179-202; P. Häberle, *Die Menschenwürde als Grundlage der staatlichen Gemeinschaft*, *in* J. Isensee & P. Kirchhof (Eds.), Handbuch des Staatsrechts 317, at 359-362 (2004); Herdegen, *supra* note 11, at 57-65; Stern, *supra* note 11, at 27-47.

[17] A Bill amending a provision in the Bill of Rights needs the assent of at least two thirds of the members of the National Assembly, and at least six of the nine provinces in the National Council of Provinces (section 74(2)). It must, however, be borne in mind that section 1 affirms human dignity as one of the Constitution's founding values. Section 1 itself is more firmly

problems of categorisation and definition. There is no reason to deny dignity the status of a right, and the danger that dignity will be given an overly restrictive interpretation is greatly reduced. At the same time, however, there is a risk that dignity might become just one constitutional right and value among many, and that the inherent dignity and worth of the human person could be sacrificed in the name of countervailing interests.

The Constitutional Court has relied on a variety of interpretive strategies in attempting to avert this danger. In the first place, it has held that where "the primary constitutional breach" is of a "more specific right,"[18] the Court will generally focus on that right. Dignity thus assumes the role of a residual right which is used to interpret and give shape to more specific rights, and which is relied upon directly only in cases in which no more specific right is available.[19] Although sensible, this approach in itself does not resolve the problem. The mere fact that the primary constitutional breach is not that of dignity does not make it more palatable that a breach of fundamental rights is condoned in circumstances where it impacts adversely on the complainant's dignity.

A second strategy is grounded in the Court's understanding of proportionality. The Court has been clear that, although no right is absolute, a serious infringement of dignity would require a particularly persuasive justification. Rather than positing a categorical ban on the limitation of dignity, this approach is sensitive to differences of degree. Limitations which go to the heart of the individual's inherent dignity and worth would seldom if ever pass constitutional muster, while limitations are allowed more readily in the case of marginal infringements.[20] However, this approach is not without problems. A first difficulty is that of distinguishing between a core of human dignity, the limitation of which must meet the most stringent standards of justification, and penumbral areas where the individual's rights might more easily yield to countervailing interests. Although certain general guidelines can be laid down (for instance, it appears as if the right not to be reduced to a mere object belongs to the very heart of the dignity guarantee, whereas the right to personal reputation is further removed from the core of human dignity and is therefore more open to balancing), they must of necessity remain rather vague, and much depends on the court's characterisation of the interests at stake.[21] A second

entrenched and requires a 75% majority in the National Assembly plus the support of at least six provinces in the National Council of Provinces (section 74(1)).

[18] Para. 36.

[19] *See* S. Woolman, *Dignity*, *in* S. Woolman, T. Roux & M. Bishop (Eds.), Constitutional Law of South Africa (2005) 36-19 to 36-25 for an analysis of the various ways in which dignity has been used by the courts.

[20] *See* S. Woolman & H. Botha, *Limitations*, *in* S. Woolman, T. Roux & M. Bishop (Eds.), Constitutional Law of South Africa (2006), at 34-116 to 34-121 for a critical analysis of the Court's use of dignity in its proportionality analysis.

[21] The object formulation, which is derived from Kant's categorical imperative and in terms

problem has been that the distinction between core and peripheral areas lends itself to conservative assumptions about choice, marriage and sexual intimacy. It has, for instance, been held that the stigma suffered by prostitutes is a result of their own choice, rather than being directly related to the role of the law in reinforcing structural disadvantage and harmful stereotypes.[22] The diminished protection granted to intimate relations that do not conform to – an idealised – model of heterosexual marriage also falls into this category.[23] A third problem is that even a severe limitation which goes to the heart of human dignity can, in principle, be justified in terms of pressing social needs.[24]

The idea of dignity as absolute and inviolable thus invariably runs into interpretive problems. It does not require a radical brand of legal realism to see that dignity cannot be insulated from limitation. And yet, the danger that severe violations of dignity would be tolerated in the name of public safety or the common good – a danger that looms particularly large in our post-9/11 world[25] – casts serious shadows over an understanding of dignity as just one right or value among many. Problems of interpretation notwithstanding, we need to hold on to the normative ideal of an inviolable core of human dignity, or else submit to the harsh logic of an economic and political order based on survival, greed and self-interest.

---

of which an individual may never be reduced to a mere object, has been influential both in Germany and in South Africa. *See*, Dürig, *supra* note 11, at 127 for the classical statement of this formula. *See also*, in the German context, BVerfGE 27, 1 at 6 (1969); BVerfGE 45, 187 at 228 (1977); and in the South African context, S *v.* Makwanyane, *supra* note 5, paras. 271, 313, 316; S *v.* Dodo 2001 3 SA 382 (CC); 2001 5 BCLR 423 (CC) para 38. However, the object formulation has been criticized for its indeterminacy and over-inclusiveness. *See e.g.* Dreier *supra* note 11, at 167-168; Herdegen, *supra* note 11, at 23; Stern, *supra* note 11, at 18-19. Since such a wide variety of laws and conduct can be said to be objectifying, it is not always clear how the object formulation, on its own, can distinguish serious infringements of dignity from less serious ones.

22 Jordan *v.* S 2002 (6) SA 642; 2002 (11) BCLR 1117 (CC) paras. 16, 74.

23 *Cf. Jordan*, *supra* note 22; Volks NO *v.* Robinson 2005 (5) BCLR 446 (CC) (exclusion of permanent life partners from benefits under the Maintenance of Surviving Spouses Act held not to infringe their rights to equality and dignity). *See also* P. de Vos, *The 'Inevitability' of Same-Sex Marriage in South Africa's Post-Apartheid State*, 23 South African Journal on Human Rights 432 (2007); R. Robson, *Sexual Democracy*, 23 South African Journal on Human Rights 409 (2007).

24 Although the Court found in Makwanyane, *supra* note 5, that capital punishment annihilates human dignity, the finding of unconstitutionality ultimately seems to turn on the state's failure to demonstrate that the death penalty deters violent crime. A different outcome might have been reached if only the state successfully crossed that hurdle.

25 *Cf.* BVerfGE 115, 118 at 151-165 (2006). In this case, a statute enabling the security forces to shoot down an aircraft which was to be used to destroy human life was held unconstitutional to the extent that it authorised the killing of innocent victims. The Court refused to balance the dignity of the victims against the lives of others who may be saved in the process.

3. Pushing Against (National and Cultural) Boundaries

The second paradox is closely related to the first. Dignity is seen as a matter of cosmopolitan right; something which is inherent in all human beings and transcends cultural barriers and national boundaries.[26] And yet its protection depends, for the most part, on the nation state, and its precise meaning and contours are culturally mediated.[27]

One manifestation of this paradox is that there are severe forms of degradation which go legally unnoticed, or which fall through the cracks separating national and international law. Consider the following two examples, which are both taken from an article by Hasso Hofmann. In the first place, a German consulate in Somalia is under no constitutional or legal obligation to provide food to starving local inhabitants. Secondly, the Federal Republic of Germany is not duty-bound to respond positively to the pleas of asylum-seekers who can demonstrate that, due to restrictions in their home country on basic economic and other liberties, they live under conditions that would not be regarded in Germany as a dignified existence (at least as long as they are not subjected to more serious violations of their dignity than the general populace). Hofmann uses these examples to demonstrate that dignity can only be realised within a concrete – and therefore particular – community based on mutual recognition.[28] While his communicative theory of dignity explains why certain individuals are excluded from a community based on the reciprocal recognition of each member's inherent dignity, it risks reducing dignity to the protection afforded to it within a particular nation-state. It is only by keeping alive the notion of dignity as a universal ideal and a cosmopolitan right that we can hope to challenge traditional ideas which effectively exclude large numbers of people from a common humanity. Only thus can we seriously engage with the limits of the existing legal order, while at the same time remaining open to the utopian possibilities inherent in the notion of an absolute and limitless human dignity.

This paradox is also evident from the divergent approaches taken to dignity in different national systems. Consider, for instance, the articulation in Germany of the values of life and dignity, the protection given to the unborn and the prohibition of the instrumentalisation of human embryos. By contrast, the early link made in the South African context between life and dignity has remained wholly underdeveloped,[29] and the recognition in Germany of

[26] Minister of Home Affairs *v.* Watchenuka 2004 (4) SA 326 (SCA); 2004 (2) BCLR 120 (SCA) para. 25 ("Human dignity has no nationality. It is inherent in all people – citizens and non-citizens alike – simply because they are human.")

[27] For a perceptive analysis of this paradox, *see* A. A. An-Na'im, *Universality of Human Rights: Mediating Paradox to Enhance Practice* in this volume.

[28] H. Hofmann, *Die versprochene Menschenwürde*, 118 Archiv des öffentlichen Rechts 353, at 365-366 (1993)

[29] S *v*. Makwanyane, *supra* note 5.

the dignity of the unborn is often explained by South African lawyers as a uniquely German preoccupation which is rooted in Germany's particular history.[30] In South Africa, the most innovative uses of dignity have come from an exploration of the intersections of dignity, equality and difference. This serves once again to confirm the influence of contingent historical factors on the shape and content given to dignity within a particular legal system.

It is important to keep these tensions alive. We can never simply step outside the confines of the positive legal ordering or transcend the cultural and historical schemata through which our understandings of dignity are invariably filtered. At the same time, we need to remain open to the utopian possibilities inherent in the notion of an absolute and limitless human dignity. Only thus can we hope to push against the boundaries – whether geographical, cultural or ideological – which tend to legitimate and normalise degradation and inequality.

4. Recognition and Material Need

The third paradox concerns the idea of human dignity as something inherent in every human being. Dignity accrues to every human person, regardless of his or her material conditions or social standing. And yet, the equal respect and autonomy to which every person is entitled is contingent on mutual recognition within a community of equals and on the material conditions needed to enable individuals to develop their capabilities.

South Africa's Constitutional Court has, in a number of cases, linked the deprivation of basic material needs (such as access to adequate housing and social security) to the impairment of a person's human dignity.[31] Drawing on this jurisprudence and relying on the work of Martha Nussbaum and of Amartya Sen, some commentators have argued that respect for dignity requires society to create the material conditions needed to enable persons to develop and exercise their capabilities.[32] However, others have criticised the capabilities approach for its tendency to suggest that persons who are denied certain material conditions lack human dignity.[33] This debate highlights the

30 *See* Christian Lawyers Association of SA *v.* Minister of Health 1998 4 SA 113 (T); 1998 11 BCLR 1434 (T) 1445I-1146A.

31 Government of the Republic of South Africa *v.* Grootboom 2001 (1) SA 46 (CC); 2000 (11) BCLR 1169 (CC) paras. 23, 44, 83; Jaftha *v.* Schoeman; Van Rooyen *v.* Stoltz 2005 (2) SA 140 (CC) para. 21; Khosa *v.* Minister of Social Development; Mahlaule *v.* Minster of Social Development 2004 (6) SA 505 (CC); 2004 (6) BCLR 569 (CC) paras. 41, 44.

32 S. Liebenberg, *The Value of Human Dignity in Interpreting Socio-Economic Rights*, 21 SAJHR 1 (2005); Woolman, *supra* note 19, at 36-16 to 36-17, 36-65 to 36-70.

33 D. Cornell, *A Call for a Nuanced Constitutional Jurisprudence: Ubuntu, Dignity, and Reconciliation*, 19 SA Public Law 666, at 667-668 (2004). Cornell is critical of attempts to justify socio-economic rights with reference to the Kantian notion of human dignity. *See also*

contradictory nature of our intuitions about human dignity. On the one hand, abject poverty offends our most basic conceptions of dignity. On the other hand, the idea of dignity as something universal and inalienable resists the notion that dignity is somehow conditional on minimum material conditions.

The Constitutional Court has also linked dignity to basic notions of respect and social citizenship. Because a person's agency and sense of self-worth are intimately bound up with recognition of her status as a free and equal member of society,[34] dignity, in the Court's view, precludes laws and official conduct which perpetuate harmful stereotypes about a particular group or category of persons.[35] Again, this raises a tension. Equal recognition is basic to our understandings of individual autonomy and self-worth. At the same time, however, we understand human dignity to extend to everyone – including those persons who lack the mental capacity to participate in a moral community of equals.

5. Contingency and Transcendence

The fourth paradox can be stated as follows: Dignity demands respect for the familial ties, communal attachments, cultural meanings, religious beliefs and discursive practices through which we make sense of our world and forge our individual identities. It rejects the notion of the unencumbered self and recognises the formative role of – contingent – cultural value patterns and institutional arrangements on our sense of self. At the same time, however, respect for someone's inherent dignity requires recognition of the person's capacity to transcend the strictures of her social background and to forge an autonomous identity.

Both the German Federal Constitutional Court and its South African counterpart have disavowed the idea of dignity as attaching to atomic individuals. The German Court has been at pains to point out that the Basic Law recognises that citizens are members of and bound to the community.[36] Human dignity is taken to vest not in the "isolated, sovereign individual",[37] but in persons who are constituted through intimate and familial relationships, communication and participation in the life of the community. The South African Court has similarly recognised the importance of the family to

K. van Marle, *'The Capabilities Approach', 'the Imaginary Domain', and 'Asymmetrical Reciprocity': Feminist Perspectives on Equality and Justice*, 11 Feminist Legal Studies 255 (2003).

34 Khumalo *v.* Holomisa 2002 5 SA 401 (CC); 2002 8 BCLR 771 (CC) [27] (human dignity includes both the "individual's sense of self-worth" and "the public's estimation of the worth or value of an individual").

35 Minister of Finance *v.* Van Heerden 2004 6 SA 121; 2004 11 BCLR 1125 (CC) [116].

36 *See* BVerfGE 27, 344 at 351 (1970).

37 BVerfGE 4, 7 at 15-16 (1954).

individual dignity and wellbeing,[38] and acknowledged the centrality of religion and culture to the identity and dignity of the person.[39] It has, moreover, tied dignity to the indigenous African concept of ubuntu, which refers to broad notions of human solidarity, respect and interdependence.[40]

These attempts to tie dignity to communitarian and solidaristic notions of interdependence and mutual respect have not been uncontroversial. Some German commentators have been critical of the idea that the Basic Law could be said to embrace a particular image of the human person. They have argued that it is highly problematical in a modern, pluralistic society to seek to entrench in the Constitution a unitary 'image of man' which is invoked as the basis of individual duties and fundamental-rights limitations.[41] Similar concerns have been raised in the South African context over the link made between dignity and ubuntu. The Court's reliance on ubuntu has been criticised, *inter alia*, for romanticising traditional African values, uncritically conflating them with contemporary constitutional norms, and negating the conflict inherent in a pluralistic society. It is feared that ubuntu, with its appeal to broad notions of interdependence and societal harmony, might be used to leaf over disagreement and difference and to induce conformity to dominant mindsets.[42]

Others have pointed out that the recognition of the role of ties of community and solidarity in forging individual identities is not at odds with individual autonomy and need not result in mindless conformity. According to Häberle, the image of man which is said to inform the German Basic Law is flexible – and contradictory – enough to accommodate a plurality of vastly different self-understandings. Encompassing both the autonomy of the individual and his/her membership of and boundedness to the community, it creates space for a diversity of ways of being in the world.[43]

A similar argument can be made about ubuntu. Ubuntu, in this view, need not foster a form of collectivism which stifles individual autonomy and

---

[38] Dawood; Shalabi; Thomas *v.* Minister of Home Affairs, 2000 (3) SA 936 (CC); 2000 (8) BCLR 837 (CC); Minister of Home Affairs *v.* Fourie; Lesbian and Gay Equality Project *v.* Minister of Home Affairs, 2006 (3) BCLR 355 (CC); 2006 (1) SA 524 (CC).

[39] Christian Education South Africa *v.* Minister of Education, 2000 (4) SA 757 (CC); 2000 (10) BCLR 1051 (CC) para. 36; Bhe *v.* Magistrate Khayelitsha; Shibi *v.* Sithole; SA Human Rights Commission *v.* President of the RSA, 2005 (1) SA 563 (CC); 2005 (1) BCLR 1 (CC).

[40] *See* Makwanyane, *supra* note 5, paras. 223-225, 307-308; Port Elizabeth Municipality *v.* Various Occupiers 2005 (1) SA 217 (CC); 2004 (12) BCLR 1268 (CC) para. 37; Dikoko *v.* Mokhatla 2006 (6) SA 235 (CC); 2007 (1) BCLR 1 (CC) paras. 68-69, 112-120; Union of Refugee Women *v.* Director: Private Security Industry Regulatory Authority 2007 (4) SA 395 (CC); 2007 (4) BCLR 339 (CC) 382D-H.

[41] Dreier, *supra* note 11, at 229-230.

[42] *See* R. English, *Ubuntu: The Quest for an Indigenous Jurisprudence*, 12 South African Journal on Human Rights 641 (1996); J. van der Walt, Law and Sacrifice: Towards a Post-Apartheid Theory of Law 109-115 (2005).

[43] P. Häberle, Das Menschenbild im Verfassungsstaat 37, 60-63 (2005).

difference, but can help to resist what Justice Sachs has called the 'hydraulic insistence on conformity' to dominant cultural and religious norms.[44] The work of Drucilla Cornell and others suggests that ubuntu could open up a rich reservoir of alternative understandings which, rather than suppressing difference, could be used to challenge dominant conceptions of the self and community.[45] Because these dominant conceptions are widely identified with Western notions of 'individualism', they tend to be taken for granted in a constitutional democracy in which the equality and autonomy of the individual take centre stage. What is, however, obscured from view is the fact that these understandings are often used to induce conformity to a set of normative expectations that are rooted in a dominant – yet contingent – worldview and culture. As Patricia Williams argues, these dominant understandings of the self and community tend to impose a 'corporate group identity' which stifles autonomy, difference and self-experimentation.[46]

Recognising the constitutive role of culture, religion and community in the formation of individual identity can thus enhance equality and freedom by providing greater space for marginal cultures, religions and worldviews; by challenging the privileged position of a particular understanding of the self and of its place in the universe; and by expanding the scope for individual experimentation. It is therefore perfectly consistent with the inherent dignity of the person. Human dignity is, however, far less accommodating of strong claims for group autonomy which rest upon a thick conception of group identity, and which assert the precedence of collective identities over individual rights. Such claims tend to frustrate challenges from within the group to dominant constructions of communal norms, deny the capacity of cultures to transform themselves, and lock their members into a particular way of life. They are also likely to entrench the material disadvantage and inferior social status of vulnerable subgroups and stifle individual autonomy and experimentation.

A recent judgment of South Africa's Constitutional Court dealing with religious and cultural diversity illustrates the Court's use of dignity to avoid both the radical individualist conception of the self that is unencumbered by social ties and relations, and a thick, essentialist view of a self that is incapable of escaping the strictures imposed by attributes like culture and religion. *MEC for Education: KwaZulu-Natal v. Pillay*[47] concerned a school rule prohibiting the wearing of jewelry. The Constitutional Court dismissed an appeal against the finding of the High Court that the school's failure to permit a learner to

---

44 Prince *v*. President of the Law Society of the Cape of Good Hope 2001 (2) SA 388 (CC); 2001 (2) BCLR 133 (CC) para. 156.

45 *See e.g.* Cornell, *supra* note 33, at 666; N. Bohler-Muller, *The Story of an African Value*, 20 SA Public Law 266 (2005).

46 P. Williams, *Metro Broadcasting, Inc v FCC: Regrouping in Singular Times*, *in* K. Crenshaw *et al.* (Eds.), Critical Race Theory: The Key Writings That Formed the Movement 191, at 194 (1995).

47 2008 (1) SA 474 (CC); 2008 (2) BCLR 99 (CC).

wear a nose stud constituted unfair discrimination. The learner in question wore the nose stud as an expression of her South Indian Tamil Hindu culture. In his judgment, Langa CJ noted the "importance of community to individual identity and hence to human dignity."[48] He was, however, quick to point out that, far from being monolithic, cultures are

> living and contested formations. The protection of the Constitution extends to all those for whom culture gives meaning, not only to those who happen to speak with the most powerful voice in the present cultural conversation.[49]

He rejected, moreover, the argument that a learner could not claim an exemption based on voluntary, as opposed to mandatory cultural and religious practices. Having pointed out that dignity demands respect for the unique set of ends of every individual, he stated: "That we choose voluntarily rather than through a feeling of obligation only enhances the significance of a practice to our autonomy, our identity and our dignity."[50] The judgment, while recognising the centrality of culture and belief to the dignity and identity of the human person, thus refuses to block out the voices of individual members in favour of a single, supposedly authoritative interpretation of cultural practices and religious beliefs.

6. Freedom and Constraint

The fifth paradox, like the fourth, concerns the relationship between dignity, the individual and community. Dignity is closely related to personal freedom and presupposes the right of the individual freely to choose her own ends. At the same time, however, respect for dignity requires us to set limits to freedom – particularly in an age characterised by pervasive private power, excessive consumerism and deepening inequality.

It is accepted in Germany that dignity serves not only to strengthen and to expand the sphere of personal freedom, but also to ground individual duties which may result in restrictions to individual freedoms.[51] In South Africa, too, the Constitutional Court has insisted that "community rights and the rights

[48] Para. 53.

[49] Para. 54. J. O'Regan in her dissent rejected the majority's approach as too individualised and subjective. It is in her view not enough to establish whether a particular belief is held sincerely. Since cultures are associative, it needs to be asked "what the cultural community considers to be a cultural practice" (para. 154), *see also* paras. 152-153. She did, however, add that cultures "are not generally unified and coherent but are dynamic and often contested" (para. 154). Although her approach insists on the need for a shared understanding that a particular practice is a cultural practice and not merely a personal habit, it is not premised on the idea of a single authoritative interpretation of any given culture.

[50] Para. 64.

[51] Häberle, *supra* note 43, at 47-50.

of fellow members place a corresponding obligation on a citizen, thereby shaping the abstract notion of individualism towards identifying a concrete member of civil society."[52]

In South Africa, as in Germany, the tension between dignity as enhancing and restricting freedom has come to the fore in cases in which individuals willingly participate in sexual acts which are viewed as degrading, demeaning or unnatural. The German Federal Administrative Court has held that peep shows violated Article 1(1), despite the fact that the women who participated did so on a voluntary basis.[53] Here, the state's duty to protect participants against being reduced to mere objects of the viewers' lust apparently trumped their freedom. This judgment has been heavily criticised for its reliance on dignity to deny autonomy.[54] South African courts have similarly invoked dignity to justify restrictions on prostitution[55] and the possession of pornography.[56] The dangers inherent in such reliance on dignity are illustrated by a High Court judgment, in which it was held that bestiality is "so repugnant to and in conflict with human dignity as to amount to perversion of the natural order" and that the state is under an obligation to "prevent any individual or group from descending to the level of the beast."[57] This reasoning risks reducing the scope of personal and sexual autonomy and conflating dignity with dignified behaviour. The link made between dignity and the 'natural order' is particularly unfortunate, as it tends to naturalise dominant assumptions about what constitutes 'normal' sexual behaviour.

Contract is another area in which respect for individuals' autonomous choices comes into conflict with the need to limit freedom in the interests of dignity and equality. South African courts tend to cling to an almost absolute conception of contractual freedom which seems strangely out of place in the twenty-first century. Although it is accepted that a term in a contract can be voided if it is against public policy, this has made no significant dent in the prevailing judicial ideology, which continues to privilege the principles of contractual autonomy and *pacta sunt servanda* over considerations of equity and fairness. Hopes that the constitutional values of dignity and equality might be used to set limits to contractual freedom have so far proved largely illusory. In fact, the Supreme Court of Appeal has invoked dignity to bolster the claims

---

52 Bernstein *v.* Bester *NO* 1996 (2) SA 751; 1996 (4) BCLR 449 (CC) para. 67.

53 BVerwGE 64, 274 at 279-280.

54 *See* Dreier, *supra* note 11, at 218-220.

55 Jordan, *supra* note 22, para. 74 (human body is devalued by its commodification through prostitution).

56 De Reuck *v.* Director of Public Prosecutions (WLD) 2004 (1) SA 406 (CC); 2003 (12) BCLR 1333 (CC) (ban on child pornography is justified, as child pornography impairs the dignity of children).

57 National Coalition for Gay and Lesbian Equality *v.* Minister of Justice 1998 (6) BCLR 726 (W) 751B-D; reasoning endorsed in *S v M* 2004 (1) BCLR 97 (O) paras. 15, 24.

of contractual autonomy.[58] And while it has been conceded that dignity and equality may have a role to play in trimming the excesses of contractual freedom[59] – for instance, in cases of unequal bargaining power[60] – the courts' actual decisions show that the exercise of this power will be confined to such extreme cases that it is likely to have a minimal effect in combating inequality and protecting consumers.[61]

What is missing in these cases is a critical engagement with the social context. Rather than situating their analysis within the context of vast inequalities of power and resources, South African courts have embraced a libertarian approach to contract which rests upon metaphysical notions of freedom. Human dignity, equality and freedom have been grounded in abstract notions which seem more at home in a nineteenth-century treatise than in a society trying to come to terms with a history of institutionalised inequality and deprivation. The courts have thus missed a critical opportunity to situate their dignity analysis within the lived reality of ordinary South Africans.[62]

7. Concluding Remarks

In this paper, I have explored five paradoxes that lie at the heart of human dignity. In the first place, dignity signals an absolute commitment to a sphere of personal inviolability. And yet, not every violation of dignity attracts – or can attract – legal censure. Secondly, dignity is seen as a universal entitlement. However, it depends on a particular legal order for its concretisation, and the precise content given to it is invariably filtered through contingent social, cultural and historical factors. Thirdly, while dignity requires ongoing challenges to misrecognition and material deprivation, it resists the conflation

---

[58] Brisley *v.* Drotsky 2002 (4) SA 1 (SCA); 2002 (12) BCLR 1229 (SCA) para. 94 ("contractual autonomy is part of freedom. Shorn of its obscene excesses, contractual autonomy informs also the constitutional value of dignity"); Afrox Healthcare Bpk *v.* Strydom 2002 (6) SA 21 (SCA) para. 23.

[59] The best statement of this view is that of J. Davis in Mort NO *v.* Henry Shields-Chiat 2001 (1) SA 464 (C) 475. In his view, the values of equality and human dignity require

> [p]arties to a contract [to] adhere to a minimum threshold of mutual respect in which 'the unreasonable and one-sided C promotion of one's own interest at the expense of the other infringes the principle of good faith to such a degree as to outweigh the public interest in the sanctity of contracts'.

[60] Afrox, *supra* note 58; Napier *v.* Barkhuizen 2006 (4) SA 1 (SCA); 2006 (9) BCLR 1011 (SCA) para. 14.

[61] In Afrox, *supra* note 58, a clause indemnifying a hospital against liability for the negligence of its staff was held not to be against public policy.

[62] *See e.g.* D. Bhana & M. Pieterse, *Towards a Reconciliation of Contract Law and Constitutional Values: Brisley and Afrox Revisited*, 122 South African Law Journal 865 (2005) for criticisms of this approach.

of individual dignity and worth with dignified economic conditions or social respect. Fourthly, dignity demands respect for the cultural and symbolic processes through which we become persons and make sense of our world. At the same time, it presupposes the ability of the individual to transcend the narrow confines of her socio-economic environment and upbringing and to forge her own autonomous identity. Finally, dignity is intimately connected to individual autonomy, yet requires placing certain limits on freedom.

Despite its paradoxical nature, dignity can constrain the range of legitimate constitutional interpretations. In the South African context, the inherent dignity of each individual has been invoked to exclude both a radical, abstract individualism and stronger notions of 'group rights' in which the collective takes precedence over the individual. Precisely because it values both the centrality of cultural practices, religious beliefs and communal ties to individual dignity and identity, yet celebrates the capacity of the individual to transcend the strictures of her own background, dignity can be used to negotiate conflicts between the individual and community in a way which neither obliterates diversity nor stultifies the dynamic processes through which community norms are generated and contested.

Allow me one last go at trying to capture the paradoxical nature of human dignity. Dignity requires absolute respect for the inherent worth of each individual. It thus demands an impossible and unlimited responsibility to respect and protect everyone's inherent dignity – regardless of national boundaries and countervailing rights and interests. At the same time, however, dignity requires meticulous attention to particular, local contexts. An understanding of dignity as something abstract and formal – like that informing South Africa's law of contract – inevitably ends up as a caricature. It is only through careful attention to the particularity of human lives that we can keep interrogating concepts, rules and institutions – state sovereignty, the market, the public/private distinction, cultural value patterns, etc. – which render degradation and abuse invisible and lend them an air of inevitability.